Elisha Benjamin Andrews

Institutes of economics

A succinct textbook of political economy for the use of classes in colleges, high schools and academies

Elisha Benjamin Andrews

Institutes of economics

A succinct textbook of political economy for the use of classes in colleges, high schools and academies

ISBN/EAN: 9783337134594

Printed in Europe, USA, Canada, Australia, Japan

Cover: Foto ©Suzi / pixelio.de

More available books at **www.hansebooks.com**

1888

By E. BENJAMIN ANDREWS

Typography by J. S. Cushing & Co., Boston
Presswork by Berwick & Smith, Boston

TO

HOF-RATH DR. JOH. A. R. VON HELFERICH

*Professor of Economics and Finance in the
University of Munich*

By his former pupil

THE AUTHOR

ἆρά γε ἡ οἰκονομία ἐπιστήμης τινὸς ὄνομά ἐστιν ὥσπερ ἡ ἰατρικὴ καὶ ἡ χαλκευτικὴ καὶ ἡ τεκτονική; ... ἦ καὶ ὥσπερ τούτων τῶν τεχνῶν ἔχοιμεν ἂν εἰπεῖν ὅ,τι ἔργον ἑκάστης οὕτω καὶ τῆς οἰκονομίας δυναίμεθ' ἂν εἰπεῖν ὅ,τι ἔργον αὐτῆς ἐστι; δοκεῖ γοῦν.

XENOPHON, *Oikonomikos*, I, 1, 2.

PREFACE

Two main motives have prompted the composition of this book, one concerning method, the other, doctrine. The most excellent manuals of Political Economy now in use seem to the author to involve two serious faults of method. One is that they nearly everywhere say too much, totally ignoring the instructor, and on most points leaving the pupil himself little thinking to do even when they stop short of positively confusing his mind in its efforts to construe the thought in its own way. The other is that they do not mark for the eye, in differences of type, any distinction between substantive and subsidiary material, their pages exhibiting principle and illustration, statement and amplification, clothed in equal dignity of form. It is believed both on psychological grounds and from much experience, that the best printed presentation of a subject for class-room purposes is the briefest which clearness will allow, leaving indispensable amplifications and illustrations to notes, and all fuller exposition to the teacher's wit or the student's search. This is the aim of the following pages. That the pupil, so soon as master of the essential idea, may be able to at once enlarge and tighten his grasp upon it through reading, most of the paragraphs are introduced by references to the best accessible authorities, more recondite works being at the same time named for the behoof of teachers. On collateral subjects of special importance the ablest convenient discussions are listed in notes. The analysis and arrangement of topics are in many particulars new, and it is hoped that some of the changes introduced will prove welcome. As the result of careful reflection, a prominence which may at first seem grotesque has been given to the paragraph-captions. Students will find this not merely a mnemonic convenience for the purposes of review and examination, but a most efficient objective help in grasping the science. Touching the doctrine of this new class-book there is less to say. As Economics is now in transition many deprecate all effort at present to summarize it afresh. This logic, strictly taken, presupposes the advent, sooner or later, of a fixedness in the science which we fervently hope will never arise, since it could not but imply stagnation in economic thought. Meantime our best texts, with all that is true, profound, and well said in them, blend not a few propositions that what may be called the general judgment of progressive economists pronounces inadequate, misleading, or erroneous. Such are especially numerous in regard to the nature of Wealth, the scope of Economics, and in the weighty rubrics of Value, Money, Interest, Wages, and Profits. Nearly all our treatises, besides, betray from beginning to end a deceptive air, a wry *ensemble*, springing from writers' too sharp sundering of Economics from general Sociology. Whether the volume now offered to the public contains in these respects aught of true amendment, those who read and use it must judge. They will at any rate find in it, not always adopted but at least sympathetically mentioned so far as these are sufficiently non-technical to be named in a work of this character, the latest views which can with any propriety pretend to be settled. The book has been written during the odd moments of a very busy year, and it will be a wonder if the critic's keen glance shall not unearth in it some inconsistencies and errors of detail. The author will be happy to be notified of any such. He is indebted to several gentlemen for their kind pains in looking over the proof sheets as they have appeared. In this, Professor J. W. Moncrief, Ph.D., of Franklin College, has rendered a peculiarly grateful service.

E. BENJ. ANDREWS.

July 3, 1889.

TABLE OF CONTENTS

INTRODUCTION

§ 1 Economics Defined (1)* — § 2 General and Private Wealth (4) — § 3 Economic Evolution (5) — § 4 Economics a Science (7) — § 5 Modern (8) — § 6 Its Origin (9) — § 7 The Mercantile System (10) — § 8 Progress (12) — § 9 Physiocracy (14) — § 10 Adam Smith (15) — § 11 The Smithian School (17) — § 12 The Historical or Aposteriori Tendency (19) — § 13 Professorial Socialism (20) — § 14 The Socialists Proper (23) — § 15 Our View (25) — § 16 Value of the Study (28) — § 17 The Division of Economics (30)

PART I
PRODUCTION
Except as Involving Exchange

CHAPTER I
THE NATURE OF PRODUCTION

§ 18 Various Views of Productivity (31) — § 19 Wealth-Increment which is not Production (33) — § 20 Production (34) — § 21 Special Remarks on Production (36) — § 22 The Conditions of Production (38)

CHAPTER II
THE ABSOLUTE CONDITIONS OF PRODUCTION
Nature — Labor

§ 23 The Materials of Nature (40) — § 24 The Forces of Nature (42) — § 25 Labor: its Necessity (43) — § 26 Its Forms (44) — § 27 Its Relation to Nature (45)

* Figures in brackets refer to pages

CHAPTER III
THE RELATIVELY ABSOLUTE CONDITIONS OF PRODUCTION
Capital — Social Organization

§ 28 Capital Defined (47) — § 29 Kinds of Capital (48) — § 30 The Place of Capital in Production (50) — § 31 Society (52) — § 32 The State (53)

CHAPTER IV
THE RELATIVE CONDITIONS OF PRODUCTION

§ 33 General View (55) — § 34 Diminishing Return and Increasing Return (56) — § 35 The Labor-Force: Extent (57) — § 36 The Labor-Force: Quality (59) — § 37 Socialism and Production (62)

CHAPTER V
THE RELATIVE CONDITIONS, CONTINUED

§ 38 Extraneous Aids to Labor (64) — § 39 Geography and Topography (64) — § 40 Material Capital in General (66) — § 41 Machinery (67) — § 42 Unembodied Invention (68) — § 43 The Organization of Industry (69) — § 44 The Same in a Special Aspect (71) — § 45 Evils and Limitations (72) — § 46 The Form of Undertaking (73)

CHAPTER VI
COST AND CONSUMPTION IN PRODUCTION

§ 47 Metaphysical Cost (76) — § 48 Mercantile Cost (78) — § 49 Consumption (79) — § 50 Waste and Thrift (80)

PART II
EXCHANGE
Except as Involving the Science of Money

CHAPTER I
THE NATURE OF EXCHANGE

§ 51 In Rude Societies (83) — § 52 Philosophy (85) — § 53 Intrinsic Advantages (86) — § 54 Reach of Influence (87) — § 55 The Perfection of Exchange (90)

CHAPTER II
INTERNATIONAL EXCHANGE

§ 56 Initial View (92) — § 57 Common Ground (94) — § 58 The Theory of Nutrient Restriction (96) — § 59 Continuation (98) — § 60 Important Specific Points (99)

CHAPTER III
VALUE: GENERAL

§ 61 Value and Value (102) — § 62 Value in Use (103) — § 63 Value in Exchange (105) — § 64 Price (107) — § 65 Normal Value in Exchange (107)

CHAPTER IV
VALUE: PECULIAR PROBLEMS

§ 66 Competition and Value (110) — § 67 Monopoly Value (112) — § 68 Values between Non-Competing Groups (113) — § 69 Complex Cases of Value (114) — § 70 A Measure of Exchange-Value (115) — § 71 The Value of Futures (117)

PART III
MONEY AND CREDIT

CHAPTER I
THE NATURAL HISTORY OF MONEY

§ 72 Barter (118) — § 73 Primitive Money (119) — § 74 Money Proper (120) — § 75 The Money Metals (121) — § 76 Mode of their Distribution (124) — § 77 Bimetallism (125)

CHAPTER II
BANKS AND PAPER MONEY

§ 78 Banks of Deposit (128) — § 79 Developed Banking (129) — § 80 Government Paper (130) — § 81 Historical (131)

CHAPTER III
THE THEORY OF MONEY

§ 82 The First Function of Money (134) — § 83 The Second Function (135) — § 84 Other Offices of Money (136) — § 85 The Value of Money (137) — § 86 Paper Money (139) — § 87 Ideal Money (141)

CHAPTER IV

CREDIT

§ 88 The Nature of Credit (143) — § 89 Credit and Crises (144) — § 90 Further Abuses of Credit (145) — § 91 Free Banking (146) — § 92 The John Law Theory (147) — § 93 Fiat Money (148)

CHAPTER V

THE CLEARING SYSTEM

§ 94 Settlements by Check (151) — § 95 International Payments (153) — § 96 Special Modifiers of the Rate of Exchange (156)

PART IV

DISTRIBUTION

CHAPTER I

THE NATURE OF DISTRIBUTION

§ 97 General Statement (158) — § 98 Categories and Shares (159) — § 99 Blending (161) — § 100 The Law of Equal Returns to Last Increments (162) — § 101 The Other General Laws of Distribution (162) — § 102 The Fifth Category (164)

CHAPTER II

RENT

§ 103 Rent in General (165) — § 104 Ground Rent (166) — § 105 Rent and Price (167) — § 106 Peculiar and Nominal Rents (168) — § 107 Controversy (169)

CHAPTER III

INTEREST

§ 108 The Nature of Interest (171) — § 109 Loan Interest (172) — § 110 The Rate on Loans (173) — § 111 Inflation and Interest (175) — § 112 Usury Laws (176)

CHAPTER IV
WAGES

§ 113 Definition (178) — § 114 Cause and Source (179) — § 115 Developed Wages (180) — § 116 The General Rate of Gross Wages (181) — § 117 The Residual Claimant Theory (182) — § 118 The Truth (183) — § 119 Concluding Points (184)

CHAPTER V
PROFITS

§ 120 Terminology (186) — § 121 Undertakers' Profits (187) — § 122 Undertaker-Talents (188) — § 123 Profits, Prices, Wages (189)

PART V
CONSUMPTION

CHAPTER I
NEED

§ 124 To Resume (190) — § 125 Elasticity of Need (191) — § 126 Fashion and Progress (192) — § 127 Legitimacy of Need (193)

CHAPTER II
ECONOMY IN SUPPLY

§ 128 Generic Principles (195) — § 129 Specific Principles (195) — § 130 Prevention of Loss (196) — § 131 Luxury and Idle Wealth (197)

PART VI
PRACTICAL TOPICS INVOLVING ECONOMIC THEORY

CHAPTER I
COIN CURRENCY IN THE UNITED STATES

§ 132 Colonial Times (200) — § 133 Earliest National Coinage (201) — § 134 The Dollar of the Fathers (203) — § 135 Remonetization (204) — § 136 The Future (206)

xii TABLE OF CONTENTS

CHAPTER II
PAPER CURRENCY IN THE UNITED STATES

§ 137 Early (208) — § 138 Thence to the Civil War (208) — § 139 Government Paper (209) — § 140 Government Banking (210) — § 141 The National Bank System (212)

CHAPTER III
OUR PAPER CURRENCY IN FUTURE

§ 142 Present System (213) — § 143 Difficulties (214) — § 144 Proposed Change of Basis (215) — § 145 Probable Outcome (216)

CHAPTER IV
TAXATION

§ 146 General Principles (218) — § 147 Direct and Indirect Taxes (219) — § 148 Norms of Direct Taxation (220) — § 149 Taxation of Income (221) — § 150 Emergency Taxation (222)

CHAPTER V
POVERTY

§ 151 The First Class of Remedies (223) — § 152 The Second Class (224) — § 153 Ultimate Help (225)

INSTITUTES OF ECONOMICS

INTRODUCTION

§ 1 ECONOMICS DEFINED

Cossa, Guide, ch. i. *Mill*, Essays, 1829, on Method in Pol. Ec. *Sidgwick*, on do., Fortnightly, 1879. *Roscher*, Grundlagen, Einl., ch. i. *Cohn*, Grundlegung, Einl., chaps. i, ii, iv. *Garnier*, Traité d'écon. pol., 682-'5.

Economics[1] is that branch of learning conversant about general **wealth,** wealth being the collective name for all those categories[2] of things, powers,[3] relations, and influences, which both result from conscious human **effort** and directly[4] contribute to human **welfare** in its **temporal** aspect. Single pieces or elements of wealth may be called **'goods'**[5] or **'values.'**[6] Notice in this definition (i) that not all wealth is of a material[8] nature, and (ii) that the mark **'exchange,'** though helpful in forming the conception of Economics, is accidental rather than fundamental[7] thereto, since a study substantially the same might exist if men did not exchange. Economics, in discussing wealth, has of course also to canvass the **conditions**[8] of wealth.

¹ Originally and by etymology, "house-management," yet not indoor merely or mainly. *οἶκος* meant "estate," "property." Macleod, Elements, vol. i, 132. Bacon still used *economia* in its classical sense. The title "Political Economy" [*Économie politique*] first by Montchrétien de Watteville, in 1615. It is still in excellent use, but "Economics" is clearer as well as briefer. Roscher, § 16, following Uhde, who introduced the word in 1849, prefers *Oekonomik* to name economic science, using *Oekonomie* to mean economic life. Few if any have followed this distinction, and Cohn, p. 5, explicitly repudiates it, sticking to *Oekonomie* as appellation for the science. Cf. § 3, below.

² Isolated articles may be wealth, though costing no labor, as an aerolite of gold falling at your door, or a pasture-weed discovered to be a specific. But the *classes* of goods in which these examples belong are gotten only by labor.

³ So far as they fall under the definition, *i.e.*, spring from man's effort and make for his welfare, *powers*, intellectual or physical, *relations*, as the good name or the custom of a business house, and *influences*, such as a great advocate's reputation gives, are no less truly wealth than houses, garments, or bread. If the definition of wealth as always material is simpler, which is certainly the case in expounding Distribution, it is less deep and truthful. Why, *e.g.*, term medicine wealth, yet deny the name to the skill able to cure without medicine? In crucial analysis, material wealth itself becomes wealth only in and through its immaterial relationships. Wheat is not wealth merely because so and so constituted physically, but because it is *here* instead of beyond reach, adapted to *our* constitution, and not repugnant to our taste. Now these relations are not material entities at all. Millions of goods that have length, breadth, and thickness, would be turned to refuse by trifling supposable changes in the psychical side of our sensibility. This is a most important consideration; though it is of course quite possible to frame a system of workable economic definitions on the material basis. So doing, we should style these powers etc. [immaterial wealth], *conditions* of wealth [note 8]. Böhm-Bawerk, *Rechte und Verhältnisse*.

⁴ There are high elements of character, perhaps also physical products, like unsalable keepsakes and family heirlooms, which are the creatures of effort and have a certain bearing upon our well-being, yet in so remote a way that it is unnatural to reckon them as wealth.

⁵ Most German writers approach the definition of Economics from the notions of "needs" and "need-satisfiers" or "goods." Cutting off non-temporal goods on the one hand and gratuitous ones on the other, they fence out the same economic field which our definition covers. Thus, —

INTRODUCTION 3

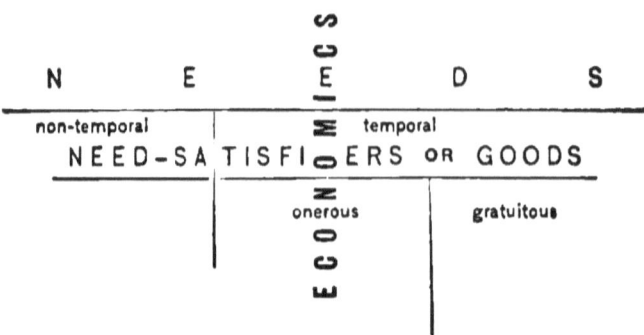

⁶ In the sense of "labor-requiring utilities," but not in any meaning which would involve the idea of *exchange*. Cf. note 7. For the force here assigned to "value," see the Chapter on this topic in Part II. Cf. Roscher, § 5 and notes.

⁷ Contrary to the "catallactics-theory" of Economics, held by Condillac, Bastiat [Harmonies, ch. iv], Whately, Macleod, and Perry [Elements, ch. iii], which builds the study entirely about the conception of exchange as centre, reducing it to an investigation of exchange-value. This procedure at first attracts by the simplicity it seems to impart, but is gravely unscientific. Exchange is not the substance of man's economic life, but an incident, though an important one. We can easily conceive a very complete set of economic phenomena, calling for investigation and offering full basis for a science of Economics, exchange being totally absent. Suppose a number of Robinson Crusoes [cf. Roscher, p. 5], some well off, some ill off. There would be *reasons* for the difference, inviting study. Pioneers in new lands exchange little, yet vary greatly in weal. So the Indians before the whites came, and so, still better, the ancient Peruvians. This is the chief objection to the theory named, but far from the only one. Mill, Principles, bk. iii, ch. i, § 1. Cf. *post*, § 3, n. 9.

⁸ "Object-phenomena of Economics," that is, is a broader conception than "wealth," including things, circumstances, etc., helpful to wealth, and things, circumstances, etc., unfavorable to the same. Original fertility of the soil, with mines, water-powers, and the other "natural" wealth of any country, would illustrate what is meant by conditions of wealth. So would the native endowments of the people which aid thrift and accumulation, and also any acquired powers having the same tendency, if built up without conscious aim. The state is a prime condition of wealth. At this point again, however, imperfect definition need not prevent clear insight.

§ 2 General and Private Wealth

Storch, Zur Kritik d. Begr. von Nationalreichthum [1827]. *Marshall, Economics of Industry*, § 7. *Hawley*, Quar. Jour. Econ., vol. ii, 365 sqq. *Inama-Sternegg, Vom National-Reichthum, Deutsche Rundschau*, June, 1883. *Neumann-Spallart, Weltwirtschaft, Jahrg.* 1883-4, pp. 8 sqq. *Schmoller, Forschungen*, VII.

General, national, or cosmic wealth is not merely the summed possessions[1] of individuals and mercantile corporations. Immaterial[2] wealth and public property must be reckoned in, and either titles or the things to which they entitle omitted.[3] Valid titles held by persons in **one** land to values in **another** are, however, part of the first land's wealth; but all such rights have to be excluded from an inventory of the **world's** wealth. In estimating general wealth the test of **exchange**[4] value has but very limited application.

[1] "The wealth of the country being the aggregated wealth of its citizens," Gannett, in Int'l Rev., vol. xii. Mulhall computes the world's wealth at about 255 billion dollars: lands and forests 84½ billion, cattle 10½ billion, railways 20, houses 61, furniture 30½, merchandise 6½, bullion nearly 5, shipping 1½, other forms of material goods nearly 20. He departs from Gannett's loose maxim so far as to reckon in public works, — at 15¼ billion. As to the rest he probably estimates by exchange value [see n. 4]. Computing as he does, and omitting public works, we may place the whole wealth of the United States in 1888 at 51 billion, the yearly earnings at from 10 to 12, the yearly savings at 900 million, and the daily [week-day] savings at 3 million. Such approaches to fact are valuable for comparison of nation with nation and section with section, still are approaches only. The same is true of the following wealth-statistics from the United States Census Reports.

Census of	Population	The Nation's Wealth: Millions of Dollars	Percentage of Increase in Population	Percentage of Increase in Total Wealth	Average No. of Dollars *per capita*
1800	5,305,937	1,072.	35.02	43.	202.13
1810	7,239,814	1,500.	36.43	39.	207.20
1820	9,638,191	1,882.	33.13	24.4	195.
1830	12,866,020	2,653.	33.40	41.	206.
1840	17,069,453	3,764.	32.67	41.7	220.
1850	23,191,876	7,135.8	35.87	89.6	307.67
1860	31,500,000	16,159.	35.59	126.4	514.
1870	38,558,000	30,069.	22.	86.1	780.
1880	50,155,783	43,642.	30.	45.	870.

² The immaterial variety is never referred to in listing wealth. The chief reason for the omission is the indefiniteness of the thought and the difficulty of appraising immaterial riches in dollars and cents. But assuredly it ought not to be ignored. Dollars cannot measure the superiority of health to sickness or of satiety to hunger, yet these differences are as thinkable and important as they are familiar.

³ If a mortgaged farm is put down for its whole worth and the mortgage too, evidently all the property covered by the mortgage is twice told. So of a railway and its stock or bonds. In case of a great corporation, if we are summing up the nation's wealth, a careful inventory would be a much safer index than the market value of the stock. A given patent or copyright is no increment to the national wealth, though a good *system* of such rights might be. Certain credit-instruments are wealth [§ 84, n. 3, § 86, n. 3].

⁴ Even Knies, *Geld*, 23, takes money-exchange power as practically his criterion of wealth. But there is a vast deal of every land's wealth whose proportion to the whole is not so much as indicated by its power, if it has any, in exchange. How little would roads and streets sell for in comparison with the contribution they make to the community's welfare? Good sewers are worth all they cost and usually much more, but could not be sold at all.

§ 3 ECONOMIC EVOLUTION

Schaeffle, Bau u. Leben d. socialen Körpers, vol. iii, 402, sqq. *Schoenberg, Handbuch d. Pol. Oek.*, vol. i, ch. i. *Cohn*, 91–93. *Hyndman & Morris*, Summary of Socialism.

In man's economic life ¹ hitherto and now the following more or less clearly defined stages or gradations ² are discernible : (i) the **hunting**,³ (ii) the **pastoral**,⁴ (iii) the **agricultural**, (iv) the **manufacturing and commercial**, and (v) that of **credit, free contract, and giant industries**. In (i), man is totally **dependent** on **nature**, hard-worked and poor. Industry has no **diversity, war** is incessant and population scant and homogeneous. **Community** of **property**⁵ prevails, and there is neither **exchange** nor money. The succeeding stages witness progressive improvement in all these particulars. In this, to a good degree, civilization consists. **Slavery**⁶ and other forms of social cleavage begin with ii, also exchange and the genuine unrest of life and growth. In iii, industry becomes greatly diversified,[7] and man, no longer her slave, largely **determines** what nature shall produce. He **settles** in **communities**. **Law** and the **state** develop, military system and new **social** formations rise. Of iv, **city** life, the **division** of labor, **exchange,** and **metallic**[8] money are the chief marks. Slavery now goes down and a **separate wages-class** emerges. Law and the state assume higher and more complex forms, and **leisure** makes possible the amassing of **intellectual** wealth. Stage v is that at which America and West Europe now are.[9]

[1] "Life" as opposed to "doctrine" [*Wirtschaft: Wirtschaftslehre*]. Of course men have always had an economic experience of some sort, but the study of this is a recent matter. Cf. § 5. Sound economic doctrine must be based upon large knowledge of economic life.

[2] "Gradations" as well as "stages," because certain peoples, the Esquimaux, Bushmen, and Hottentots, *e.g.*, do not seem to improve at all.

[3] Fishing tribes are on substantially the same plane with hunters, both these being "occupatory" industries [*occupare* in Roman law = to take possession of], but fishers are usually the better off, have the denser populations, sometimes own slaves, and are apt, instead of becoming shepherds and farmers, to grow first into pirates, then into ocean-carriers.

[4] Pastoral peoples are always nomadic as well, driving their herds from place to place to find the best pastures [Genesis, ch. xiii].

[5] Except perhaps in personal clothing and each man's kit of utensils for taking and skinning animals, etc., and for war.

[6] Hunters could utilize slaves only by giving them arms, which would render them dangerous; but shepherds may employ them for herdsmen.

[7] That is, though agriculture forms the staple calling, the lower kinds of industry still continue. Besides, many ancillary trades are now demanded, as those of smiths and wood-workers.

[8] Metal money has been found among pastoral nations, gotten probably in the way of exchange with those more advanced. Cattle [so *pecunia*, from *pecus*. "Cattle" and "capital" are originally the same word, from *caput*

through *capitalis, e*] are their common medium of exchange. Slaves, too, are so used. In stage i barter prevails. For the difference between barter and money, see in Part III. Ancient society at this general level (iv) differed from modern. It did not reject slavery, and its cities sprung from commercial not from manufacturing necessities. Greece and Rome had no factories, whence to form cities like Lowell or Paterson. There were at Athens, indeed, immense workshops, where thousands of slaves wrought, but apparently they did not exist to secure division of labor. Blanqui, vol. i, 31.

[9] The stage on whose phenomena all the current English works in Economics are based, — Adam Smith, Ricardo, Mill, Senior, and the numerous manuals which have been published this side the Atlantic. Only quite recently have economists seen the need of a broader historical outlook. Cf. §§ 11, 12. For a graphic comparison between xivth and xixth century society, see H. C. Adams, Outline of Lectt. upon P. E., 67 sq.

§ 4 ECONOMICS A SCIENCE

Marshall, Ec. of Ind., § 2. *Mill*, Logic, bk. vi, ch. iii, cf. ch. vi. *Schurman*, Eth. Import of Darwinism, ch. i. *Wagner*, in Quar. Jour. Econ., vol. i, 117 sqq. *Cohn*, *Einl.*, ch. ii. *Roscher*, *Einl.*, ch. ii. *Cossa*, pt. i., ch. iv, pt. ii, ch. i. *Newcomb*, Princt. Rev., Nov. 1884. *Cairnes*, Logical Method, i, ii.

As Economics canvasses phenomena in **classes**, and ascertains and expounds their underlying **laws**, it may, however inexact and as yet incomplete, justly be regarded a **science**.[1] In this character it is partly **deductive**, partly **inductive**, the first as applying certain already admitted laws of human nature and of physics, the second, inasmuch as by the aid of observation, experience, statistics, and history, it sets forth the concrete working of these laws and finds out others.

[1] See Mill, as above, ch. vi, also chaps. ii, x, xi. It has been objected that Economics cannot be a science because man's will is free. But freedom and action under law are not incompatible. The notion that there is no science but exact science is as vicious as it is common [*der über den Strang der " Exactheit" schlagender Naturforscher*, Schaeffle, Letters, 15]. A science may be called exact when the causes and laws with which it deals are not only knowable but known. Pure mathematics approaches

this character nearest. A potentially exact science, whose causes and laws are in their nature knowable but not yet studied out, as meteorology and tidology at present, might be styled "incomplete." "Inexact" are those sciences where occult causes, whose working the human mind with its present powers is unable to trace, more or less perturb the action of the knowable and known causes. All the social sciences, including Economics, are of the last order, as, in a degree, are all those which have to do with *life*. Study § 15 [and notes] along with this one.

§ 5 MODERN

Ingram, Hist. of Pol. Ec., chaps. i, ii. *Perry*, Elements, ch. i.

The science is of **recent** origin. In ancient, and even in mediæval times, while many true notions regarding it were advanced, as by Plato, Aristotle, Xenophon and the Roman lawyers,[1] its facts were too little observed and reduced to order to constitute a science. The **real springs** of public prosperity were either **unperceived or not investigated**.[2] **Slavery** was universal, the accumulation of **wealth decried**.[3] **Industry** and the mechanic arts were **despised, wars** continual, and, as to property, far more destructive than now, subjugated lands laid waste, and no means recognized of enriching one country but **plundering** others.

[1] Thus Plato has these worthful *aperçus:* gold and silver not valuable *in se;* too much gold possible; the advantage of the division of labor [the last, shared by all the ancients above named]. Aristotle distinguishes utility from value and natural wealth from artificial. Xenophon descries the true nature of wealth, of money, and of prices, Demosthenes that of capital [ἀφορμή, ἔρανος]. D. extends the notion to cover incorporeal capital. Ulpian neatly defines property [not wealth] as what can be bought and sold: *Ea enim* RES *est quae emi et venire potest*. But all these writers, to mention no more of their false ideas, believe in slavery and over-value money. Is Horace consciously arguing against the bullion theory [§ 7, n. 3] at Sat. I, i, 40–45, "Unless you reduce your gold-pile it has no beauty"? On the Roman authors of economic ideas, Ingram, 18 sqq.

[2] The only wealthy nations of antiquity which bred minds capable of pursuing such a study were Athens and Rome, precisely the ones whose entire economic development was artificial. They became rich by exploiting, one the Confederacy of Delos, the other the world.

[3] Cicero, *de officiis*, i, 42, perfectly sets forth in this matter the spirit of the classical world: *Illiberales autem et sordidi quaestus mercenariorum omnium, quorum operae, non artes emuntur. Est autem in illis ipsa merces auctoramentum servitutis. Sordidi etiam putandi, qui mercantur a mercatoribus quod statim vendant, nihil enim proficiant, nisi admodum mentiantur. Nec vero est quidquam turpius vanitate. Opificesque omnes in sordida arte versantur; nec enim quidquam ingenuum habere potest officina. . . . Quibus autem artibus aut prudentia major inest, aut non mediocris utilitas quaeritur, ut medicina, ut architectura, ut doctrina rerum honestarum, eae sunt iis, quorum ordini conveniunt, honestae. Mercatura autem, si tenuis est, sordida putanda est; sin magna et copiosa, multa undique apportans, multaque sine vanitate impertiens, non est admodum vituperanda. . . . Omnium autem rerum, ex quibus aliquid acquiritur, nihil est agricultura melius, nihil uberius, nihil dulcius, nihil homine libero dignius.*

§ 6 Its Origin

Blanqui, chaps. xiv-xxx. Ingram, ch. iv. Laughlin, ed. of Mill, Int. Sketch.

The necessary new thought was turned to economic facts mainly through: i **Commercial** activity during and after the Crusades,[1] and especially after the period of **discovery** began. ii **Rise of prices** incident to the increased bulk[2] of the precious metals consequent upon opening the **American mines.** iii Frequent **debasement of monies** by monarchs.[3] iv New need of **revenues** and the changed **mode** of **raising** these, attending the transition from feudalism to modern states.[4] v Questions of trade arising in the application of the European **colonial system.**[5] vi Enlarged acquaintance with the economic conceptions of the **Roman law.**[6] vii The development and organization of **credit.**

INTRODUCTION

¹ The greatness of the famous merchant cities, Venice, Genoa, Pisa, and Amalfi, now began. Commerce and business were henceforth reputable, and men engaged in them could be raised to the nobility. The Hanseatic League dates from about 1260, ten years before the last crusade. On this see Blanqui, ch. xvi.

² The general law is, the more money in circulation the less the purchasing power of each piece, and the higher the range of prices. See the discussions of Part III.

³ Their regular resort for centuries so often as impecunious. The usual mode was, while leaving the face of the coins unchanged, to abstract part of the true metal, putting baser in its place. Not seldom they would force the money so debased into circulation at its face value, and accept it only at its real value. So did Emperor Ferdinand II in Bohemia, 1620.

⁴ This change involved paid armies, costly ministries and embassies and the expensive pomp and circumstance of great courts. Systematic taxation and fiscal machinery had to be resorted to, enforcing economic study.

⁵ See Blanqui's excellent chapter [xxiii] on this. Every nation which had colonies regarded and used them simply as means for enriching the mother state. There were three different plans for accomplishing this: i Spain and Portugal kept colonial trade in the hands of the government. ii Holland, Sweden, Denmark, and France till 1720, placed it exclusively in the power of a gigantic stock company. iii England [Lecky, Eur. in xviiith Cent., vol. ii, 8 sqq.], also France after 1720, effected a national monopoly by navigation laws practically to exclude foreign vessels from visiting their colonies. Here again was necessity for study.

⁶ Roman law was at no moment in the middle age disused or unknown, but the discovery, at the sack of Amalfi, 1135, of the Florentine copy of the Pandects immensely stimulated the study.

§ 7 THE MERCANTILE SYSTEM

Ingram, ch. iv. *Ad. Smith*, Wealth of Na., bk. iv, ch. i. *Roscher, Gesch. d. Nat. Oek. in Deutschland*, 228 sqq. *Perry*, Elements, ch. xiv. *Blanqui*, chaps. xxvi-xxix. *Schoenberg*, vol. i, 63 sqq. *Cossa*, Guide, 119 sqq. *Cohn*, 94-100.

While much vigorous economic thinking¹ was done in the middle age, especially by the **canon lawyers,** the earliest serious efforts to arrange economic data as an orderly whole were made in **France,** resulting, provisionally, in the so-called Mercantile System.² This, neglecting agriculture, magnified other businesses, and commerce in particular, yet, regarding money as the most real form of wealth,[3] insisted that in order to profit by trading, a nation must have the 'balance of trade'[4] in its favor, work mines, tax imports, subsidize exportation, and conduct its whole policy with the view of amassing the greatest possible hoard of the precious metals. To this end ubiquitous governmental regulation of industries was necessary, with privileges and monopolies to all inland business deemed important, also encouragement to domestic shipping, discouragement to foreign. These notions, while more explicit in France, were common to all Europe, and determined the character of economic and international politics for centuries. Not even yet are they fully overcome.[5]

---

[1] Particularly upon money and the problem of a fair price [*justum pretium*]. The latter was discussed by every great theologian from St. Augustine down. This renowned doctor condemns the man who would *vili emere et caro vendere*, and after him the whole mediæval church taught that such a practice was wrong. By *justum pretium* was meant *cost*, including labor and time of the salesman in getting, keeping, and selling his ware. The principle of supply and demand as price-determinant was, so far as recognized at all, denounced as necessarily unrighteous. Far clearer was mediæval thinking on the subject of money. Nicolas Oresimus, bp. of Lisieux, † 1382, has left us a sermon containing a theory of coinage almost exactly modern in its ideas. From the schoolman, Gabriel Biel, we have another monetary discussion of decided worth.

[2] Sometimes styled "Colbertism," after Colbert, the distinguished minister of Louis XIV. On Colbert's views, Roscher, as above, 229, and Blanqui, ch. xxvi. The latter will have it that the system was Italian in origin, and brought to honor by Spain, and that in spirit Colbert was not a mercantilist at all. His mercantilist views were certainly more moderate and sensible than most of those advanced by his school. Cromwell was the chief, though far from the only, English ruler to push the mercantilist policy. Frederick the Great, also his father, did the same for Prussia.

[3] The "bullion theory." Blanqui [i, 223, ch. xviii] dates Mercantilism from 1303, when Philip the Fair forbade the exportation of gold and silver from France. An English law of Edward III's time swears inn-keepers in seaport towns to search their guests to prevent the exportation of money or plate [H. Spencer, The New Toryism, S]. Even Locke strongly advocated the policy of piling up gold and silver in the country. All nations had laws to effect this. Yet Ad. Smith, bk. iv, *ad. init.*, Garnier, "Physiocrates," in Lalor's Cyclop., and most critics state it too strongly when they accuse the mercantilists of really identifying money with wealth. No men could ever be so foolish. They greatly overvalued it, however, relatively to other wealth, just as thoughtless people do now. For the error of this view, see § 9. It arose partly from the ready serviceableness of money for all purposes, partly from the need which each nation then felt of a great hoard of gold and silver for war, and partly from mistakenly comparing a nation to a manufacturing town, taking in raw material to be worked up and sold for money [next note].

[4] Thomas Mun said: "The secret means to enrich the nation is to sell each year to foreigners more wares than we consume of theirs," receiving the balance in money, of course. The older mercantilists believed that money should never, under any circumstances, be permitted to go "forth of the realm." Mun and the newer school held differently. They regarded its exportation sometimes profitable, as a means of getting back much more, and likened the outgo and return to seed-time and harvest. The Emperor Charles V forbade Spain to export precious metal or raw material. An imperial decree in Germany, 1500, commanded tailors to work up none but domestic cloth.

[5] Daily one may read in the newspapers expressions to the effect that fortune is smiling upon us if we happen to be importing gold, frowning if the same is leaving us. As if a land could not be money-poor ! Or as if it were possible for all our money to desert the country ! And Mercantilism at large is spoken of even by competent economists as, for past times, "relatively justifiable."

§ 8 Progress

INGRAM, 51 sqq. *Garnier*, " Physiocrates," in Lalor. *Horn, L, Écon. Pol. avant les Physiocrates.* *Cohn*, 101-107. *Cossa*, pt. ii, ch. iii.

During the XVIIth and XVIIIth centuries, economic topics were discussed by many **German** writers, commonly in a narrow, mercantilist spirit,[1] yielding few

valuable insights, and mostly without discovery of the
nexus between these. More advance was made in
England. Sir William Petty,[2] b. 1623, argued that
value originates in labor, and demonstrated the advantages that flow from the division of labor. He likewise
anticipated Ricardo's law of rent and theory of wages.
Sir Dudley North, 1691, affirmed that the whole world
is, as to trade, one nation, that laws cannot fix prices,
that money is merchandise, subject to glut as well as to
scarcity, and that all special governmental favor to any
one interest is an abuse, cutting off so much benefit from
the public. Locke, 1690, 1695, noted the distinction
between utility and value, and denied the ability of governments to fix the purchasing-power of money. Hume[3]
showed, 1752, that wealth consists not in money but in
the supply of wants, and that the prosperity of one land
is the prosperity of all. Berkeley, in his Querist,[4] 1756,
questioned 'whether it were not wrong to suppose land
or gold and silver either to be wealth.' While, till
Hume, no English writer appreciated Petty and North,
similar views were championed with exceeding zeal in
France by Boisguillebert,[5] Vauban, Fénelon, Montesquieu, and Cantillon.

[1] Zincke, 1692-1769, was the only noteworthy exception. See Ingram, 80.
[2] On Petty, see Wirth, in Braun's *Vierteljahrschrift*, 1863, pp. 110 sqq.
He was one of the most versatile of men: — pedler, sailor, physician,
draughtsman, inventor, scientific writer, land-surveyor, organizer of businesses. His education was but ordinary, gotten mainly at the grammar
school of Romsey, in Hampshire, his native town, though he had studied a
little at the University of Caen, Normandy. In youth distressingly poor,
he became rich, leaving an ample fortune to his son, who was created
Baron Shelburne, and founded the Landsdowne family. Petty, so early,
ably discussed, and answered negatively, the question so much agitated
still, whether government can establish a permanent value-relation between

gold and silver. This in ch. x of his Pol. Anatomy of Ireland, published in 1691 among his posthumous works.

[3] Ad. Smith's personal friend and chief British forerunner as an economist.

[4] First published in 1735.

[5] On these Frenchmen, see Ingram, 57 sqq. Fénelon's Télémaque did more than anything else to popularize the new views in France. Cantillon was a French merchant of Irish extraction. He is hardly distinguishable from the physiocratic writers. Jevons accounted him the founder of that school and so of economic science. He deserves this eminence no more than Bois-guillebert. Both differ from the regular physiocrats in relative failure to array their insights as a system, and in making less of the *law of nature* [see next §].

§ 9 PHYSIOCRACY

Ad. Smith, bk. iv, ch. ix. *Garnier*, " Physiocrates," in Lalor. *Blanqui*, ch. xxxii. *Cossa*, pt. ii, ch. iv. *Batbie, Turgot, Condorcet*, do. *Tissot*, do. *Cohn*, 101-107.

This, the next system,[1] also French in origin, went to the **opposite** extreme from Mercantilism, making **land** the only source of income, and **agriculture** alone productive. The physiocrats maintained that : i Gold is never the **end** of trade, but only a means. ii A nation cannot in the long run sell more than it buys, and would not be benefited if it could. iii All governmental **privileges** and **monopolies** relating to business and commerce are wrong. iv Trade, both domestic and foreign, should be **free,** state interference with business affairs reduced to a minimum.[2] v The sole tax should be a **direct** one, upon land rent.[3] These principles they connected with their doctrines of natural rights and a condition and law of nature,[4] which they expounded in a way to belittle the state and exhibit all conscious action of society as necessarily artificial. This theory is remarkable for its influence upon Adam Smith, and in hastening the French Revolution.

¹ We may speak of this one as having rallied a *school* to its support.

² The "*laissez faire*" doctrine, which, with that of natural law, forms the heart of Physiocracy. The phrase was first used in an economic sense, though doubtless not with full physiocratic meaning, by a merchant in a conversation with Louis XIV. The formula *laissez nous faire* was employed by Legendre, the geometrician, in 1680, disputing with Colbert. The phrase *laissez faire* was introduced to scientific literature in 1736, by the Marquis d'Argenson, finance minister to the Duke of Orleans, Regent of France after Louis XIV's death. Dr. Gournay was the earliest physiocrat to utter it, which he did with the addition, "*et laissez passer.*" From him this language became the physiocrats' watchword [not, however, separating "*faire*" and "*passer*" as if they meant respectively " produce " and " exchange "]. See on this, Pol. Sci. Quarterly, vol. ii, 706.

³ At a good remove, however, from the thought of Henry George. i The physiocrats would tax improvements on land: George not. ii They expected revenue mainly from country sections and from fertility of soil: he has regard to unearned increment from the growth of cities, towns and villages. iii They taxed the product of labor, and because it was such: he sedulously exempts this.

⁴ "The state of nature was the reign of God." Pope, Essay on Man, Epistle iii, line 149. This essay is a great piece for the doctrine of a state of nature and for the ethics of the XVIIIth century. The thesis of Ep. iii is that the interest of one is the interest of all. Sir H. Maine, in his Ancient Law, traces the history of the " law of nature " conception. The distinction between man's condition under the minimum of society's influence and that amid the play of fully developed social forces, is real and important. One may, for lack of nicer descriptives, name these, as the physiocrats did, respectively the state of nature and the state of culture. Only it is senseless to account the latter as of necessity depraved or perverse. It, too, is in its way a state of nature. This admission should not, however, carry us to the counter error of praising all past acts or states of society as alike good simply because they have had place in history. Into this fallacy fall those [§ 7, n. 5] who attempt to justify Mercantilism.

· § 10 ADAM SMITH

Ingram, 87 sqq. " Smith, Adam," in the Cyclopedias. *Cossa*, pt. ii, ch. v. *Cohn*, 107-115. *Buckle*, H. of Civilization, vol. i, 152 sqq., 602 sqq.

But Economics can hardly be said to have attained scientific rank till the publication, in 1776, of Adam

Smith's Inquiry into the Nature and Causes of the Wealth of Nations, — a truly epoch-making[1] work, far the most important single treatise ever devoted to the science. The material, so rich and large, which Turgot, Hume, and others had gathered and partially systematized, it at the same time utilized, purified, and arranged. Smith's central thought, instead of commerce on the one hand or agriculture on the other, is **Industry,** which he makes include both. In his system **labor** is the one source of value and ultimate determinant of prices. Productive labor, which is here, against the physiocrats, extended to include manufactures and commerce, though not '**services,**'[2] as of teachers, physicians, *savans, etc.*, is declared to be the real creator of wealth. Smith agrees with the physiocrats that, as a rule,[3] industry ought to be **unimpeded** by governmental action, left to free competition under the benign spur of individual self-interest. Like them, too, he continually appeals to what is **natural.**[4] The exceeding merit of Smith's performance lay in his exhibition of the **laws** governing economic phenomena, and in his facile and copious presentation of **historical** proofs. His book also contains a number of discussions, masterly and never yet equalled, of certain weighty specific questions, as taxation, the advantages of the division of labor, the causes of the diversity in wages, and the difference between money and other capital. His refutation of the bullion theory it would be as hard to improve as to impugn.

[1] How far Smith was a creator will be debated always. He raised few new problems, and the scope of his actually fresh insight was not large. But he saw in every direction somewhat that was new, and saw clearly

what he saw, whether at first or at second hand. Withal he knew how to expound felicitously, keeping up interest amid the dreariest details. His position as to Economics is much like Plato's touching philosophy. Each had numerous and great forerunners, yet succeeded in making himself forever the necessary point of departure for every intelligent student and writer in his line. Whole pages and chapters in the most recent treatises, however remote the writer's standpoint from that of Smith, read as but transcripts from the old master's book.

² He does not, in naming them unproductive, deny the usefulness of such services. They may be even indispensable. Productive is labor which creates wealth, and it is Smith's habit to restrict wealth to material entities. Useful abilities, however, he designates as capital, and hence, it would seem, must have thought them wealth as well. The two lines of representation appear inconsistent.

³ He approved England's navigation policy [§ 6, n. 5], as a means not to national wealth, but to the naval power so necessary for England in facing other nations. Smith was far from going the physiocrats' length in denouncing all governmental touch of industry.

⁴ See preceding §, n. 4.

§ 11   THE SMITHIAN SCHOOL

Ingram, 110-195.   *Brentano*, *Die klassische Oekonomie* [1888].   *Lunt*, Pres. Cond. of Pol. Econ.   *Cohn*, 115-123.   *Sidgwick*, Principles, Int.   *Bagehot*, Ec. Studies, iii.

The influence of the Wealth of Nations upon economic thought was very great. Hundreds of keen minds turned to the new science; minor **points** of its **theory** were worked out; its tenets began to shape **legislation.**¹ Ricardo was the next noted general expositor in England, J. B. Say in France. Ricardo powerfully impressed James Mill, Senior, and J. S. Mill, through whose able presentations of the subject he silently became for all lands its accepted interpreter. Adam Smith was still praised much, but read less and less. His narrowness and errors were perpetuated, and his abstractions, untempered by his regard for history and concrete fact, taken literally as universal truth. **Dogmatism, apri-**

orism, and passion for crisp **formulæ** prevailed. No side of man was studied but the economic, and this was assumed to have presented itself **always** and **everywhere** as in England during the early XIXth century.[2] Like defects marked the evolution in France,[3] Italy, and America. Such an exhibition of Economics,[4] dry, eccentric and partial, rather than in the full sense false, continued till yesterday the dominant one. Authors belonging to this Orthodox School have, however, always differed among themselves not only upon lesser but upon fundamental doctrines. Such have been: i the degree and location of the **scientific character** attaching to Economics, ii the proper **limits** of **laissez faire,** iii the theory of **Population,** Malthus and his critics, iv that of **Rent,** Ricardo and his, v that of **Wages,** vi that of **Money.**

[1] As in England the Factory Laws and the abolition of protective duties.

[2] The misapprehensions, it will be seen, were mainly three, those of i) 'perpetualism,' ignoring the change in human nature and society from age to age, ii) 'cosmopolitism,' ignoring the differences among various peoples at the same time, and iii) assuming an 'economic man,' when in fact no man's motives are ever solely economic. [*Rümelin, Red. u. Aufsaetze*, I, p. 13.] The first of these errors was the worst.

[3] Only here with more originality and variety. Bastiat [§ 1, n. 7] was the ablest French writer after Say and had wide influence in France and outside. His, especially, is the doctrine of economic optimism, that the highest social weal is attained when each individual follows his own interest. English economic masters have never urged this.

[4] One sees how far just and how far unjust it is to call all this 'Smithian.' 'Ricardian' would be a stricter designation. German writers refer indiscriminately to the 'English School,' 'Manchester School,' 'Apriorists,' 'Dogmatists,' 'Cosmopolites,' as holding these notions. J. S. Mill had before his death, in 1873, emancipated himself at many points into a more truthful manner of viewing the science; and the other writers here reviewed were by no means so absolutely out of the way as has often been

represented. No critic has yet succeeded in judging between these and the newest writers with satisfactory impartiality and insight. Sidgwick, Principles, does best.

§ 12 THE HISTORICAL OR APOSTERIORI TENDENCY

Sidgwick, Principles, Int., iii. *Ingram*, ch. vi. *James*, Pref. to Ingram. *Roscher*, § 26 sqq.; Prelim. Essay, in Eng. Tr. *Cohn*, 157-180. *Smith* [R. M.] and others, in " Science Economic Discussions."

Inevitable reaction came, taking chiefly two shapes, a **Socialistic** and an **Historical**, the former attacking more the **laissez-faire** doctrine, the latter the **apriori** character previously ascribed to the science. Hildebrand,[1] Knies, and Roscher[2] were the pioneers in the historical path, and their spirit and method have more or less affected nearly every economist in the world.[3] Hence, (i) the greater insistence now on **historical** and **statistical** knowledge in interpreting and applying economic laws, and (ii) the inclination in many quarters to see in Economics **nothing universal** or of the nature of law, but only a **phase of history**,[4] a product of times, localities, and national peculiarities, requiring different maxims for different peoples. Man and society, it is urged, essentially alter with centuries and climes. Economic theory itself as well as economic practice is matter of **historical evolution**, growing up in 'living connection with the entire organism of a period in the life of humanity and of peoples, with and out of the given conditions of time, space, and nationality, in fact consisting in these, and passing on with them to new developments. Even the **general laws** of Political Economy are nothing but an historical explication, an advancing manifestation, of the truth, a mere generalization of the facts recognized up to any given point, and cannot as to either sum or formulation be declared unconditionally complete.'[5]

[1] Died in 1878.
[2] In the history of Economics and in economic history the most learned man living. He is commonly referred to as head of the historical school, but Knies is a far more radical opponent of the English method.
[3] Cf. § 3, n. 9.
[4] But by no means all aposteriorists go as far as this. Roscher himself does not, his exposition agreeing in the main rather with Adam Smith's. He decidedly alleges Economics to be a science, based on laws. So, indeed, does Knies, but he minimizes more than R. the resemblance of these [social] laws to those of physics.
[5] Knies, Pol. Oek., p. 24. This he opposes to the 'absolutism of theory' which he charges upon the apriori economists. The quotation goes on: 'The absolutism of theory, whenever it does happen to display validity at a certain stage, is simply a child of that time, and characterizes but a particular period in the development of the science.' This is easily seen to be the development hypothesis of general philosophy applied to Economics.

§ 13 PROFESSORIAL SOCIALISM

Cossa, Guide, 196. *Laveleye*, Socialism of To-day, ch. xii. *Rae*, Contemp. Socialism, ch. v. *Ely*, French and German Socialism, ch. xv. *Held, Grundriss für Vorlesungen*, 25 sqq. *Schmoller, Ueber einige Grundfragen*, etc., 31-50, also 93 sqq. *Meyer, Neuere Nationalökonomie*, 227 sqq.

This expression names a bold and popular phase which, since 1872, economic theorizing has assumed especially among professors of Economics, and in Germany. In that land this is now the ruling school, and an increasing number of the foremost English and American economists are its adherents. The professorial socialists,[1] like the aposteriorists, have little faith in any natural or universally valid laws of Economics, and insist on the relativity of its doctrines to time, place, and history. They indeed differ from writers like Roscher,[2] less in virtue of any strict principle than through peculiar emphasis upon certain points. i They make 'wealth' distinctly subordinate to 'man' as the **central economic conception,** refusing to sunder Economics sharply from sociology in general.[3] ii They assert a vital relation between **ethics** and Economics, insisting that human nature is essentially **altruistic,** and that, so far from self-interest, in whatever sense,[4] being the sole economic motive, wealth is always in large part a product of **moral** and religious factors. iii They ardently oppose *laissez faire* as presumptive maxim,[5] and **deny Bastiat's** contention that harmony of interests must accompany free competition. iv Believing that economic law is very much the creature of **legislation,** they freely recommend **governmental intervention** to assuage inequalities of fortune [6] and social ills of nearly all sorts. v They rebuke the inclination of the older economists to identify Economics with the mere **production** of wealth, and urge attention to questions of **distribution** as even more important.

[1] This name, *Kathedersocialisten*, or socialists of the [teacher's] chair, was first applied in derision, to ridicule the alleged proposal of the new theorists to settle the social question 'by university lectures.' The movement originated in Schaeffle's *Capitalismus u. Socialismus*, 1870, Wagner's *Rede ueber die Sociale Frage*, 1871, and Schoenberg's treatise entitled *Arbeitsaemter*. October 6 and 7, 1872, a convention was held at Eisenach, and the next year the *Verein für Socialpolitik* formed in the interest of the new views. Besides the three writers named, Brentano, Held, Nasse, Schmoller, and von Scheel, have been prominent as socialists of the chair. The men who share this tendency, by no means agree in details or even in all the doctrines which themselves consider important. See next note.

[2] Some of them, as Schmoller and his pupils, go very much farther than Roscher in denying to Economics the character of a science. A few practically reduce it to the mere empirical knowledge of trade and industry

[Descriptive Economics]. Cf. Wagner, in Quar. Jour. Econ., vol. i, 113 sqq., and Nasse, ibid., 503 sqq.

³ There is a cluster of subjects, e.g., the prevention of vice, the management of criminals, sanitation, divorce, charity, no one of which perhaps is yet worthy to be regarded a science by itself, and which it is customary to group together as departments of the general science of sociology. The latter title is also used generically, as including several branches of knowledge recognized as sciences, law, politics, and ethics among them. It is the habit to rank Economics with these last: professorial socialists incline to place it rather in the less differentiated class. They mock at the assumption of an "economic man," and see danger in attempting to separate its economic elements from the rest of human nature even for analysis and study. Schmoller makes a point of distinguishing between a *natural* order in the economic life [such as § 15, n. 4, refers to], the reality of which he fully admits, and a moral, social, or psychological order, race-customs, the spirit of times, etc.; and he complains that the Smithians ignore this realm. He expects economic reform to come largely from the building up of new customs and social ideas, more favorable to the laboring classes, which shall, when necessary, though by no means all of them, congeal into laws.

⁴ I.e., whether as downright selfishness or as a self-regard in accord with general warfare. Adam Smith's most famous followers were wont considerably to overlook or belittle man's natural regard for his kind, and their representations need correction [§ 15, n. 1]. Their meaning on the point has, however, been in part misunderstood. Often what they affirm is not so much man's selfishness, whether in a worse or in a better sense, as it is his individualism, his dependence for greatest efficiency in action, upon his own rather than upon society's initiative.

⁵ See § 15.

⁶ Here socialists of the chair approach pure socialism [next §]. Wagner goes so far in this direction as to favor the public ownership of land in cities, and the use of taxation as a means of equalizing wealth. Schmoller [*Einige Grundfragen*, 97] quotes with delight an expression of Frederic the Great, to the effect that taxes have among other ends that in particular " of establishing a sort of equilibrium between rich and poor."

INTRODUCTION 23

§ 14 The Socialists Proper

Schaeffle, Quintessenz d. Socialismus. Laveleye, Rae, and *Ely,* the works mentioned at § 13. *Kirkup,* Inquiry into Socialism. *Osgood,* Pol. Sci. Quar., vol. i, 564 sqq. *Marx,* Capital. *Adler, Rodbertus ;* also his *Grundlagen d. Marx'schen Kritik. Kozak, Rodbertus-Jagetzow's Ansichten. Dietzel, Karl Rodbertus. Cohn,* 133-157. *Dawson, German* Socialism and Lassalle.

These are the most pronounced foes of Adam Smith's system, set especially against the principles of **private property** and **free competition** in work and trade, regarding them the roots of all social misery. Scientific socialism pleads for an economic régime wherein all **land and material capital**[1] shall be **public** instead of private property, the **state**, not the individual capitalist, being the employer of laborers, and production and the distribution of products not left as now, subject to speculation and to the law of supply and demand, but **regulated** justly and by authority, according to the wants of the **whole body** of consumers, so that no one need be idle, uncared for, ignorant or poor. Saint-Simon, Fourier and Owen[2] had each developed a kind of socialistic scheme, but Louis Blanc was the first[3] to expound socialism as a thorough-going new political order. Proudhon, his contemporary, advanced the thesis that property is theft, though he subsequently retracted this. But no strong scientific grounds for socialism were presented till Rodbertus and Karl Marx, two able German thinkers, whose reasoning has commanded the attention of the economic world. From one of their favorite premises, Adam Smith's doctrine of **labor** as the **sole source** of wealth, they argue that the laboring class **deserves far more** than it gets; while from another, viz., Ricardo's '**iron law**' of wages, they conclude that such injustice must **inevi-**

tably continue so long as the means of production remain in private hands.[4]

[1] Socialists must be distinguished from anarchists, who believe that government, as contrasted with administration, can and should be abolished, and from communists, who wish possession and enjoyment in common, as well as production. In opposition to the anarchist, the socialist proposes to continue some form of real political authority; contrary to the communist, he does not expect or desire complete levelling in social place or economic condition. Henry George is not a socialist. He indeed proposes state ownership of land, but his entire conception of the social body and its mode of true growth is Smithian, at the farthest possible remove from that of socialists.

[2] Saint-Simon, 1760–1825, wished society reorganized into a grand coöperative commonwealth, under the masters of industrial science and administration as governors; but he gave only the vaguest hints how to accomplish this. Late in life he gathered a few brilliant enthusiasts into a school. This survived him, but perished in 1832. Fourier, 1772–1837, and Owen, 1771–1858, both devised schemes of coöperating communities, numbering from a few hundred to a few thousand members apiece, each occupying a huge barrack [or 'phalanstery,' to use Fourier's word], and carrying on all the necessary industries with the fullest aid of coöperation and improved machinery. Owen wanted products enjoyed in common; Fourier did not wish to abolish private property, but planned, after assuring a minimum to the least productive workers, to assign $\frac{5}{12}$ of the rest to labor, $\frac{4}{12}$ to capital, and $\frac{3}{12}$ to talent. Owen and Fourier, like the anarchists of to-day, hoped that all humanity would adopt this organization. Fourier started a phalanstery, which utterly broke down. Owen began several — one of them at Harmony, Indiana — with no better success. The chief result of these ideas was great stimulus to coöperation, of which system Fourier and Owen may be styled the founders.

[3] Blanc, 1811–1882, urged that the state should open workshops for the unemployed, expecting these to succeed so well as to raise the level of wages and gradually come to monopolize industry. Blanc put forth his first great work, *L'Organization du Travail*, in 1840, and Proudhon, 1809–1865, uttered his famous words, *la propriété c'est le vol*, in the same year. This thought was not original with Proudhon, but had been advanced long before by Brissot de Warville, the Girondist leader in the French Revolution. Proudhon was however the first to proclaim the

feasibility of just distribution by means of "labor-time" wages and prices, ideas which Marx borrowed from him.

[4] Marx, 1818–1883: Rodbertus, 1805–1875. Partly their premises, taken from Smith and Ricardo, are unsound; partly they reason from them illogically. Full discussion falls under Distribution, but see §§ 15, 37. Ricardo's 'iron law,' as interpreted by the socialists, is to the effect that by the present economic order all wages necessarily tend to the starvation level.

§ 15 Our View

Newcomb, Princeton Rev., Nov., 1884. *Molinari, Les Lois naturelles de l'écon. pol. Sidgwick*, Principles. *Lunt*, as at § 11.

The **Historical School** merits thanks for insisting on what, though well known, is rarely felt in proper force, that Economics, when applied, becomes a mere science of **tendencies,** and that no one of its specific laws can safely be pronounced operative in any concrete case without fullest study of **local and temporal conditions.** It has refuted the old notions of human nature and social institutions as **fixed creations,** and shown society to be an organism, subject to **evolution**[1] no less than are the other realms of biology; thus incidentally revealing, further, how **meagre** must be a system of economic truths valid for **all** ages and peoples. To the **Socialists,** whether partial or complete, be it granted that (a) *laissez faire*[2] is **no absolute** principle, (b) its application has nowhere brought social millennium,[3] (c) existence of thorough natural harmony in interests between different social classes is **not proved,**[4] (d) government can **do much** for the betterment of economic conditions without attacking the property right or becoming dangerously paternal, (e) within these limits **it should labor** in this direction to the utmost, (f) with increase of morality and intelligence, its sphere may in this respect possibly be enlarged. Yet we maintain that : i **Certain general laws of absolute and universal validity and no less 'natural' than those of physics, underlie the science of Economics, viz., those laws of the physical world and of man's constitution which determine man's temporal weal.**[5] ii **In all economic activity the presumption is in favor of individual liberty and free competition [laissez faire], rightfulness of public intervention in no case admissible save after proof.**[6]

---

[1] Society an organism (i), subject to evolution (ii) — these are the main insights for which we are indebted to the aposteriorists. The nominalistic, individualistic idea of society, making it a mere chance aggregation of individuals, must be surrendered. Society as such and by itself has aims, tendencies, a life entire, which are more than generalizations from the experiences of John, Richard, and Peter. With this better view of man as member of a social cosmos has naturally come a sounder ethics. Self-regard is seen not to be the whole duty of a moral agent [§ 13, n. 4]. Neither is the self-seeking of A, B, and C that sure way to the general good which Bastiat thought it [§ 13, iii], except in the sense that one best serves self by devotion to others. The second truth, social evolution, must also be recognized. Human nature, unless the notion be made ridiculously meagre, is not the same in different generations but changes from age to age. On the whole matter of this note, cf. Ward, Dynamic Sociology.

[2] This maxim, never authoritatively defined, has been used with great latitude of meaning. See Garnier, "Laissez Faire," in Lalor. English writers have meant less by it than French. Sidgwick, Principles, 22. As usually applied it has signified that government should restrict its agency to the protection of men in their "natural rights," to life, liberty, and property. But no government has ever yet been able to proceed upon so narrow lines. Nor ought governments to attempt this. If legislation is often a hindrance economically, it may be also a great, even an indispensable help. Its work in gathering statistics is invaluable. So are its coast and other surveys and its meteorological reports. Forests, fisheries, and

ocean and river dikes, to cite a few obvious cases, government alone can supervise in accord with the economic interest of all. For other benefits from the state's positive intervention, see Shaw-Lefevre, opening Addr. bef. the British Social Science Cong., Birmingham, Sept. 17, 1884 [in ans. to II. Spencer's Man and the State]. Cf. Mill, bk. v, ch. i, and Schmoller, *Grundfragen*, 95.

³ In England, e.g., where industrial freedom is most complete, but poverty still dire and stubborn.

⁴ More nearly is it disproved. The immediate interests of different men and classes certainly clash continually. The permanent good of individual or class is surer to accord with that of society; though it by no means always does so, unless a higher than economic good is meant, or "permanent" taken as reaching beyond time. Thus, riches are acquired in the liquor trade, in gambling, and by selling obscene literature and pictures — businesses which curse humanity [§§ 18, n. 5, 21, n. 7].

⁵ See Cohn, 69-78, and Senior, Pol. Econ., 26-81. That men must eat to live, and work in order to eat, that they prefer pleasure to pain, and seek to attain their ends [whether selfish or unselfish] by the least onerous processes, are specimens of such laws. The tendency of population to outrun subsistence [Malthusianism] is another. De Molinari's law that the price of a commodity falls or rises in a geometrical ratio as its amount increases or diminishes in an arithmetical, may be cited as still another example, valid universally so soon as exchange begins, though in a less definite way than his presentation would imply. We name, too, the law by which the precious metals distribute themselves. If they are peculiarly plenty high prices [of other things] prevail and the money flows off to effect purchases at remote centres. If they are scarce the counter phenomena have place. The law of diminishing returns, however checked here and there, is as universal as the industries, agriculture and mining, to which it relates. Knies's scruple [Pol. Oek., 356], to call some of these 'natural' laws, on the ground that they do not relate to "things corporeal and subject to sense-perception" seems fanciful. Whatever objection may lie against regarding as 'natural' the purposive movements of society, the unconscious play of psychical and social forces may assuredly be so styled. The idea of a world's text-book on Economics is therefore not absurd, though the principles which such a work could lay down would be few and general. Cairnes, Logical Meth., i.

⁶ Sidgwick, Principles, p. 22; Mill, bk. v, ch. xi, 7; Schmoller, *Grundfragen*, 47. Notice that the maxim is not announced as certainly valid for all past or possible states of society.

§ 16 Value of the Study

Laughlin, The Study of P. E. *Cumming*, Value of P. E. to Mankind, Cobden Club Prize Ess. for 1880. *Roscher*, Prelim. Ess. to English Tr. *Cossa*, 23. *Buckle*, Hist. of Civilization in Eng., vol. i, 150 sqq. TENNEMANN, *Gesch. d. Philos.*, 1, 30.

In fitness for place in an educational curriculum,[1] Economics perhaps surpasses all other studies, through the remarkable combination which it involves of **mental discipline** with practical **utility**.[2] Each of its propositions requires careful thought, while certain of its reasonings challenge the **highest** powers of **mind**.[3] On the other hand, though it is a science, not an art,[4] its truths touch every **human life**. Among a great deal else of obvious importance which acquaintance with Economics incidentally makes clear, may be mentioned : (i) the **fallacy** of many prevalent notions about **wealth**,[5] (ii) the **failure** and even positive **cruelty** of much intended **charity**,[6] (iii) the sure and widespread effects of **waste**,[7] (iv) the inevitable **interdependence** of individuals, classes, and nations, and (v) striking evidence of **intelligence** and beneficent **law** as reigning in the universe. A time comes in the history of every cultivated people, when social comfort, to say nothing of social progress, depends absolutely upon knowledge of economic principles. Europe is at this point already ; we shall soon be.

[1] Whether more *liberal* or more practical. It is perverse to limit science to exact science [§ 4, n. 1]. Equally so to suppose the best education attainable by drill in the exact sciences alone. That is important but often carried relatively too far. Not only do action, conduct, life, all lie in the domain of inexact science, making training in this indispensable to every educated person, but even looking from the point of view of an exclusively liberal education, it is a higher attainment, a finer feat of mind, to be expert in the inexact than in the exact sciences.

[2] The advantage of this, considering the study as a branch of liberal culture, lies in the zest it imparts. It is a help, too, that the pupil is sure to possess beforehand a certain familiarity with the subjects to be considered. This, however, in spite of the best instruction, sometimes breeds slovenly analysis and looseness of view. A kindred difficulty arises from the use in Economics of many ordinary words in a technical sense. Students suppose themselves thinking the correct thought because they attach a more or less definite meaning to the word. From the same cause is also most of the economic sciolism so common among persons not students at all, who yet discuss rent, profits, wages and whatever other topic is named by a familiar title, with all the assurance of an Adam Smith.

[3] As those upon money and foreign exchange. Not here alone but throughout the science the data have a peculiar mutual relativity which renders them elusive. The ποῦ στῶ is for many an argument difficult to fix. Premises can often be made definite only by a piece of abstraction which the course of reasoning shows to have been incorrect. We have then to amend them and rethink our work with scrutiny to see whether, and if so where and how far, the change has vitiated it. No other sort of exercise will test and develop the mind like this.

[4] As Adam Smith, in the main, conceived it. We investigate its facts not primarily to use them, but to know them. Yet their character lends a special interest to the work. Here at least it is not true, if it is or ever has been anywhere, that science cares, in the strictest sense, only for truth, regardless of truth's worth in life.

[5] In reference to its nature [§ 1, n. 3], and its importance to happiness and civilization. How many consider wars, fires, and floods as blessings because they 'make work.' Cf. n. 7, below. Read Bastiat's bright essay [*Œuvres*, vol. v, 336 sqq.] on That which is Seen and that which is Unseen. A writer in the Pop. Sci. Monthly for 1885, estimated the loss by fire in United States during 1884, at $160,000,000.

[6] Mill, bk. ii, chaps. xii, xiii. By misplaced alms, not only is wealth wasted which might have supported honest productive labor, whose product might in turn have gone to support labor in further production still, and so on indefinitely; but a vicious, lazy habit is engendered in the object.

[7] Could we prevent the waste from uneconomic housekeeping alone, the fund resulting would far more than suffice to feed all the hungry. "Whoever can teach the masses of the people how to get five cents' worth a day more comfort or force out of the food which each one consumes, will add to their productive power what would equal a thousand million dollars a year." See § 49.

§ 17 The Division of Economics

Cossa, pt. i, ch. ii. *Garnier*, *Traité*, 18-20.

Our science is most commonly presented under the four general heads of Production, Exchange, Distribution, and Consumption.[1] This arrangement is illogical, since all Exchange and an important part of Consumption are branches of Production. As, however, Production, exhibited so in its strict integrity, forms a most bulky topic, overshadowing the others and giving to the parts of the discussion a very unequal size, we may consult convenience along with logic, and lay out our matter as follows : Part I, **Production,** except as involving Exchange. Part II, **Exchange,** except as involving Money. Part III, **Money.** Part IV, **Distribution.** Part V, **Consumption.** Part VI, **Practical Topics** touching upon Economic Theory.

[1] So Wayland, F. A. Walker, Mangoldt and Garnier, exactly, also most other French writers [Leroy-Beaulieu, Levasseur], only placing Distribution before Exchange [*circulation*]. Roscher, too, has the order given in the text, save that he injects after Production as coördinate with the other four, a Part [ii] on Freedom and Property. Chapin's Wayland strangely alters the order to Production, Consumption, Distribution, and Exchange. M'Culloch, Principles of Pol. Econ., is exactly logical : Production, Distribution, Consumption. Mill and Fawcett both say Production, Distribution, Exchange. Laughlin and H. C. Adams have these same topics, but reverse the order of the last two. Senior divides into the Nature, Production and Distribution of Wealth. Cherbuliez has Production, Circulation, Distribution, treating Consumption as sub-topic of Production. Except in the last point Held agrees with him [*Production, Verkehr, Vertheilung*]. Quite original is Cohn's marshalling, into the *Elements,* the *Form-taking* [*Gestaltung*], and the *Processes,* of the Economic Life. With a similar motive, to emphasize the dynamic aspect of the science, F. H. Giddings suggests treating it under the rubrics of Descriptive Economics, and Economic Physics, Politics, Biology, Psychology, and Evolution. The purpose is a good one, but can, we believe, be carried out as logically, and, for the purposes of a treatise like the present, more profitably, by handling the material as the text proposes.

PART I

PRODUCTION
EXCEPT AS INVOLVING EXCHANGE

CHAPTER I

THE NATURE OF PRODUCTION

§ 18 VARIOUS VIEWS OF PRODUCTIVITY

Roscher, §§ 48-52. *Mill*, bk. i, ch. iii, § 3; *Essay* iii on Unsettled Questions. *Garnier*, *Traité*, ch. ii. *Ad. Smith*, bk. ii, ch. iii.

The **mercantilists** regarded industry productive only in proportion as it tended to swell the nation's stock of money. They deemed manufactures more productive than agriculture, their finer forms more than the coarser, active[1] and direct commerce more than passive and indirect. The **physiocrats** identified productive toil with the extraction of useful **raw material**, stigmatizing other occupations[2] as '**sterile**,' because sustained only by overplus gained through work upon the land. **Adam Smith** and **Mill** styled unproductive all exertion, however useful, not taking form in some useful **material object**, placing in the unproductive list in fact more callings[3] than their own definition required. Their classification has been followed by most writers of the **English School**. Not by the **French**,[4] who, even when disciples of Adam Smith, have usually reckoned as productive all labor imparting economic modifications to the **immaterial** nature of man. Roscher goes further still, and defines every sort of activity as productive which society is willing to **pay for**.[5] This is now the prevalent doctrine.

[1] Cf. § 7. "Active" commerce = preponderance of export = favorable balance of trade: "passive" = preponderance of import = unfavorable balance of trade [Roscher, § 48].

[2] Cf. § 9. They believed manufacturing to do nothing but change the form of things, whatever value it added being just the sum of the raw materials consumed by the laborers in the process of manufacture. Quesnay indeed saw that not all the new worth added by manufacturing could be so explained, but considered the rest the outcome of natural or legal monopoly. Trade too the physiocrats thought "sterile," merely passing wealth from one hand into the other. What merchants won was at cost of the nation. On all this, and the easy refutation of it, Roscher, § 49, and n. 2. These men supposed, as did so clear a head as Locke, that what one party to a trade gained the other must lose — a perfectly patent error [§ 20, n. 4]. Boisguillebert made clear the productiveness of exchange, by supposing three men bound to stakes one hundred paces apart, the first with a stock of victuals but naked, the second with a huge pile of fuel but no food, the third with a superfluity of clothing but no supply besides. Could they exchange, all three would be happy: as they cannot, all die.

[3] Not only the frivolous occupations of opera-singers and ballet-dancers, but the important ones of statesmen, judges, clergy, physicians, army and navy. I.e., violin-making productive, but violin-playing not, though the sole end in making the violin is that it may be played [Garnier]! Training of swine productive, educating men unproductive [List]! The churl who scares crows from cornfields productive, soldiers who bar out invading armies unproductive [M'Culloch]! Roscher, who cites the objections just given, notes that the Smithians have to own certain industries as productive though affecting material objects only indirectly, and that government officers, physicians and the like, certainly contribute at least indirectly to much material production.

[4] J. B. Say, Dunoyer, Garnier, Sismondi. The last speaks of government and army as "guardians, who *produce* security" [Garnier, p. 34]. Bastiat went so far as in effect to make all production immaterial, calling

commodities a form of services. J. B. Clark [Philos. of Wealth, ch. i] precisely reverses this, interpreting the essence of a *service* to be always of a material nature. The wealth which the orator produces in speaking, or the *prima donna* in singing, consists in the exhaled air vibrating so and so, etc.

⁵ See his § 52. "Every business whose service is *rationally* sought for and duly paid for." By inserting "rationally" he would hint at the mal-productiveness of lucrative trades which curse mankind. In 1853 there were said to be in France 3500 colporteurs of immoral literature and pictures, selling yearly nine million copies and getting for them six million francs [$1,200,000]. Such businesses are formally rather than really productive. "No *rational* labor is unproductive" [Garnier]. "The union of the word *labor* with the word unproductive is nonsense" [Rossi]. "The only labor that is really unproductive is that which fails to attain its purpose" [H. C. Adams].

§ 19 Wealth-Increment which is not Production
Mangoldt, Grundriss d. Volkswirtschaftslehre, §§ 12-15.

While the classes of entities making up wealth come by man's deliberate **exertion**, certain contributions to wealth are free.¹ Such may spring from: i Changes in the **objects** of wealth, as gratuitous abundance at harvest owing to propitious weather, or advance in landed or other wealth by the natural growth of a community.² ii Changes in the **subjects**³ of wealth, as the increase of their needs in compass, kind or intensity, larger knowledge of the means for supplying them, or fuller power to utilize these means. iii Changes of **relation** between the subjects and the objects of wealth, as by better laws or government,⁴ or progress of the community in morality.

¹ § 1, n. 2. This truth socialists ignore, a defect which vitiates Marx's "Capital" almost entirely. While wealth, speaking generally, originates in labor, the amount of wealth in a thing is usually a very inexact measure of the labor bestowed on it.

[2] The two cases are unlike. When a generous rain adds a million bushels to the wheat-yield for the year, no part of the gain is due to human agency. Rise in the amount of wealth embodied in its land and buildings by the growth of a city is a result of what men have done, yet one not consciously purposed. It therefore does not fall under our definition of wealth [§ 1]. In speaking of land value here we make no reference to the original properties of land, or to mere *place*, both of course gratuities and therefore conditions of wealth rather than wealth; but to improvements upon land. Obviously unearned increment may attach to these as well as to the uncreated, primordial qualities. It is natural to call the increment in the one case wealth, since it is an addition to wealth, and in the other for an analogous reason, condition of wealth.

[3] See Mangoldt, § 14. Human beings are of course meant. With advance of culture man experiences ever new need and comes upon ever new objects for its satisfaction, — both, in numberless cases, as in many inventions and discoveries, accidentally, without any purposive action of his own. The benign outcome of such new knowledge has sometimes very wide sweep. The discovery of spinning and weaving must have greatly enhanced the value of sheep, wool, and all fibre-producing plants. As acquaintance with the earth and its products increases, insight into the useful properties of things and into ways for using them becomes increasingly a matter of study, so that discoveries occur more from purpose. Then the search, if successful, is genuine production.

[4] Making *ownership* a surer thing. But so far as the betterment in law or administration proceeds from economic motive, more and more the case as governments grow better, the generation of new value thereby is out and out production.

§ 20 PRODUCTION

Mongredien, Wealth-Creation. *Roscher*, § 30. *Mangoldt*, as at § 18. *Mill*, bk. i, ch. 1.

Production consists not in the creation of new material, a deed beyond finite power, but in the origination by conscious human act,[1] of wealth or of direct gratifications such as commonly proceed from wealth. We originate wealth by so **shaping, combining** or **placing** given elements or forces of the universe or of man's nature as to bring forth, impart or increase **util-**

ity. Immaterial wealth is produced by the development or training of **intellectual** power, skill, sleight, or habit, or by putting human beings into new **relations** [1] one to another. Material wealth is produced, (i) by '**occupying**'[2] spontaneous natural elements or products, (ii) by **extracting** minerals from the earth, (iii) by **growing** vegetable or animal products through use of nature's forces, (iv) by **transporting** things from place to place, (v) by **changing** their mechanical or chemical forms,[3] or (vi) by **exchanging** them between different owners.[4] All **prevention** of decrease or destruction, in wealth may be called **negative production.**[5]

[1] See § 1, and its n. 3. "Relations" here means not only those referred to by this word in § 1, but also the "influences" had in mind there; these last too being relations, though of a peculiar kind. On relations as wealth, see the art. "Copyright," in Lalor.

[2] Appropriating, that is. For this nice sense of *occupare* see § 3, n. 3. Hunting, trapping, gathering wild fruits, and the like, taking water gratis from springs or streams and purveying it to people in towns at a price, would illustrate.

[3] Mechanical, cloth-making; chemical, soap-making. The pupil can multiply examples.

[4] One man owns a dray-horse but needs a roadster; another needs a dray-horse but owns a roadster. They exchange and both are richer. So is the world. This and the case of production by transportation excellently bring out the essential idea. Roscher refers to the ice trade between Boston and the W. Indies. So early as 1843 55,000 tons were sent. Uncut it cost 25 cents a ton, packed in the ship, $2.55, and brought at destination over $65 a ton, an advance of more than $3,561,250, — almost entirely due to transportation alone. Carloads upon carloads of hides go from N. Y. city to Chattanooga to be tanned and returned as leather. In the latter case travel is not the cause of the added value but the condition, it being necessary in order to utilize the excellent tanning properties of the chestnut burr oak of Tennessee [Atkinson].

[5] No inconsiderable part of the work of clergy, judges, army and police. Legitimate speculation falls here [§ 21, n. 7. Cf. Mangoldt, § 37]. Pro-

duction is not negative simply because [like washing clothes] it begets no new thing or form, or because it simply does away with obstacles. In this last, strictly, all production consists [Cannan, Elementary P. E., 7, 8].

§ 21. SPECIAL REMARKS ON PRODUCTION

Roscher, § 50. *Garnier*, ch. ii. *Cannan*, Elementary P. E., pp. 9 sq. *Clark*, Philos. of Wealth, ch. i. *Mangoldt*, § 26.

i The dignity of production is not determined by either the duration,[1] or the dispensableness[2] of the product, but by its total and final effect upon the nature of man.[3] ii The real product in activities like oratory, music, and teaching is either a temporary gratification or a more or less permanent addition to immaterial wealth,[4] the tones and words being instrumental only. iii 'Directly and indirectly productive' is a purely relative distinction, as every productive process has the one or the other phase according to your point of view. The policeman produces security directly, the hatter hats; while each's work indirectly helps into existence the other's product. So in all cases.[5] iv Distinguish 1) technical or formal production, which neither increases nor diminishes wealth whether general or private,[6] 2) production which adds to private wealth only and perhaps detracts from general,[7] and 3) that which at first and visibly swells general wealth alone, advancing individuals' possessions merely in the ways all public benefits[8] do. v Inasmuch as national and cosmic wealth, like private and general, are partially susceptible of antagonism, 'we should denominate as absolutely productive only such industries as promote the wealth of mankind.'[9] vi There can be no such thing as general overproduction, viz., an all-round glut of products, because the desires of men, intrinsically satisfiable economically, are unlimited in number, indefinite in degree, and forever increasing.[10]

[1] Bread may last two days, lace two centuries, yet bread-making is, if we distinguish at all, the higher service. Roscher observes that labor upon *persons* and *relations*, though in compass and duration less mensurable than other, is apt to rank highest in power to multiply and propagate itself.

[2] We could get along without music or works of art better than without cloth, but real civilization demands both. Roscher justly rebukes the habit of regarding any general department of industry more honorable than another on this score. Agriculture gives us tobacco, from manufacture come playing-cards, from commerce rum, while " among *services* belong the indispensable ones of educator and judge, as well as the dispensable ones of rope-dancer and bear-exhibitor." Cf. Knies, *Dienstleistungen d. Soldaten.*

[3] Often to be ascertained only by extra-economic inquiry, in æsthetics and ethics.

[4] In agreement with Garnier and Dunoyer, and against J. B. Say, who considered [in case of a teacher] the lecture the product. For Clark's notion, see § 18, n. 4. He will not term any property of man economic product [wealth], lest we confound wealth-creating abilities with the product resulting from the exercise of them. But no confusion need arise by naming both wealth, any more than by applying this term to a machine, which is at once wealth and wealth-producer [capital]. Exactly how we define here is however not a vital point.

[5] Thus a wagon is now used for pleasure, again to transport goods, and a meadow serves partly for beauty, partly to grow grass.

[6] Making things which do no one any good.

[7] Like the business specified at § 18, n. 5. Cf. above, n. 3. To this add the general manufacture and sale of liquors, very profitable trades to most engaged in them, 99 per cent of whose effect, however, is a palpable impoverishment to the community, i) withdrawing capital and labor from admittedly productive channels, ii) diminishing men's productiveness, partly day by day, partly by shortening life, iii) vastly increasing public expenses by multiplying paupers and criminals, iv) breaking down characters and swelling the misery of human life. This is not denouncing the existence of intoxicants or declaring the use of them never justifiable. Gambling at best ministers only to private wealth. Every cent which A gains, comes from B or C. Worse than this, the habit breeds a temper

most deleterious to thrift and industry. Gambling in stocks, wheat, cotton, etc., is precisely as condemnable economically as faro or bluff. Not so speculation with genuine intention to transfer the goods. This tends to steady prices and hence is negatively productive [§ 20, end]. Betting on futures, which a vast amount of speculation in the various exchanges essentially is, does not have this tendency but just the reverse.

[8] Many, not to say most, new railroads have caused loss to their first owners; few if any of them have failed to benefit their localities. Good public works require taxes, but more than repay these, being a blessing to every citizen, whether enhancing the selling value of estates [the usual result] or not.

[9] Roscher. A nation may enrich itself at the expense of the world, as I at the cost of my neighborhood. This not necessarily by arms, nor even by its own act at all. Great Britain has for years had cheap sugar partly as a gift at the cost of the continental states, through the operation of their sugar bounties. Cf. § 36, n. 7.

[10] George, Soc. Problems, 90, 164 sqq. Cannan, § 1, Perry, 126 sqq. Mill, bk. i, ch. v, § 3: "The limit of wealth is never deficiency of consumers, but of producers and productive power." This truth is against writers like Malthus, Chalmers, and Sismondi, who have alleged unproductive consumption to be a good, without which wealth would accumulate beyond needs and run to waste. Crocker, in Quar. Jour. Econ., vol. i, 362 sqq., essays to show the same. He of course fails, not seeing that to prove actual over-production in many departments — which is easy — is far from proving *general* over-production.

§ 22 The Conditions of Production

Garnier, ch. ii, IV. *Roscher*, bk. i. *Mangoldt*, bk. ii, ch. ii. *Mill*, bk. i, ch. i.

These may be grouped in three classes, as follows : i The **absolute**, without which **no production** whatever could occur. They are **Nature** and **Labor**, and their formula, *sine, non*. ii The **relatively absolute**, in whose absence production, possible indeed to a very limited extent, must ever be too **meagre** to result in civilization. These are **Capital** and **Social Organization**, and the formula for them is *sine, minimum*. iii The **rela-**

tive, all those circumstances, too many to enumerate, whose presence in **greater** or **less** degree makes production abundant in proportionally greater or less degree The formula for these is *quanto plus, tanto plus.*

CHAPTER II

THE ABSOLUTE CONDITIONS OF PRODUCTION

NATURE — LABOR

§ 23 THE MATERIALS OF NATURE

Roscher, §§ 31-37. *Mangoldt*, §§ 19, 20. *Leroy-Beaulieu, Précis,* pt. i, ch. i. *Schoenberg, Handbuch,* vol. i, 194 sq.

These are nature's[1] passive contribution to production, the stuff and basis with which the process begins. They are important according to: i Their abundance and distribution.[2] ii The number and intensity of the needs which they serve and the perfection of such service.[3] iii The expense in labor and capital of rendering them available.[4] iv The durability of their products.[5] Of these materials some are wholly appropriable,[6] some partially so, some not at all. Those equally appropriable, in any given degree, are appropriated the more fully the better their value becomes known, the fewer they are in proportion to the need for them, and the more the use of them presupposes exclusive possession.[7]

---

[1] Human nature included. "Materials" here not = "matter"; hence one may speak of immaterial materials. All nature is meant so far as its static aspect extends [§ 24, n. 1], the subject for all known forces, the groundwork for all the phenomena of the world. But for the peculiar original endowment of man as distinguished from the brute, production would be little more than the passive reception of nature's gifts. Brutes do not to any extent utilize [external] nature to exploit nature. The use

THE ABSOLUTE CONDITIONS OF PRODUCTION 41

of a stone by a monkey to break a cocoanut is referred to as a wonder. So the bird's nest, the beaver's dam and the squirrel's supply for winter.

² Iron will illustrate. Were it with all its valuable properties as scarce as jade-stone, or plentiful, yet only at a few mines, it could not possess the same significance for the world's work as now. The world's production of iron in 1882 amounted to 9 million metric tons, in 1885 to 7¼ million. That of steel was in 1882 6½ million, in 1885 about 6 million. That of coal was in 1882, 377,707,000, in 1884 375 million [Neumann-Spallart, *Uebersichten d. Weltwirtschaft*].

³ So coal is of more consequence than nickel, or even gold. Wood could be used for nearly all the services which coal performs, but many of them it would not render as well.

⁴ Distant or deep mines or quarries, compared with those close by and near the surface. Magnificent timber may grow so far away or so high up mountains as to have little worth. A marsh may be potentially the best land in all its vicinity, yet in fact good for nothing because of the cost of draining. The bronze age in pre-historic times preceded the iron age for the reason that bronze, though a compound [then of about nine parts copper to one of tin] could be extracted and fused much more easily than iron. On 'labor' and 'capital' see the following §§.

⁵ Ledges of granite, other things being equal, are far more a treasure than those of marble; these more than those of ordinary sandstone. Iron is for the same reason giving way in many directions to steel, and wood to iron.

⁶ As land, with its birds, animals, timber, mines and quarries, most of its waterfalls and many of its waters. The edge of the ocean is appropriated, by nations to the distance of three miles seaward, and, by the individuals owning adjacent land, so far out as it is available for any useful purpose [oyster-beds, *e.g.*]. Open ocean, tides, air, climate and sunlight cannot be subjected to ownership. Roscher makes the possibility or impossibility of this the basis for his classification, perhaps a more natural one than Mangoldt's, which the text follows.

⁷ It was for the last two reasons that the products of the land were made private property earlier than land itself, and the movable ones earliest of all.

§ 24 THE FORCES OF NATURE

Mangoldt, § 21. *Roscher* and *Schoenberg*, as at last §.

In these nature aids production actively.[1] They vary in importance, according to abundance, availability and necessity,[2] much as the materials do, the most noteworthy special circumstances being a) their kinds and degrees,[3] b) their stability and regularity,[4] and c) their transportability.[5] For economic purposes the forces of nature are conveniently classed, sometimes (i) as **organic**[6] and **inorganic**, the former partly psychical and partly physiological, the latter partly mechanical, partly chemical; sometimes (ii) as **spontaneous**, needing only to be **applied** and **directed** by man, and **non-spontaneous**, requiring first to be **developed**[7] as well; and sometimes (iii) as **inappropriable**, because characterizing whole districts or lands,[8] and **appropriable**, as properties, now of fixed, now of movable objects.

---

[1] Whether or not matter is at bottom anything but force, Economics has no need to inquire. Nature in her dynamic aspect [§ 23, n. 1] is here our theme. Some of the items referred to in §§ 23, 24 connect themselves about as well with the one phase of nature as with the other. Mangoldt mentions mineral treasures and land-fertility under "forces."

[2] See § 23. As to availability we may recall that the arc principle of electric lighting was known so early as Sir Humphry Davy's experiments in 1813, but no method of generating electricity cheaply enough to make the discovery valuable was invented till about 1878, in Brush's dynamo. The incandescent principle too was understood for years previous to the application of it by Edison, which made it a commercial success. Nearly every one of men's most precious insights into nature has thus lain sterile for a longer or a shorter time.

[3] Many merely do what men could at some rate do, others, the same in kind, transcend in degree the utmost reach of human energy. Nature's

chemical forces, as also the propensities and many of the powers of brutes, are intrinsically unlike any which unaided man could supply.

⁴ A brook's value as a water-power is greatly lessened if it habitually dries up in summer. Wind sometimes drives sailing vessels faster than steamers can go, but it is not to be depended on. Hence windmills are used only for irregular work or where trustier motors fail or are very costly.

⁵ Water-power has to be used *in situ*. Coal can be carried far, though with difficulty and expense. Suppose it were but a hundredth as heavy or bulky as it is! It is estimated that could the power of Niagara be transported thither it would furnish all the light, heat and power needed by New York City. This may one day come to pass by turning the force into electricity, carrying it either stored or by means of conductors, and reconverting it as needed.

⁶ Belonging to human beings, lower animals, plants. Among the physiological do not overlook the reproductive forces of animals and plants, on which the evolution of varieties depends.

⁷ This difference well illustrated by a water or a wind mill on the one hand and a steam mill on the other. As civilization and man's mastery of nature go forward, the spontaneous forces lose in relative importance and the developed ones gain.

⁸ Winds, tides, navigable streams, the sun's heat and light.

§ 25 Labor: its Necessity

Mill, bk. i, ch. i. *M'Culloch*, pt. ii, ch. i. *Garnier*, ch. iii. *Clark*, Philos. of Wealth, ch. ii. *Schoenberg*, vol. i, 196 sqq. *Robinson*, Thoughts on W. and its Sources.

Labor is the **exertion**[1] of **human** beings directed toward productive or **economic** ends. It consists in 'the action of spirit on itself and on matter,'[2] always involving an **intellectual** as well as a **physical** element. Labor is equally with nature a **fundamental**[3] requisite to wealth. But for it 'mankind would necessarily perish off the face of the globe even if all soils were fertile and all climates temperate.'[4] On the other hand it is, however important, a **means only**,[5] not an end.

[1] Sometimes it is said to be the 'voluntary' exertion, etc., this word being added to exclude slaves' work. But it is far more natural to call

this labor than to rank it with the energizing of brutes. Labor is exertion, "and it is necessary to include in the idea not only the exertion itself but all feelings of a disagreeable kind, all bodily inconvenience or mental annoyance connected with the employment" [Mill]. Not all human activity is labor. Activity may have merely the aim of enjoyment. Yet sport engaged in with the express aim of rendering one's self efficient in labor might itself be classed as labor.

[2] Roscher. So J. B. Clark: "To a large and controlling extent the mental element is present in the simplest operations. With the laborer who shovels in the gravel-pit the directing and controlling influence of the mind predominates to an indefinite extent over the simple foot-pounds of mechanical force which he exerts." On the other hand no labor is purely mental. Pen, tongue, or at least brain must be employed in every kind. Mill, after Bacon, rightly resolves all physical labor into an impartation of motion to some portion of matter.

[3] More truly so than capital, as we shall see.

[4] Cannan.

[5] This to warn against such common vagaries as that whatever 'makes work' must be a blessing and whatever lessens it a bane. Conflagrations make work: machines and inventions save work.

§ 26 Its Forms

Mill, bk. i, ch. ii. *Roscher*, § 38. *Cohn*, 290–298. *Clark*, as at § 25. *Held, Grundriss*, § 5.

The chief forms assumed by labor are[1]: i **Invention and discovery.** ii **Getting in possession** nature's spontaneous gifts, either by mere **occupation** or by **extraction.** iii **Creating** raw materials by the manipulation of nature's forces, as in agriculture and stock-rearing. iv **Manufacturing** the crude effects of ii and iii into higher forms. v **Distributing** things already formally produced. vi **Exchanging** the same. vii Imparting **instruction.** viii Securing **protection.** ix **Directing** the labor of others. x Making **laws.**

[1] The classification is nearly that of Roscher, as above, only dividing his one class of "services" into our vii, viii and x, and inserting ix, which

he omits. We shall find that the function of the *entrepreneur*, contractor, undertaker, or middle-man is at bottom but a species of labor. Clark's arrangement of labor-products in four classes: elementary utilities, form utilities, place utilities, and time utilities, is good as far as it goes, but is meant to allow for material wealth alone. With this § cf. § 20.

§ 27 Its Relation to Nature

Mill, bk. i, ch. i, § 3.   *Leroy-Beaulieu, Précis*, pt. i, chaps. i, ii.   *Roscher*, § 37.

In **no form** of production can one of these factors be strictly pronounced **more important** than the other, since each is absolutely indispensable.[1] Yet if **measured by bulk** different products display the presence of the two ingredients in very various degrees,[2] the general[3] rule being that the labor-element in wares predominates in proportion to removal from their crude state. Intellectual wealth too is built up with less or greater labor according to richness of native endowment in its subject. Nor if **measured in dollars' worths** do equal amounts of the different species of wealth embody labor equally,[4] though the correspondence is in this case much closer.

[1] "The part which nature has in any work of man is indefinite and incommensurable. It is impossible to decide that in any one thing nature does more than in any other. One cannot even say that labor does less. Less labor may be required, but if that which is required is absolutely indispensable, the result is just as much the product of labor as of nature" [Mill]. He adds that when two conditions are thus equally necessary to a result, the endeavor to fix their relative proportions of contribution is like attempting to decide which blade of a pair of scissors is the more efficient; or whether 5 or 6 is the main factor in their product, 30. On the impossibility of ascertaining with any exactness the mass of labor which has entered into any commodity, Mill, bk. i, ch. ii, § 1.

[2] A ton of steel and a ton of needles or of watches. The average production of the Torrid Zone, taken bulk-wise, contains far less labor than that of the North Temperate.

³ General, not by any means universal, since mere occupation is sometimes, as in the case of diamonds, an affair of much labor. A buffalo robe stands for several times more labor now than in 1850. The extraction of ores often requires the finest appliances of mechanic art, to be had and used only at immense outlay. Of different petroleum wells, costing each the same amount to bore and work, one has been known to yield, for a considerable period, oil 2000 times beyond the average product of other wells which were still pumped with more or less profit.

⁴ This against the labor-value fallacy of Adam Smith, Marx and the socialists generally. Cf. Mill, as cited in n. 1, above. The dollar measure is of course the same as that of exchange value. The correspondence to amounts of labor would be no more perfect were goods to be rated according to their degrees of *utility*, or according to their *values proper* [onerously created utilities: § 1, n. 6].

CHAPTER III

THE RELATIVELY ABSOLUTE CONDITIONS OF PRODUCTION

CAPITAL — SOCIAL ORGANIZATION

§ 28 CAPITAL DEFINED

Ad. Smith, bk. ii. *Mill*, bk. i, ch. iv. *Marshall*, Economics of Industry, bk. i, ch. iii. *Roscher*, § 42. *Sidgwick*, p. 143. *Clark*, Cap. and its Earnings, Papers of Am. Ec. Ass., vol. iii. *Leroy-Beaulieu*, pt. i, ch. iii. *Cossa, Saggi di Economia Politica*, pt. iii, 1. *Supino, Il Capitale nell' Organismo Economico. Schoenberg*, vol. i, 206 sqq. *Knies, Geld*, I. *Böhm-Bawerk, Kapital u. Kap.-zins.*

Capital[1] is the name of all products, material or immaterial, which are engaged in or devoted to[2] the mission of helping labor to create further products. It is thus one great department of wealth. Sharply to be distinguished from it are, (i) **non-capital wealth**, viz., the portion of wealth destined for immediate consumption, and (ii) property which is **not wealth** at all but a condition of wealth, like land[3] apart from improvements thereon, and the original endowments of slaves. The boundary between capital and other wealth often wavers and is sometimes untraceable, an article's place on this or that side of the line frequently depending on the owner's **varying intention**, and many things being used **now for gain, now for pleasure**.

[1] There have been and still are many different conceptions of capital: i The classical, mediæval and mercantilist, making it the same that is now called " principal," as opposed to interest, — in Greek, κεφάλαιον; in Latin, *caput*, or *capitalis pars debiti*. ii The physiocratic, by which capital

means massed, reserved or stored material products of any kind [not money alone], whatever their destination. Knies still defines thus. iii The modern, taking it to include all means of production whatever their origin, *i.e.*, land as well as capital. iv The most modern: capital consisting only of produced means of production, land excluded therefore, and regard had to both origin and end. iii and iv afford each a still further division according as capital is thought of as material only or as in part immaterial also. The text gives iv in its second phase. H. George's definition [Prog. and Poverty, bk. i, ch. ii, end], capital = wealth in course of exchange, is practically equivalent to iv in its first phase.

² Products may be 'devoted to' further production yet temporarily idle, as in a factory or foundry during hard times. Such property may be called 'dead capital,' and in this sense alone is capital usually styled 'dead.' But 'dead' would not be an inapt appellation for it when only technically productive [§ 21, n. 4]. Capital is by no means dead simply because passive and inert like an instrument, instead of living and growing like animals and trees, though this distinction is worthy of notice [Prog. and Pov., 162 sqq. Cf. Bastiat's fable of the plane, in his pamph. on *Capital et Rente, Œuvres*, vol. v, 43 sqq.]. Things made for sale but which no one wants are not capital at all: nor, as a rule, are they even wealth, but waste rather. H. George [bk. iii, ch. iv] speaks of 'spurious' capital, meaning partly values, like land, that are miscalled capital, partly those employed, as in gambling, productively perhaps for A or B but not for society.

³ For ruling out land [proper], see H. George, Social Problems, 183 sq., Prog. and Pov., bk. iii, ch. iv; also Cossa, as above, 162.

§ 29 Kinds of Capital

Roscher, § 42. *Ad. Smith*, bk. ii. *Schoenberg*, vol. i, 212 sqq.

Roscher has well classified the various forms of capital as follows: i Improvements upon **land.** ii **Buildings,** streets and roads. iii **Tools,** instruments and machines.[1] iv Useful domestic **animals.** v Materials for **manufacture** which will **reappear** visibly in the product.[2] vi Materials to aid manufacture which will **not** thus **reappear.**[3] vii **Food and clothing** for the support of laborers while they labor. viii **Stocks of goods** for sale.

ix **Money**. x **Incorporeal** or immaterial capital. To this list we have only to add **weapons** and means of **transportation**. Capital is often conveniently classified more briefly, as a) **materials** to work up, b) **tools**[4] to work with, and c) **subsistence**.[5] Very important is the distinction between **free** and **specialized**[6] capital, and still more so that between **fixed** and **circulating**.[7]

[1] An *instrument* is passive in nature, a *tool* [perhaps from same root as 'do'] active. A saw-buck is an instrument, a saw a tool. When an extra-human force is joined to either or to the two combined we have a machine. Historically such motors have been applied in the order of i brute strength, ii water, iii wind, iv steam, v electricity. For pulverizing grain, hammers were first used, then, in order, hand-mills, ass-power mills [Matthew 18, 6], water-mills [which Roscher dates from Cicero's time], wind-mills [from 9th century] and steam-mills [since 1782].

[2] As wool, cotton, flax, and coloring matters in cloth, leather in shoes, etc., also all sorts of ornamentation.

[3] As coal, bleaching material, lubricants.

[4] Here taken in the largest sense, including machinery and buildings.

[5] Clothing and houses as well as food being meant.

[6] According as it is not or is so bound up with a given kind of production as to be applied to another only with much difficulty and loss. Destruction of the free variety is dollar for dollar more disastrous than that of the specialized. Cf. H. C. Adams, Outline, §§ 18, 19.

[7] Capital which, *e.g.*, mills, machinery, etc., exists a considerable time in any one relatively permanent form, aiding repeated processes of production, belongs in the former category; that which fulfils its entire function as capital of a given kind [changes its nature: is used up] in a single process of production, comes under the latter. Raw material and all goods kept for sale well illustrate circulating capital. A grindstone lying in a hardware store is circulating; revolving in a shop, fixed. So of all machinery. Money is fixed capital for society, circulating for the individual. This distinction is relative, as no capital is absolutely 'fixed.' Even money wears out : *namque in ipso usu adsidua permutatione quodammodo extinguitur* [Instt. of Justinian, II, 4]. The proportion of fixed to circulating capital in any community increases with the advance of civilization.

§ 30 The Place of Capital in Production

Marshall, as at § 28. *Mill*, bk. i, ch. v. *George*, Prog. and Pov., bk. i, ch. v. *Cairnes*, Leading Principles, 164 sqq. *Senior*, Pol. Ec., 58 sqq.

The following propositions touching capital are **fundamental** and of first importance : i All capital is the **result of labor** and secondary thereto,[1] and all material capital the fruit of **abstinence**[2] and **economy**. ii On the other hand all labor is **dependent** for its **efficiency** on capital.[1] iii The real **support** of labor consists in the **capital** which it employs and not in **demand** for the commodities or services it yields.[3] iv Material capital is a **good** only as it ministers to **consumption**,[4] and it is itself destined to be **consumed**.[5]

---

[1] Sir William Hamilton's elucidation of the intimate relations between speech and language, by citing the operation of tunnelling through a sandbank, is to our point here. As the digging must precede the shoring of plank or brick, yet can only just precede, and as thought must exist in advance of speech but only be a little in advance, so labor is the absolute *prius* of capital, and still totally dependent upon capital for any considerable development.

[2] A function quite distinct from labor, and very important. See Senior, as above. This subject will emerge again when we discuss Interest, in Part IV. Cf., too, § 46.

[3] Mill, bk. i, ch. v, § 9, needlessly obscures this important truth, yet is clearer than Laughlin, who, in his edition, has substituted his own for Mill's exposition. The idea is simply that no matter how great the demand for a commodity, unless it were of an extremely simple order, labor would not be encouraged to attempt the production of it so long as no one willed to supply capital to aid. Any increase to the stock of [non-specialized] capital increases the demand for labor, and [barring increase in number of laborers] elevates the level of wages. On the contrary, any such application of wealth as merely to act on demand and not to swell the stock of capital, robs labor of so much support. Demand alone, however, [efficient demand is of course meant, i.e., *wish* backed by money] *is* competent to

change the *direction*, the department, in which labor shall apply itself. It might conceivably, by some peculiar concourse of circumstances, set capital free in such a way as to render it more serviceable than in its previous form, thus, without being increased at all, actually furthering the interests of labor. Fresh production of capital will *result*, but only as a *consequence* of the encouragement given to labor. Thus, suppose $1000 are spent for liquors, and the money placed by the liquor-dealer in the bank, whence of course it is at once loaned out to aid industry and so labor. Mill ignores this possibility. It would confessedly be better still for labor had the money been applied in the first instance as supply instead of as demand, which is all that Mill shows. But if his statement is not valid quite as unqualifiedly as he supposed, this fact detracts not a whit from its importance. The *law* is as he declares. Nor does this admission bind us to accept his theory of wages [see Wages, in Part IV].

⁴ Not that consumption *in se* is a good. It is only a means to a good, viz., the gratification lying beyond. But as it is an indispensable means, men being constituted with needs which only economic consumption can supply, production becomes worthful for consumption's sake. Could the end be reached without consumption, the latter would at once cease. A machine which could do its work and never wear out, would be a prize. Hence the search for perpetual motors. Hence, too, the more fruitful quest for instruments which will do given amounts of work with the least motive power and friction.

⁵ Why, then, is it so valuable? the pupil might at first ask. If it must return to nothing, why call it into being in the first place? Because capital, though perishable, is still indispensable. If it perished twice as fast, were we forced to spend double the time we now do in replacing it, we should have no choice but to toil for it as at present. Material capital more than pays for itself during its brief life, and besides may be so consumed as to reproduce itself, and more. Thus individuals die, but the race lives and spreads. Far the greater part of the capital at any moment existing is less than a year old. Almost trifling in quantity is that which is over ten. But the entire bulk of capital in man's possession now was aided into being by that long since consumed. Every nail in England can be traced back, directly or indirectly, to savings made before the Norman Conquest [Senior].

§ 31 Society

Clark, Philos. of Wealth, ch. iii. *Weeden*, Social Law of Labor, Int. *Bastiat*, Harmonies, ch. i [*Œuvres*, vol. vi, 24 sqq.]. *Spencer*, Principles of Sociology, pt. ii, ch. ii. *Villey*, *Rôle de l'état dans l'ordre écon.*

To be in the least degree **copious**, production requires the existence of **society**. Man is by nature a **social being**.[1] The individual of himself does **not** form a **totality**. Society must **complement** him. Except as parcel and facet of the social body he can be nothing but a **fragment**. Now society is an **organism**, its units so **vitally related** that, as in a tree[2] or in the animal frame, each is both **end** and **means**, at once **serves** and **is served** by all the rest. Not only are the productive powers of the individual as such **incapable of development** without a **human environment**,[3] but even if developed they would be **useless**, having no **scope** for action.[4] Social **organization**, the interplay of **supply and demand**, the right mutual **relations** between **producers** and **consumers** would be needed.

---

[1] A "political animal," as Aristotle calls him. Genesis, II, 18: "not good for man to be alone," has the same meaning. It does not refer to marriage simply.

[2] "The rootlet of a tree shares with the remote leaf the nutriment which it absorbs from the earth, and the leaf shares with the rootlet that which it gathers from the sunlight and the air. This universal interdependence of parts is a primary characteristic of social organisms; each member exists and labors, not for himself but for the whole, and is dependent on the whole for remuneration. The individual man, like the rootlet, produces something, puts it into the circulating system of the organism, and gets from thence that which his being and growth require." Clark, as above, 38 sq. Cf. *ante*, §§ 12, 13, 15, and notes.

[3] This side of the truth Bastiat in his fine discussion overlooks, as do all the writers, like Adam Smith and his disciples, whose notion of society

came from eighteenth century liberalism. They have been too apt to conceive the individual man as complete in himself, and society as a mere aggregation of such individuals, sustaining to one another, indeed, relations the most complicated, but not organic [§ 15, n. 1]. Rousseau's "Social Contract" is the classic for this theory of society.

⁴ Bastiat, as above, computes that through social co-operation and the consequent amassing of wealth, one man may by his own efforts enjoy now more satisfactions than he could earn in ten centuries were he obliged to begin and work without such aid. "If the causes of a man's economic weal or misery once lay in what he himself did, now they are to be found as well in what is done and experienced by those a) for whom he produces, b) whose products he desires, c) who produce for others in the same line as he, and d) desire from others the same product as he" [Knies, *Pol. Oek.*, 164 sq. Cf. Ely, Past and Pres. of P. E., p. 50]. Take an operative in A's cotton factory, earning $1.50 per diem. That wage is conditioned upon the existence of: i The factory, with its owner and his capital. ii Builders of factories and machinery, with their respective plants and groups of workmen, insuring to A the possibility of repairing or replacing his plant were it injured by fire, storm or earthquake, — each man in all these groups being bound in the same mesh-work of relationships as the operative in question. iii Men working southern cotton-fields, every one dependent in this same way. iv People similarly circumstanced engaged in the manufacture of implements for cotton-raising. v Still others, so circumstanced, building and running steamboats and railways to transport the various wares mentioned. vi Human beings in all lands who wish cotton fabrics and have means to buy them. vii Morality, customs and laws, making possessions and traffic secure. viii Teachers, writers, legislators, judges, police and army, giving sustenance to vii, each enabled to fill his place only by a complex congeries of action and reaction like this which we are tracing.

§ 32 THE STATE

Wagner, Lehrb. d. Pol. Oek., § 161. *James, et al.*, in Science Economic Discussion, 26–43. *Schoenberg*, vol. i, 197, 255 sqq. *Spencer*, Prin. of Sociology, pt. v.

Every separate permanent human community spontaneously[1] assumes more or less **authority** over its members, forcing each, within certain limits, to obey the **collective will.** This is **inevitable.** Such authority always has been exercised, and **always will be,**[2] however high a degree of moral, political or economic advancement may be reached. In its character as asserting and exercising this eminent domain society becomes **the state.** Society is in principle no less **indispensable** economically in this aspect than in that of an organism merely. Not alone **anarchy** but the slightest real insecurity to life or property will **paralyze production.** Even among the best-meaning citizens there must be some **authoritative tribunal** to settle honest disputes. Besides, nearly all peoples have **vital interests** of a purely **economic** nature which only the **state** can administer.[3]

[1] We see this from what occurs in mining camps and caravans, and among pirates. Government does not originate in contract any more than life does, though a particular *form* of polity may thus arise.

[2] Contrary to the belief of the anarchists, who expect to take out of government the whole element of authority, reducing it to mere administration [§ 14, n. 1]. This cannot be. It is not the wickedness of men, which may in time abate, but the permanent finiteness of their knowledge, that renders anarchy impossible of realization.

[3] See § 15, n. 2; § 36, n. 7. Cf. Villey, as at § 31. Thus, England never had an efficient express system till Fawcett, as Post-Master General, introduced the Parcels Post. Then all the railways took up the business and accommodations of this sort became good.

CHAPTER IV

THE RELATIVE CONDITIONS OF PRODUCTION

§ 33   General View

Mill, bk. i, chaps. vii–xiii. *Mangoldt*, pp. 20–44. *Garnier*, pt. ii, sec. iii. *Cannan*, §§ 5 sqq. *Held*, p. 48. *Schoenberg*, vol. i, 198–262. *Roscher*, 103–209. *Ad. Smith*, bk. i, ch. i. *Cossa, Elementi*, sec. ii, ch. iv. *Bagehot*, Ec. Studies, vi.

All four of the preceding conditions being given the production of wealth will ensue, but will be **more or less abundant** according to a multitude of **further circumstances**. The chief of these are now to be discussed. They include whatever **increases** the **amount** or the **efficiency** of either **capital** or **labor**, viz., those things[1] which somehow (i) promote man's **power** to save wealth, (ii) quicken his **will** to do the same, (iii) prompt the **determination** to **labor**, (iv) better the **quality** of labor, (v) strengthen the **labor-force** of the country or countries in question, or (vi) enable men to **make the most** out of a **given amount** of labor. The progress will take place through such an application of the **free capital and labor** available from time to time, as shall not only **make good** all **consumption** involved but also create a **surplus**.[2] This may occur in either of three ways: 1 **Increase** of **product** without proportional increase of expense. 2 **Diminution** of **expense** without proportional diminution of product. 3 Increase of product **along with** diminution in expense. The **result**, like the **aim**, will be a continual **reduction** on the whole,[3] in the amount of human **toil** necessary for a unit of product. Human needs being expansive, however, and the utmost possible supply to them limited, labor can never become unnecessary, nor decrease in absolute quantity, but only relatively to product.

[1] The power to save depends on good government, industrial liberty, thrift, etc.; the will to labor or to save, on morality, freedom, private property, culture, high rate of interest, and the like; the labor force, on numbers, favorable climate, health, strength; the quality of labor, on such considerations as intelligence, education, and practice. Chief aids to the ability to make most out of a given amount of labor are **machinery and the organization of labor.** See on all this §§ 35 sqq.

[2] Sir William Petty, Political Arithmetic, ch. i, names this process of progressive increase to wealth, 'superlucration' — not a bad term.

[3] 'On the whole,' because although, as pointed out in § 34, agriculture and mining follow another law, the disadvantage thus arising bids fair to be offset for an indefinite time to come by the greater and greater cheapness of manufactured articles.

§ 34 Diminishing Return and Increasing Return

Marshall, bk. i, ch. iv. *Sidgwick*, 151 sqq. *Walker*, Wages, 89 sqq. *Cairnes*, Log. Meth., 50, 51, n. *H. C. Adams*, Principles to Control State Interf. in Industries.

The **general** rule of growth in production is: the more **effort** applied to nature, the more **product,** effort including capital also, as hoarded labor. If, however, a long period of time is considered, two important **variations** from this are perceived to hold. In **agriculture** and, with modifications, in **mining,** the law of **diminishing return**[1] prevails, that, in the long run, increase of effort secures a **less** than proportional increase of product. The operation of this law in agriculture may sometimes be temporarily postponed and even disproportionately large returns secured, by (i) increase of **population,**[2] (ii) improved **machines and methods,**

(iii) bringing, in a new country, more fertile or convenient **land** under cultivation.[1] **Manufactures** on the other hand are, as a class, subject to a law of **increasing return,** the creation of their products growing steadily less and less costly per unit.[3] Increasing return characterizes in a marked manner all **special industries** which, while ministering to wide, regular and decided needs, enjoy some sort of a **monopoly**,[4] natural, governmental, or based on vastness of capital.

[1] This law forms the basis of Malthusianism [§ 15, n. 5]. H. C. Carey supposed that in demonstrating [iii], above, he had refuted the law, and Malthus's doctrine along with it. He did neither.

[2] There is a certain point up to which the greater the population on a given territory the greater its *per capita* yield; and beyond which additions to population will have the reverse effect. This may be called the point of 'saturation.'

[3] Cf. § 33, n. 3.

[4] In proportion to the firmness of the monopoly, cost of production [§§ 47, 48] will cease to fix prices, these rising higher and higher till checked by lessened demand. But if the products are necessaries of life prices will go very high before demand will be greatly affected.

§ 35 The Labor-Force: Extent

Mangoldt, 23-44. *Mill*, bk. i, ch. x. *Smith* [R. M.], Statistics and Economics, pt. i [pubb. of Am. Ec. Ass'n, vol. iii]. *Block, Statisque*, ch. xv. *Cohn*, I, i-iii.

To the point of **saturation**,[1] a country or community is productive, other things being equal,[2] according to the **extent** of its **labor-force**.[3] This is great for any period in proportion as: i **Population** is large. ii There is **excess**[4] of **births** over deaths. iii Such excess is maintained more by **paucity of deaths** than by multitude of births.[5] iv **Emigration** is prevented and **immigration** encouraged. v The people are **hardy** and temperate. vi **Males, yet not too greatly, outnumber females.**[6] vii **Working hours** per day are **long and holidays infrequent.**[7] viii **Idle, helpless, and inefficient** persons are few.[8]

---

[1] § 34, n. 2.

[2] Bear this condition carefully in mind.

[3] Not population alone is meant, nor the number of persons who commonly, or ever, work; but the tale of hours' works, say, in a year. Quality is treated in § 36.

[4] This, with consideration iv, determines whether population is *growing* or not. A decreasing population is abnormal, yet not so rare: the American Indians [Andov. Rev., Aug., 1886], the South Sea Islanders, the Irish in Ireland, the French in certain districts of France. Smith, as above, p. 45. In Ireland the deficit is from emigration, in France from excess of deaths over births.

[5] Since if by the latter, much sickness is involved, calling from work not only the patients but also their attendants. Take Norway and Bavaria. B. has much the larger birth-rate, 37.3 per 1000 inhabitants yearly, to N.'s 34.7. But it also has very much the more rapid death-rate: 30.4 to N.'s 18.9 [the lowest known]; so that its yearly increase per 1000 is less than half N.'s, viz., 6.9 to 15.8. France has a very low birth-rate, 26.2; also an exceedingly moderate death-rate, 23.9, only Belgium [23.7] and Norway [18.9] having lower. But Belgium has a considerably better birth-rate, 23.7, so as to increase 7.9 per 1000 each year to France's 2.3.

[6] In the world at large 106 males are born to 100 females, and the preponderance continues till about the age of puberty. After that, the numerical relation is reversed, and holds so through life. More work commonly done by women can be done by men, than *vice versa*. For women to perform tasks fit only for men, in time weakens the entire population. But too great excess of men would mean slow, or no, numerical growth.

[7] *I.e.*, the more hours of work the greater the production, *provided energy is maintained* [§ 36]. But as human endurance is limited the *per diem* task must be, and a holiday now and then works well. The observance of Sunday is undoubtedly an immense aid to a people's productive power. Where the Greek or the Catholic religion prevails, on the other hand, holidays are too numerous for utmost productiveness [Walker, Wages, 20].

[8] Those who cannot or do not support themselves. Here are usually reckoned all persons under 15 and over 70, the remainder constituting the

population of productive age. In France 68.6 per cent are of this age; in England, 61.2; in Germany, 62.7; in the U. S., 59.6. The more slowly a population increases the larger will be its proportion of adults. Then there are the defectives, constituting, of each 100,000:

IN	Blind.	Deaf Mutes.	Idiots.	Insane.	Total.
Italy	105	74	65	99	343
Germany	87	96	139	88	410
Great Britain . . .	98	57	129	178	462
Norway	136	92	119	185	532
Sweden	80	102	39	176	407
Belgium	81	43	50	92	266
France	83	62	114	146	405
United States . . .	96	66	152	182	496

To be added are the idle aristocracy, of blood or of wealth, monks, nuns, superfluous clergy, soldiers, and various classes of servants. Spain, under Philip III, had 988 nunneries and 32,000 mendicant monks. In 1787 it had 188,625 religious persons, 480,589 nobles, and 280,092 people at service. Beggars certainly increased the number to a million, while the exclusively productive classes then were under 2½ million. Portugal in 1800 had 200,000 religious to 3 or 3½ million inhabitants [Roscher, § 54]. Sir W. Petty, Pol. Arithmetic, ch. iv, argues that France, about 1665, had 250,000 needless clergymen, each consuming 18 pence worth a day, which he says was triple what a laboring man required. In contrast with these cases, by the U. S. census of 1880, of the 17,392,099 persons in gainful callings here [being 34.68 per cent of the entire population], only 4,074,238 were engaged in personal and professional services. The others wrought at agriculture [7,670,493], trade and transportation [1,810,256], and in manufacturing, mechanical and mining operations [3,837,112].

§ 36 THE LABOR-FORCE: QUALITY

Mangoldt, as at § 35. *Mill*, bk. i, ch. vii. *Roscher*, bk. ii. *Cherbuliez*, bk. i, ch. v, sec. ii, iii. *Walker*, Wages, ch. iii. *Brassey*, Work and Wages. *Marx*, Capital, ch. xv.

The **efficiency** of labor may vary greatly between two communities whose hours of work per annum are equal, one excelling the other in the **skill, spirit,** and **vigor** with which the work is done. Superiority in these traits will turn upon : i The native **strength, enterprise,** and **will-power** of the people.[1] ii Their habitual **diet.** iii Their **moral** development.[2] iv Their **intelligence,** natural and acquired. Industrial and technical training are here of incalculable importance, yet not more vital, on the whole, than is general education.[3] v Favorable **relation of workmen to product.** The self-employed are usually the most diligent and earnest, co-operators next, then piece-wage-workers, then time-wage.[4] High pay begets zeal; low, apathy. vi Reasonable **work-hours,** daily and weekly, neither too few nor too many,[5] fewer for women than for men, fewest for children. vii Honorable **political status**[6] of the laboring population. Serfs will out-toil slaves, free men do better still, those with the electoral franchise best of all. viii Good **government,**[7] equitable and stable laws, fiscal and other, just and firm administration.

---

[1] In all which prevail differences so great as at first to seem incredible. Thus, the lifting power of a Van Dieman's Land native and that of an Anglo-Australian differ as 50 to 71 [Batbie, cited by Walker]. Peoples near together too are often extraordinarily unlike in these qualities. An English laborer is said to do double the work of a French. Some of the peculiarities are inexplicable, lost in the mystery of race-idiosyncrasies at large; others traceable to national experiences and habits, favorable or unfavorable [Mangoldt, § 25].

[2] Conscience favors (i) fidelity to appointed work, (ii) care for materials, (iii) obedience to law. In all these ways expense for oversight and police is obviated. Conscientiousness also implies contentment and hope, industrial qualities of first moment. To all co-operative forms of industry, to all organization of labor, it is absolutely indispensable.

[3] Not only acquired industrial abilities, a form of capital [§§ 28, 29], are needed, but large, diversified, and widely distributed intelligence whatever its source. The point is not that this will tell in the level of a people's enjoyment — of course true; but that high productive efficiency itself is

conditioned upon it. On industrial education, see Monographs of the Industrial Ed. Ass'n., N. Y. City.

⁴ Roscher, § 39. Here is a table illustrating this, adapted from H. C. Adams:

UNDER	THE WORKMAN HAS		CONSEQUENTLY
Slavery,	No rights, civil or political; pay determined by animal wants.	No interest in quantity or quality of work done; no care for material.	Only low-grade industry possible.
The Ordinary-Wages system,	Civil and perhaps political rights, but no legal property in product; pay determined before work is done.	No direct interest in quantity or quality of work done, or in care for material.	High technical skill possible, but no guarantee of continuous or contented industry.
The Piece-Wages system,	Civil and perhaps political rights, but no legal property in product; pay determined by work done.	Interest in quantity only; otherwise same as above.	Greater encouragement while work lasts; otherwise same as above.
Profit-Sharing or Co-operation,	Civil and perhaps political rights; also property in product; pay determined by work done.	Direct interest in both quantity and quality of work done, and in care for material.	An ideal system wherever applicable. Marshall, bk. iii, ch. ix.

That they are usually better paid in America is among the chief reasons why our immigrants achieve more here than in their old homes. Not always have they this advantage. We cannot infer it from their mere nominal wages. On real as distinguished from nominal w., see under Wages, in Part IV.

⁵ Cf. § 43, n. 5.

⁶ Cf. note 4. This too is a most powerful cause of their improved productivity on coming hither from the old world.

⁷ The *form* of government has much effect. See notes 4 and 5. Nearly or quite as important is its solidity. Witness the industrial backwardness of Mexico, Central America, Peru, Turkey. Laws should be clear, certain, and not changed except for good cause. They should be just to all men and classes, partial to none. Judicious bankruptcy, currency and poor laws are of especially vital consequence. Still more so are those touching taxation. The world is at this moment probably suffering more from bad taxation than from all other governmental ills together. And lastly, "The true test of a good government is its aptitude and tendency to produce a good

administration" [Alexander Hamilton]. In western continental Europe from the 13th to the 17th century farmers could not keep sheep on account of the unbridled rapacity of noblemen and their retainers. Only in England was the king's peace firm enough. Hence England became the great wool-raising country, and could collect from the continent an extensive export-duty [Th. Rogers, Ec. Interp. of Hist., 9].

§ 37 Socialism and Production

Gronlund, Co-operative Commonwealth. Also the works listed at § 14. *Cohn*, II, ii. *Schoenberg*, vol. i, 107-124. *Hyndman*, Hist. Basis of Soc'm in Eng.

Partly *a priori*, partly from the observed effects of co-operation, socialists argue that **land** and **material capital** should be made **collective property**, private fee simple in them being abolished. It is urged that an indefinitely more copious **production** would thus result, making it safe heavily to bond the country, if necessary, to pay off present proprietors. The improvement is expected to come in part from a **more perfect organization**[1] of industry, saving **waste** of labor and of capital; but mainly from the fresh **hope and courage** which would inspire the laboring masses. All **wishing work** might have it. Thirst for **inordinate wealth** would cease. Every commodity or service could be had at precisely its **cost**[2] in labor. Society would no longer be **robbed by gambling** in stocks or produce, or industry palsied by **fluctuations** in the **value of money**. **Commercial crises** would be unknown, and corporations' passing away would render impossible the **frauds** of their managers. Henry George and his followers deem that the essence of this beneficent reform would follow **nationalization of the land**[3] alone. It is likely that the introduction of socialism would **to some extent** quicken productive energy, though by no means in the degree alleged. But we see insuperable **obstacles** to the launching of the system as advocated, and insufferable **evils** sure to spring from it if launched. It would (i) dangerously **concentrate power**, (ii) **abate thrift** in some while promoting it in others, and (iii) **repress** that marvellous **inventiveness, enterprise, and daring** in industrial undertakings which only the hope of great **personal profit** will at present induce in men.[4]

[1] This point naturally connects itself with the discussions of Chapter V. Co-operation and the George reform also both have this double face: they propose to inspire and hence increase labor, and at the same time to organize or apply it better, so that a given measure of it may amount to more than now.

[2] By a system of labor-time money for the payment of wages, and of labor-time labels on commodities to show just how much time in labor each required for its manufacture [§ 14, n. 3]. You work, and are paid in certificates of labor-time, having a face value just equal to the number of hours you have wrought if at unskilled labor, or twice, thrice or ten times that number if at skilled. Each hour of face value in these tickets purchases at any of the public bazaars commodity that it has taken an hour's labor to produce. *Money* and *markets* disappear. The scheme is ingenious but impracticable. See, further, under Distribution [Part IV].

[3] § 14, n. 1.

[4] Cf. § 46.

CHAPTER V

THE RELATIVE CONDITIONS, CONTINUED

§ 38 Extraneous Aids to Labor

Roscher, bk. ii. *Bagehot*, Ec. Studies, vi. *Mill*, bk. i, chaps. vii–xiii. *Cohn*, I, i, iv, v, II, III, i. *M'Culloch*, pt. ii, sec. ii.

Another immense and generic class of the conditions to production touches the ways and means of getting the **utmost possible** out of a **given amount of labor**.[1] The principal circumstances which contribute to this result may be grouped in four clusters: (i) **physical and topographical** advantages, (ii) material **capital in general**, (iii) labor-helping and labor-saving **inventions** in particular, and (iv) the **organization** of labor itself.

[1] Those canvassed in §§ 35–37 have to do with labor intrinsically considered, *i.e.*, its quantity and its quality. We now suppose a certain quantum of labor, its quality so or so, and notice that it avails more or less abundantly according to the place and manner of its application.

§ 39 Geography and Topography

Cohn, 213–229. *Roscher*, §§ 30–37. *Schoenberg*, vol. i, 198 sqq. *Knies*, § 11.

A people's **habitat** is a prime determinant of its economic welfare. It will be helpful or the reverse according to: i Its territorial **extent**,[1] ii Its **superficial aspect**, as mountainous, hilly, or plain.[2] iii The nature of its **earth-crust**, as (a) **soil**[3] well or ill rewarding cultivation, (b) a theatre of much or little **spontaneous production**, in **forests, wild birds and animals**,[4] and (c) a magazine of abundant or scanty **raw materials**, as **coal, stone, and metals**. iv The plentifulness, location and character of its **waters**. Are **springs, brooks, ponds, and lakes** numerous and well distributed? Do they furnish sufficient drink, irrigation, and water-power? Are **rivers** many and navigable far inland?[5] Is **seacoast** extensive, offering frequent and commodious **harbors**?[6] Are **fish**[7] in rich supply? v The salubrity of its **climate** and the favorableness or unfavorableness of this to production. **Temperature, rainfall,** humidity, and the strength and regularity of **winds** have here to be taken into account. vi Its location in **relation to the territories of other peoples**, and the character and resources of those peoples.

[1] It may at any given time be too great or too small for the people.

[2] How important, *e.g.*, to the ease or expense of building railways and canals.

[3] Fertility and good drainage are the main qualities.

[4] Ostrich-feathers, ivory, game [including supplies for menageries and zoölogical gardens], peltry, and guano are, in places, important sources of wealth. The presence in a country of desirable beasts, birds, insects and plants is of great importance, as is the absence of noxious ones. In Russia twenty-five million squirrels are killed yearly for their skins [Mulhall]. The Eng. gov't in Cyprus expends $15,000,000 yearly in destroying locusts. Block Island has the great advantage in poultry-raising that no foxes, skunks, or weasels are found there.

[5] Nor do railroads strip this item of consequence. It is also of much moment whether the land is subject to floods or not.

[6] Note England's advantage herein over the Continent. Its harbors are not only thick, but well situated. Tides and the Gulf-stream mostly sweep past them instead of straight in, which so fills up those beyond the Channel. The economic influence of the Gulf-stream on the Atlantic coast of Europe is obvious but immeasurable.

[7] The late Spencer F. Baird regarded an acre of ocean equal to six of land in ability to produce food for man. Seals and porpoises as well as fish might be mentioned among the valuable gifts to us from the sea.

§ 40   Material Capital in General

Mangoldt, §§ 30, 31. *Mill*, bk. i, chaps. v, vi, xi. *Ad. Smith*, bk. ii. *Roscher*, §§ 42 sqq. *Bagehot*, Ec. Studies, vi. *Rae*, Prin. of P. E. [Bost., 1830], 123 sqq.

Speaking broadly, production will be large in proportion as material **capital is plenty**.[1] Laborers must have food, clothing, shelter, working-gear and stock. Labor-force not supplied with these becomes a **burden**, and labor-force can **increase** only as these multiply. Mere abundance for present needs is **not enough**. Healthy production requires an actual or potential **surplus** against emergencies. Capital in the form of roads, canals, dikes, piers, and public buildings may aid production through hundreds and thousands of years.[2] The **proportion**, in capital, of kind to kind is hardly less important than **bulk**. Aside from cases of specific over-production, either fixed or circulating capital may exist in **vicious disproportion**[3] to the other. Preponderance of circulating is the **lesser danger**, owing to the larger possibility of adapting it to a variety of uses.[4]

---

[1] On *intellectual* capital as a condition of production, see § 36, iv, and n. 3. The richest importation the U. S. ever made came encased in Samuel Slater's head. The present § is to be brought into relation with §§ 29, 30, *ante*. In those §§ our thought was primarily a static one. Here we have in view the dynamics of production.

[2] Though most capital, however 'fixed' [§ 29, n. 7], is ephemeral. The average life of an English locomotive, costing £2,000, is only 15 years, no subtraction being made for repairs. The average total run is 200,000 miles [Mulhall]. American machines, the term being reduced according to amount of repairs, average to live but 5.07 years. The cost is $8,000. A box car costs $450, lives 9.05 years; a flat lives 8.15 years [W. C. Fisher].

[3] The main cause of the hard times in 1857 was probably the locking up of too much capital in the form of new railways.

[4] *I.e.*, it is less specialized [§ 29, n. 6].

§ 41 Machinery

Ad. Smith, bk. i, chaps. i-iii. *Cherbuliez*, bk. i, ch. vi. *Roscher*, 'Machinery,' in Lalor; also *Ansichten*, etc., vol. ii. *Mangoldt*, § 36. *Senior*, 3 Lectt. on Wages, etc. *Schoenberg*, vol. i, 218 sqq. *Marx*, Capital, ch. xv. *Cossa, Elementi*, 31.

The ability of **tools** and **instruments**[1] to help production is **infinitely multiplied** by harnessing to them some agent with **superhuman power,** as brutes,[2] water, steam, or electricity. **Machines** then result, which (i) **make possible much production** not so without them,[3] (ii) in forms of production intrinsically possible without,[4] **enormously spare** the **health,** strength, and morale[5] of laborers, (iii) in other cases render products **better, cheaper,** and **vastly more plentiful.**[4] Through these advantages, in spite of **temporary misfortunes**[6] often occasioned by the introduction of it, machinery becomes an **inestimably** valuable **auxiliary** to labor in creating wealth.

[1] On the difference between tools, instruments, and machines, § 29, n. 1.

[2] The first cotton mills in America were driven by horses or oxen.

[3] Partly by the fineness and regularity of their work, as mowers, reapers and steam ploughs; partly by sheer power, as in heavy hauling, lifting and pumping. Sometimes their force is not beyond what united human effort might yield, but has to be applied in a place [a mine, *e.g.*] where not enough men can 'get hold.' But the earth's population were insufficient to do a tithe of the work which machinery now performs. The world's horse-power in steam alone aggregated [Mulhall] in 1880, 28,952,000. Each horse-power being equal to 12 men's power, we have steam doing the work of 347,424,000 men. But engines, furnishing power alone, represent but a small part of the work of machinery. Competent estimates

regard machinery as doing in Great Britain alone the work of 700,000,000 men, a number probably in excess of the entire laboring population of the globe. Cf. n. 4. Notice, further, that machinery, like labor [§§ 43, 44], gains in efficiency by *organization*, piece standing in rightly complementary relations to piece.

⁴ A sewing-machine does the work of 12 women. A Boston 'bootmaker,' with one workman, makes 300 pairs of boots daily. In 1880, 300 of these machines were at work in various countries, and turned out 150 million pairs. Glenn's California reaper will cut, thresh, winnow and bag the wheat of 60 acres in 24 hours. The Hercules ditcher removes 750 cubic yards of clay per hour. The Darlington borer enables one man to do the work of 7 in tunnelling, and reduces the cost by two-thirds [Mulhall]. One boy with a knitting machine does as much work as 100 persons could 100 years ago.

⁵ It imbrutes as well as kills off men to do work which constantly tasks their physical power to its utmost. Cf. § 35, n. 6.

⁶ Capital suffers, as each new piece renders more or less old property worthless — a process continually going on. Usually, of course, the new gear soon more than recoups this loss. Much sadder is the displacement of labor which an important novelty in machinery always effects. Laborers no longer young are ruined for life, their hard-earned skill going for nothing. Even the young suffer painfully. No state has ever yet, as Sir James Steuart advocated, sought to make good these losses. Yet after all, how mad to prohibit machinery! Nor does it on the whole advantage the capitalist more than it does the poor.

§ 42 Unembodied Invention

M'Culloch, pt. ii, sec. iv.

By no means all special ideas, helpful economically, thus take form in tools, instruments or machines.[1] An immense proportion of the most valuable applied science does not. We instance: i **Chemical** information and skill in washing, dyeing, tanning and the like.[2] ii **Geological** knowledge of leads, layers, etc., used to guide mining operations. iii Nearly the whole science of **engineering** in its various departments[3] and branches.

iv Science as utilized in **agriculture, stock-breeding, and the propagation of fishes**. v That **vast body of practical maxims**, the growth of its whole past, which exists in every department of human industry, touching the most efficient conduct thereof.

[1] A weighty truth, which economic writers have too much overlooked. *Connaissances* of this kind really form one of the main departments of capital. Observe that what we here discuss is not the same as the *intelligence* mentioned in § 36, iv, though the two are closely related.

[2] "Mr. Walter Weldon, chevalier of the Legion of Honor, who died in England, Sept. 20, 1885, was one of the five men, and the only foreigner, whom the French Société d'Encouragement has deemed worthy of its grand medal. To him we are indebted for the process by which alone bleaching powder is now made. The peroxide of manganese employed to liberate chlorine from the hydrochloric acid obtained in the first step of the soda manufacture was formerly thrown away. By a very simple process, Mr. Weldon recovered from 90 to 95 per cent of the manganese in a form available for renewed use, and thus saved nearly £6 on every ton of bleaching powder made, quadrupled the total manufacture, made the industrial world the richer by some three-quarters of a million sterling per annum, and as the French chemist, J. R. Dumas, publicly observed, cheapened every sheet of paper and every yard of calico made in the world."

[3] Civil, mechanical, electrical, marine, mining. Each has its numerous branches. Cf. *Annales des Ponts et Chaussées*, 1887, 2, p. 389 [on org'n of railway train movement in U. S.]; and p. 522 [on use of certain waste salts for clearing streets from ice].

§ 43 The Organization of Industry

Marshall, bk. i, chaps. vii, viii. *Mangoldt*, §§ 28, 29. *Roscher*, § 56; *Ansichten*, vol. ii. *Mill*, bk. i, ch. viii. *George*, Soc. Problems, ch. i. *Schoenberg*, vol. i, 203 sqq.

System is imparted to labor in two ways: I **Composition**, whereby several persons, uniting either contemporaneously[1] or successively[2] in the same acts, **accomplish more** than they could singly. II **Division**, which secures the same advantage by assigning to different parties different portions of one and the same greater or smaller task. This distribution is partly spontaneous,[3] partly the result of conscious purpose. It has three phases: i **Local,**[4] each nation or vicinity engaging in the industry giving it the **greatest relative advantage** as to climate, raw material, markets, etc. ii **Generic,** every several **body of producers** busied with the sort of work best adapted to its powers.[5] iii **Personal,** the division of labor in the narrower sense, each individual doing the particular thing which he can do most easily and perfectly.[6]

---

[1] As in lifting a heavy weight, loading logs, pulling stumps, and other jobs for which farmers "change works." In many such cases — we add proof-reading to the number — the work could not be done at all except co-operatively. In any kind of toil the union of several persons lends a peculiar inspiration, which is usually worth taking into account.

[2] As where two or three men hammer the same hot rivet, the better to head it ere it cools. Where three [even five may so combine] pound on the same drill, division of labor also comes in. The drill goes no faster than with the same number of blows from one man, but the holder of it is worked to better advantage. See next §.

[3] The local phase, at least so far as it pertains to nations, is mostly spontaneous. It is only minor and specific businesses which they formally adopt by legal encouragement. The establishment of quinine production in India through the agency of the British government, and of beet-sugar production in France, Germany and Austria, are examples. Subordinate districts adopt industries much more easily, and often, — now at a loss, now to their great benefit. In agriculture, experiment with this in view has yet to go much farther. It is not at all to be assumed that the crops grown from time immemorial in a given locality, are the only ones suited to it.

[4] Thus London, Manchester, Liverpool, and the wheat section of America supplement each other, forming an industrial group, much as do foreman, cutters, crimpers, lasters, heelers, etc., in a shoe factory. Cf. Roscher, § 57. Europe and Asia co-operate in the same way. More still

the Torrid and Temperate Zones. The importance of this international division in labor will be shown under Exchange. Tariffville, Conn., was found to be superior to Thompsonville as a site for carpet manufacturing, because the water there made faster dyes. The special excellence of West English cassimeres is said to be due to a peculiar humidity of the air, rendering the fibre tractable while wrought.

[5] Heredity of industrial tact and taste is as valuable as it is striking. English woollen spinners and weavers inherit a pronounced adaptability for their trade. So the silk workers of France, and the fishermen of Nova Scotia.

[6] This is the form discussed in next §.

§ 44 THE SAME IN A SPECIAL ASPECT

Plato, Rep., bk. ii. *Ad. Smith*, bk. i, chaps. i, ii [cf. in Playfair's Ed., supp. ch. iii]. *Roscher*, § 58, and the other authh. cited at last §.

The economic benefits[1] springing from the personal division of labor are **extraordinary**, and have been well discussed in nearly all the books since Adam Smith. They consist in: i Laborers' improved **dexterity**.[2] ii A better **distribution of abilities**[3] among the various departments of the work. iii Inventiveness and **inventions**.[4] iv **Economy of time**, employing the least possible in changing tools and place. v **Prevention of waste** in stock,[5] whether raw material or fixed capital. vi **Saving of interest**[6] and insurance.

[1] Ad. Smith's favorite illustration [bk. i, ch. i] is pin-making. It involved in his time about 18 distinct operations, each, in the best works, performed by distinct hands. He estimated that the product by this distribution was from 240 to 4800 times as great as if each workman had wrought separately and with no special education for the trade. Cf. Perry, Elements, 129.

[2] A blacksmith not specially used to nail-making turns out 200-300 a day; one used to it, yet with his hand out through other work, 800-1000; a boy, even, who has never done anything else, 2,300 [Ad. Smith]. Each pupil can multiply instances.

³ Skilled laborers need be had only for work which they alone can do, simpler parts being left to apprentices or green hands. In making needle-points children beat adults.

⁴ Though Arkwright began as a barber, and Cartwright, the inventor of the power-loom, was a clergyman, far the larger part of the inventions which have blessed the world, were worked out by mechanics. To the cunning stored in the steam-engine of to-day, Watt is hardly the thousandth part contributor. The rest is mainly from unknown men.

⁵ As a rule, waste of material will be small in proportion to the rapidity with which it is turned into product. Buildings, machinery, tools, and all fixed capital would of course better be worn out in productive use than by decay. A mill with never so few hands must have a full complement of gear. This is a strong argument for long work hours, and for night work, provided orders are heavy enough.

⁶ This, as a consideration separate from the preceding, relates to the materials used in production. The shorter this process the less time is money invested in them and the less time have they to carry insurance.

§ 45 Evils and Limitations

Roscher, §§ 59 sqq. *Mill*, bk. i, ch. viii. *Ad. Smith*, bk. i, ch. iii.

The division of labor, carried to such an extreme in the monster undertakings of recent decades, has its **dark side**. The workman's life lacks its old **diversity**.[1] Narrow, it cannot but be **monotonous** and **irksome**. The man is more **dependent** on his single art, possessing at once **less ready knowledge** and **less ability** to acquire. In two ways the system **favors strikes**. By making laborers **clannish** it **fosters union** among them, while it gives a few power to stop the work of all. Fortunately there are activities which only to a limited extent allow labor to be divided, the check lying for some in the **nature of the business**,[2] for others in a **contracted market**.[3] In all trades whatever, organization is repressed by lack of capital,[4] and ceases to be profitable[5] when in compass and complexity it **transcends available superintending ability.**

[1] All have heard the proverb that in Lynn, Mass., centre of the ladies' shoes industry for this country, not a shoemaker is to be found.

[2] In agriculture, *e.g.*, the work manifestly cannot be parcelled out among ploughmen, herdsmen, reapers, mowers, choppers, etc., but each hand has commonly to do more or less at all these. House-building and painting in cold latitudes present the same difficulty. Roscher lays down the principle that the possibility of dividing labor bears exact proportion to the degree in which, in the different kinds of industry, labor contributes to production.

[3] Read, best, Ad. Smith, as above. Cabinet-making is intrinsically susceptible of great division, yet in a country place no one can live by this craft alone. The cabinet-worker must here be carpenter, joiner and wood-carver, too. Every country blacksmith is also copper-smith and locksmith. Notice how cheap transportation, by turning many little markets into one of large size, makes possible much new division of labor. Formerly the furniture, coffins and wagons for every village had to be made there, usually by the same man, so meagre was the demand for each. Now those wares are carried thousands of miles, and even coffins can be gotten up in such numbers under one roof as to admit of the most perfect division of abilities. Frontier settlements still show the old order of things.

[4] For plant and stock. So far as thorough oversight can be secured, there is advantage in large undertakings, even in the industries referred to in n. 2, above; but if this condition fails, smaller establishments, though missing many of the advantages which fuller organization would give, will lead [Cherbuliez, vol. i, 120 sqq.].

[5] *I.e.*, ceases to be truly *productive*. But a trust or ring which has a monopoly may, though far too large to be economically managed, and hence not a help to general production, still, by raising prices, be very profitable for those interested. Cf. § 21, iv, (2).

§ 46 The Form of Undertaking

Cossa, Elementi, II, vi. *Mill*, bk. i, ch. ix. *Weeden*, Soc. Law of Labor, 30. *Walker*, P. E., 244. *Mangoldt*, §§ 33-35. *Schoenberg*, vol. i, 220 sqq. *Cohn*, 447-87.

Very many goods are produced by the identical persons or families who are to consume them: numerous others for exchange, but in petty ways. Respecting the remainder, intended for **exchange on a large scale**, it is important where, for any given line or centre of production, the sovereign **directorship and risk**[1] are located. Their seat may be: i In the **state** — public co-operation.[2] ii In isolated **groups or partnerships**[3] of men, working unitedly and on a level one with another — private co-operation. iii In **individual undertakers** or contractors — the single *entrepreneur* system. iv In **joint stock companies** as undertakers — the collective *entrepreneur* system. Each of these is useful in **special fields**; neither will do for the whole range of industry. There are species of production which the **state must assume**, and its function in this way **enlarges** with the growth of civilization.[4] Co-operation works excellently where keenest **oversight** and large, intricate **combinations** are not indispensable.[3] Single undertakers secure to the **superintendence** the maximum of **diligence and energy**, but **lack capital** for colossal works. For these, stock associations are best fitted, and the **mammoth enterprises** of the age fall more and more to them. With their endless **capital** they can command the first quality of **superintending talent**, while utilizing to the utmost the **division of labor**. But to this Titan form of undertaking attach certain evils: 1 **Irresponsibility** of managers to stockholders. 2 **Baneful political influence**. 3 Tendency to **monopoly**, making their own, and denying to the public, the benefits of cheapened production.[5]

[1] These being the chief elements in the function of "undertaker," *entrepreneur*, or middle-man — the man who harnesses labor and capital together to the work of production. We second the example of H. C.

Adams in effort to restore the word "undertaker" to its good old English and American use as the exact equivalent of *entrepreneur*, *Unternehmer*, and *imprenditore* [Alexander Hamilton, Report on Manufactures]. 'Capitalist' is too indefinite, meaning also, and usually, the *owner* of capital, which the undertaker, as such, is not. See, further, in Part IV.

² Which, made general, would be socialism [§§ 14, 37].

³ Covering private socialistic and communistic societies, co-operators, and partnerships. A partnership is in essence nothing but a case of co-operation, though the two are usually separated. Co-operation is destined to enlarge its scope, greatly to the aid of production, but not to become the general form of undertaking. Even had it enough capital — it might command much — it lacks the concentration of energy and the industrial generalship required for enterprises of much magnitude. See § 36, n. 4; Marshall, bk. iii, ch. ix; Mill, I, viii; Holyoake, Hist. of Co-op'n; Yves Guyot, bk. iv, ch. ix; Walker, Wages, ch. xv; Quar. Jour. Econ., vol. ii, 210, 446.

⁴ Professor Wagner has shown this. *Lehrbuch*, vol. i, §§ 171-178.

⁵ See § 45, n. 5.

CHAPTER VI

COST AND CONSUMPTION IN PRODUCTION

§ 47 Metaphysical Cost

Cairnes, Leading Principles, pt. i, ch. iii. *Sidgwick*, 201 sqq. *Jevons*, Theory, 159 sq. *Macleod*, Econ. Philos., 331. *Marshall*, bk. ii, ch. xiii. *Bagehot*, Ec. Studies, vii. *Macvane*, Quar. Jour. Econ., vol. i, 481 sqq.

The **real cost** of any product consists in the **effort** or **sacrifice** required to obtain it. 'It represents what man **parts with** in the barter between him and nature.'[1] Three elements compose it: i **Labor,** this being important to the result in proportion to 1) **time,** and 2) **intensity.** ii **Abstinence,** this being necessary in order to the supply of capital[2] for the support and utilization of the labor. Abstinences can be compared in the respects of duration and temptation, the latter arising from the power, as subjectively viewed, of the wealth abstained from to gratify, and in this sense corresponding to the amount[3] of that wealth. Labor-exertion is more an **individual** experience than abstinence, which is largely **social.**[2] iii **Risk,** a hardship inseparable from the exercise of either labor or abstinence.[4] The cost of a product as thus estimated is, of course, a highly **indefinite** notion, and different costs are but roughly commensurable.[5] Infinite complexity is added to the indefiniteness if we attempt to trace cost in any case to its **original elements;** since the sacrifice attending this or that piece of production depends upon the **development of man and the arts** at the time, which in turn depend on an unthinkable series of similar sacrifices, reaching back to the beginnings of human history. The **ultimate cost** of any particular item of wealth, therefore, wholly **defies computation.**[6]

[1] Cairnes, 57. In this chapter Cairnes shows how superficially Mill expounded cost of production by resolving it into wages and profits [interest]. Such an analysis is truthful enough from the business man's point of view, but does not bring to notice the final consideration which society pays for wealth. Comparing the next § with this, one sees how far, and how, Cairnes and Mill may be reconciled upon the perplexing topic before us.

[2] See § 30, n. 2. Did men use at once the results of all labor, there would obviously be no capital. It is harder to see that the abstinence demands effort. Yet it does. Witness the poverty of savages, for lack of the self-control which this effort requires. Very wealthy persons save with a minimum of sacrifice, sometimes, perhaps, with none at all. But in society as a whole, wealth cannot be maintained without it.

[3] Macvane, as above, thinks that Cairnes, in asserting abstinence to be measurable [in part] by the "quantity of wealth abstained from," defines in a circle, since the "quantity of wealth" is gauged by its value, which, in turn, depends on cost of production, the very thing which C. is seeking to define, and on wages and profits, which, C. declares, are not elements in cost. The point is ill taken, as C. means the "amount of w.," only as subjectively estimated. But Cairnes, unwilling to let go the conception of normal value [see this topic in Part II: cf. n. 1, above], does err in representing the measurement which is possible here as more definite than it can in fact be made.

[4] Risk is a separate thing from abstinence. Abstinence would call for some exertion even were we absolutely sure of enjoying the fruits of it by and by.

[5] Still, Sidgwick notwithstanding, they are commensurable. Even the socialists' proposal to reduce hours of skilled labor in its various grades to so many more hours of ordinary labor, treating this last as a common denominator for all labor, is not absurd in nature, though measurements of this sort would be painfully general.

[6] § 27, n. 4. Mill, bk. i, ch. ii, § 1.

§ 48 Mercantile Cost

Mill, bk. iii, chaps. iv, vi. Also same authh. as at § 47.

Corresponding[1] in a general way to the metaphysical cost of a thing, and furnishing for moderate lengths of time a tolerable measure of this, is the **expense** to which a **given undertaker** is put in producing that thing. Such expense may be named the **mercantile cost**. Aside from the relatively minute elements of **taxation** and **rent**, its components are (i) the **wages** of the necessary labor, and (ii) **interest** on the necessary capital. Either of these two factors remaining constant, the mercantile cost of the production in question varies closely with the variations of the other. i **For wages,** the actual expense will be determined by 1) **the rate,**[2] as high or low; 2) **the material**[3] used in payment, as dear or cheap; and 3) **the efficiency**[4] **of the labor,** as small or great. ii **For interest,** the outlay will be fixed by 1) **the rate,** higher or lower; 2) **the period,**[5] longer or shorter, needed for turning the capital into product; and 3) **the speed,** greater or less, at which the capital **deteriorates** during this process.

---

[1] The two costs must correspond, for the undertaker has no means of securing the production but to give to the laborer on the one hand, and to the capitalist on the other, a remuneration sufficient to induce in each the needed sacrifice. For the same reason one cost vaguely measures the other for any limited period. But with less and less exactness the longer the time, since, as the industrial arts improve, the metaphysical cost is less and less in proportion to the total product, while mercantile cost keeps pace with product [Cairnes, 49 sq.].

[2] To see correctly the bearing of these six main factors in mercantile cost, it is well to consider each by itself and suppose no change for the time in the other five. Thus, provided wage-material, efficiency of labor,

rate of interest, turning-period and rapidity of deterioration are the same in two different establishments, but the *rate of wages* the higher in one, production will be the costlier in that one. So with every other of the five elements. See n. 4, below.

³ Depreciated paper, silver, gold, or paper at par with silver or with gold. The principle holds also if payments are made barter-wise, or in products. The pupil will learn in Part III that the standard monetary unit itself, whether it be of gold or of silver, can suffer decided variations in value.

⁴ What was said in note 2 does not, of course, assert that low wages necessarily imply cheap production, for the *efficiency* of high-wage labor may be and very often is enough greater to render that the cheaper.

⁵ The aging of liquors requires in this trade a long investment of capital. Old brandy will bring three times as much as new. Whiskey is often kept seven or eight years, and is thought to improve constantly through even twenty. Manufacturers esteem it a great hardship that they must pay the excise on it when three years old, since the aging is in their view part of the process of production. The same question (when does production end?) arises in respect to certain other articles, *e.g.*, cigars and cheese, which improve by mere keeping. But manufacturing in the strictest sense varies greatly in time, and that in the same line. To tan a skin is the work in France of a year, in the United States of a month. Suppose all the other components of cost the same for both countries, French tanning is evidently the more expensive.

§ 49 CONSUMPTION

Mill, 2d Ess. on Unsettled Questions. *Patten*, in Science Economic Discussion, 123 sqq. *Cherbuliez*, bk. i, ch. x. *Clark*, Philos. of Wealth, ch. iii. *Cossa*, *Elementi*, iv.

i Consumption in Economics is **not the destruction of matter, but an immaterial** process. It relates to **utility**, consisting either in the total or partial **annihilation** of this, or in **change of its form**. ii Consumption is either **destructive**, not yielding any advantage, direct or indirect, to any one, or **economic**, which is the voluntary destruction of utility for the sake of advantage. iii Economic consumption, synonymous with use, may be **unproductive**, destroying utility to secure immediate satisfaction of need, or **reproductive**, the utility reappearing under other forms. Reproductive consumption is merely a **phase of production**[1] itself. iv Consumption is not necessarily **destructive**, or even unproductive, because it leaves no tangible or measurable result. The use of luxuries, intellectual or æsthetic entertainment, and the like, may **create wealth indirectly,** or a good that is not wealth, but better.

[1] This and waste [§ 50] are the only phases of consumption which it is logical to discuss in Part I. The general question of the legitimate final destination and fate of wealth we reserve for Part V.

§ 50 Waste and Thrift

Mangoldt, § 31. *Roscher*, § 45. *Cherbuliez*, bk. i, ch. ix, § 1.

But a vast proportion of consumption is **destructive** in nature, pure, unremunerative **waste,**[1] the annihilation of so much precious wealth, which men must dispense with, thus remaining **poorer,** or re-create with **toil and pain.** Such deficit mainly occurs through either (i) **carelessness,** or (ii) **thriftlessness.** To the **first cause** is due much **deterioration** of animals by overwork, ill food, and inattention, much **decay** of buildings and machinery, and fully half of the enormous **losses** each year by **fire.**[2] The **second cause,** too, contributes to the above, yet is chiefly influential in other ways. **Laziness, intemperance,**[3] ill choice of **dress, food,**[4] and modes of **cooking,** slovenly **tillage,** neglect of **accounts**[5] and of **little sums,**[6] may illustrate. The ill results do not end with the owners of the wealth that perishes. All destructive consumption tends to **injure**, and nearly always does actually injure, the **entire public**. In the aggregate, it is an incalculable detriment to mankind. Thrift is promoted less by a **high rate** of **interest** than by (i) **morality**, (ii) **good government**, rendering savings safe, (iii) strong **family ties**, prompting parents to plan for their children's best, and (iv) a **proper distribution** of wealth. Very poor persons cannot save, the very rich lack powerful motive for so doing. People of **middle rank** are the great builders of wealth, the more when gentle **gradations** among them stimulate the **desire to rise**.

[1] § 30, n. 3. Let no one suppose this to be waste any the less because it may invoke particular new applications of industry. *E.g.*, " the broken pane," in Bastiat's illustration, Ess. on P. E. [Putnam's Ed., 72 sq.]. The glazier has more work: is not the accident a blessing? Not at all. Suppose the pane had remained whole. The money which the glazier has received would have gone [say] to the shoemaker, whose prosperity is no less important to the community than the glazier's, while he who had to pay for the pane would be richer by a pair of shoes. Study this till perfectly clear.

[2] Estimated to reach in the entire United States over $100,000,000 per annum, and in New York state alone $15,000,000, — the latter sum exceeding by $6,000,000 the whole burden of taxation for state purposes, and being considerably over one-seventh of the annual increase in the state's taxable property. It is thought feasible, through increase of precaution, to reduce this destruction, national and state, by fully one-half. Fire losses to factory property have already been cut down much more than this, viz., 75 per cent, mainly in ways pointed out by the late Zachariah Allen, of Rhode Island, and Edward Atkinson, of Boston. Insurance rates have fallen accordingly. It is uncertain whether insurance decreases or increases fire losses, but it very helpfully distributes the burden which they entail.

[3] § 21, n. 7.

[4] § 16, n. 7.

[5] A very prevalent and unfortunate fault of farmers — worse among them than among other industrial classes of like intelligence.

[6] In the savings banks of the United States are, in 1889, $1,200,000,000 or $1,400,000,000, almost or quite as much as all the other banking institutions of the country contain. A great part of the sum has been deposited by persons of quite moderate means. Suppose the whole laboring populace to save as these have! Thrift should be enjoined as a duty. The introduction of school savings banks is a worthful reform, and promises much.

Part II

EXCHANGE

EXCEPT AS INVOLVING THE SCIENCE OF MONEY

CHAPTER I

THE NATURE OF EXCHANGE

§ 51 In Rude Societies

Laveleye, Primitive Property. *Maine*, Anc. Law, ch. viii. *Schoenberg*, vol. i, 27 sqq. *Hyndman*, Hist. Basis of Socialism in Eng., 104, 109. *Morgan*, 'Montezuma's Dinner,' N. A. Rev., Apr., 1876; Ancient Society, pt. ii, ch. vii.

We have already often had occasion to advert to the phenomenon of **exchange**: it now demands detailed study. Exchange is not, as is sometimes taught, a **strictly necessary** feature of economic life.[1] Among **primitive men** the distinction of *meum* and *tuum* hardly arises. Their property is mostly **common**,[2] their production wholly for **their own immediate consumption**. In the village communities of **India**, in **Polynesia**, **Australia**, and over large parts of **Africa** may even now be seen families and **groups** of families **producing all** that they consume, and **consuming all** that they produce, exchange practically unknown.[3] Society in ancient Mexico and Peru is believed to have been communistically organized, no exchange being had save trifling trade of tribe with tribe and village with village. In England, so late as the fifteenth century, exchange was, outside of towns and cities, not indeed absent but entirely insignificant[4] as an economic resource, families producing for the most part what they themselves consumed and no more. It was much the same in the American colonies, and so continued in the remoter portions of the states till the railway era opened. There remain to this day isolated sections[5] in the West and South where the play of exchange is extremely limited.

[1] See § 1, n. 7. Mill, bk. iii, ch. i, § 1, shows that it will not do to take *exchange* as the exact correlate of *wealth*. It is hence both illogical and confusing to place an exposition of exchange at the threshold of a course in Economics.

[2] See § 3. Maine, Laveleye, Cliffe Leslie and others have proved that private property, in land at least, originated in comparatively recent times. So far as can be traced, land was among all peoples, at first and for long, common property. When severalty-holdings arose they reached only to house lots and gardens. Nor was community-property confined to land, but extended to all movables as well, with such exceptions as each family's clothing and kit of utensils for hunting, fishing and the like. Even in these cases property-right was not then regarded absolute.

[3] Contrary to frequent representations, simple division of labor does not of necessity involve or imply exchange. Division of labor presents itself in every family, exchange rarely. So in Shaker communities.

[4] This, too, in an age of prosperity for the common people as great, on the whole, as was ever known in England.

[5] Our communistic societies might also be mentioned. But, though no exchange goes on within each, they do traffic with the world outside, and get gain.

§ 52 Philosophy

Ad. Smith, bk. i, ch. ii. *Mangoldt*, bk. iii, ch. i. *Cherbuliez*, bk. ii, ch. l.

Yet **exchange is natural**, in the same sense as are **development and civilization.** i Different human[1] beings possess **tastes and aptitudes** for different pursuits, nearly every individual having a **peculiar** fitness for **some one line** of production, his efforts most availing if confined to that single line. The talent may be **original, acquired,** or partly either. ii The **environments** of men are about equally various,[2] fixed so in the very constitution of the earth, and these affect their **producing power** much as their unlike abilities do. iii At the same time each man has the capacity and desire to **enjoy all** or nearly all **sorts of products,** and will enjoy them if he can obtain them.[3] iv From these multitudinous **needs** of men, coupled with the extreme diversity in the **advantages** which they possess relatively to each other, springs **exchange,** whereby one, with his special product or kind of products, **purchases** for the satisfaction of his own numerous desires, the **various products** of his fellows. The process **extends its scope**[4] according as **wealth, culture, needs,** the **division of labor,** and man's **mastery of the earth** increase.

[1] Adam Smith, as above, places exchange among the marks which especially differentiate man from the brute. He and others have raised the question whether or not there is innate in man a specific *propensity* to exchange. None pertains to the race as such. The tendency is acquired — a growth consequent upon the great good which exchange confers on society. *I.e.*, people would not long exchange did they not find their account in it.

[2] One man lives near a prolific gold mine, a second where cattle are fattened for the tending, a third where valuable game is easily taken, a fourth by fine waterfalls or rich coal beds, tempting to manufacture, a fifth on the seashore, catching fish enough in a day to feed a hundred people, a sixth owns a fertile farm, and so on.

[3] The tendency is: specialty in production, universality in consumption. But for exchange, here would be a fatal fracture in the frame of society.

[4] Cf. § 54.

§ 53 INTRINSIC ADVANTAGES

Mangoldt, bk. iii, chaps. i, ii. *Cherbuliez*, bk. ii, ch. vii. *Perry*, ch. iv.

Suppose that a tailor can make a coat in one day, a hat only in six days, and that a hatter can make a hat in one day, a coat only in six. Without exchanging, each must work seven days for a hat and a coat. By exchanging, each can obtain both articles for **two** days' work, and **wealth will gain** five coats and five hats. Such saving is the **tendency** of all spontaneous exchange. This illustration teaches that: i There is no necessary reason why, in any exchange, **both parties** should not **gain**. If the contract is intelligently and freely made, both do gain.[1] ii The **greater the diversity** of relative advantage between the parties, the **greater the profit** of exchanging. Thus every man's special **fortune, skill, talent,** or **felicity of situation** is through exchange a **benefit to the public**[2] in spite of him. iii Any **abridgment to liberty** of exchange, whether between persons, sections or nations, must, at least in the first instance, **inevitably produce loss**. Whether the hindrance can in this or that case **prevent greater loss**, or set in train **compensating** causes, is often an important question.[3]

[1] Take the men supposed at § 52, n. 2. Confine each to the direct fruit of his own toil, and, however diligent they are, all suffer from poverty. Let them exchange, and every one of them will better his condition a hundred fold without an additional stroke of labor. They can well afford to pay the merchant and the teamster who mediate the transfer.

Even if you are unfortunate, and in this sense compelled to buy or sell, your act is best for you *under the circumstances*. How is it in stock gambling? Here, too, the law holds, since, in a very true sense, the contract is blindly made.

[2] A fine illustration of the benevolence wrought by Nature into our very constitution. Cases are meant, of course, where the advantage has not been won *at any one's expense*. We may mention here the super-economic blessings: religious, moral, æsthetic, intellectual, which attend exchange — the broadening of men's horizon, aid to Christian missions, prevention of war, national and international charity in famines and pestilences. Commerce is the prince of civilizers.

[3] In some instances to be answered affirmatively, in others negatively.

§ 54 Reach of Influence

Mangoldt, as at last §. *Roscher*, § 89; *Nationalök. d. Ackerbaues, Einl. Cherbuliez*, bk. ii, ch. v.

With the progress of exchange the entire face of the **economic world becomes transformed**, while civilization[1] attains a **loftier** level and a **richer** diversity. i A special class of **merchants** or middlemen arises, whose contribution[2] to social weal consists exclusively in furthering the necessary exchanges between original **producers** and final **consumers**. ii **Communities** and **classes** ascertain their **fittest places** in the nation's economy, **nations** theirs in that of **the world**. iii Not only is **production**[3] **immensely increased** in the aggregate, and still more **relatively to effort**, but much of it takes place in mammoth establishments, corresponding to the **enlarged markets**, entailing division of labor[4] with its good and its evil accompaniments

iv Increasingly vast grows the mass of **goods which are produced for exchange**. In tendency thus to seek consumption indirectly, articles vary greatly, according to, 1) **acquaintance of peoples with peoples** and sections with sections, 2) the **desire**, both **intensive** and **extensive**,[5] of parties for each other's wares, 3) the quality of these as **preservable** or **perishable**,[6] 4) their **size and weight**,[7] 5) the presence or absence of the **necessary means of exchange** or of **transportation** and of social and legal **restrictions** thereto. v New **modes of communication and transportation** are called for and developed, which radically **change the distribution** of manufacturing and commercial[8] centres. The proportion of **urban** to **rural population** mightily swells.[9] Great cities rise, and, efficient political administration being now possible on a grander scale, **petty states** give way to those of the **colossal** order.[10]

---

[1] As a single illustration, the complicated instruments for scientific investigation could neither be made by their users nor used by their makers. The susceptibility of a nation's wealth, as a whole, to be passed from hand to hand gauges the grade of culture [England and Russia]. Species of wealth vary quite remarkably in this. Cf. notes 6 and 7, below.

[2] *I.e.*, their work as *producers*, for normal exchange is an act of production. See § 18, n. 2, § 20, vi, and n. 4. Enough of these mediators is important, too many a loss. They tend to multiply unduly, an evil analogous to overproduction.

[3] Fresh facilities for exchange quicken production, this reacts upon those, and so on, each cause ceaselessly and in ten thousand ways influencing the other.

[4] See §§ 43, 44, 45.

[5] A person, a locality, a country, may need but little of another's commodity, yet need that little very much [as quinine]. Or the need may have wide incidence, yet be little urgent [luxuries]. Regularity of demand is an important consideration.

THE NATURE OF EXCHANGE 89

⁶ With progress in the arts of preserving and handling, many products, as ice, milk, fruit, fresh fish and meat, are at present open to far exchanges, which once were not so. There is progress in these processes year by year [strawberries, oysters, clams]. There are regular shipments of fresh game from St. Petersburg to Paris, arriving in from three to five days. Articles of food as a class decay quicker than other categories of wealth.

⁷ Roads, docks, most buildings, also certain cumbrous pieces of machinery, have to be constructed where wanted. Heavy wares, lead, iron, copper, are carried only with great expense. In many such cases the mobility is considerable and on the increase. Houses are gotten up in parts and shipped afar. So water and drive wheels of largest sizes. Pig iron, copper and lead, steel rails, ties and beams cross oceans and continents. But all this costs.

⁸ Nearly all the largest cities are still accessible to heavy shipping. Berlin, however, [1,315,297 inhab.], is not, and a large and growing number of cities of the second rank, as Manchester and Birmingham, Eng., are not.

⁹ In the United States, the percentage of urban [dwellers in cities of 8000 or over] to total population has increased as follows:

1790	3.3	1840	8.5	In the 50 largest American cities in 1880, 43 per cent of the workers were engaged in manufacturing and mechanical industry, 24 per cent in trade and transportation.
1800	3.9	1850	12.5	
1810	4.9	1860	16.1	
1820	4.9	1870	20.9	
1830	6.7	1880	22.5	

In England the percentage of people in cities of 20,000 or over was 51 in 1851, 54.5 in 1861, 56.8 in 1871, and 59.6 in 1881. England and Wales in 1881 had 66.6 per cent of their population in places containing 3000 or more inhabitants. Further on this, Smith [R. M.], Statistics and Economics, 28 sqq.

¹⁰ Roads gave the Roman empire such eternity as it had. It is nearly certain that but for railway and telegraph the United States could not have continued till now a single nation. Significant that before 1870 no solid general government ever existed in Germany, nor, after Justinian, in Italy. Every nation of first rank has since 1850 either extended or strengthened its sovereignty, or both.

§ 55 The Perfection of Exchange
Mangoldt, §§ 43 sqq. *Schoenberg*, vol. i, VII-X.

Exchange becomes **freer and more complete** in proportion to improvements in : i Means of **preserving perishable goods**.[1] ii Facilities for **transporting** intelligence, persons, and freight.[2] iii Institutions which **bring** would-be **buyers and sellers together**, such as fairs,[3] market seasons,[4] market cities or towns, market places in the same, exchanges, stores, shops, travelling salesmen, international expositions, and the like. iv **Weights and measures**, wherein accuracy,[5] simplicity,[6] and universality[7] are the foremost desiderata. v The **mobilizing of property**, by stocks, bonds, certificates,[8] or other titles. vi **Money** and the system of **credit**.[9] vii **Knowledge**,[10] commercial legislation and administration, international **law**[11] and comity.

[1] See § 54, n. 6.

[2] See § 54, n. 7. Telegraph and telephone have immensely cheapened production by rendering it unnecessary for retailers or ordinary wholesalers to keep so extensive stocks as formerly.

[3] Traffic was the original purpose of fairs, and still remains that of the great fairs at Leipzig.

[4] Certain hours of the day, certain days of the week or month. It marks an advance when any commodity, not having previously been so, is *regularly* on sale in a given locality.

[5] Absolute accuracy is unattainable, yet modern standards are incomparably more exact than those prevalent so recently as two centuries ago. See 'Weights and Measures' in Am. Cyclop. and in Encyc. Brit., also Jolly, in Schoenberg. An Act of Parliament, July 30, 1855, decreed "That the straight line between the centres of the transverse lines in the 2 gold plugs in the bronze bar deposited in the office of the Exchequer shall be the genuine standard yard at 62° F." The U. S. yard is supposed to accord with the above, but is in fact about $\frac{1}{1000}$ of an inch longer. Practically, the metric basis, too, must vary with places. Ordinary instru-

ments for weighing and measuring, ill made and roughly used, betray great discrepancies.

⁶ The metric system, with binary modifications for small dealings, is far the best yet devised. The Dutch savant, van Swinden, working for the French Academy, originated the idea of it, and the system was incorporated into French law in 1795. All other civilized nations have since adopted it save Great Britain and its colonies, the U. S., Russia, Denmark, and Switzerland.

⁷ According to Kolb, cited by Mangoldt, there were in Europe at the end of the last century, more than 400 different pounds, and in the Grand Duchy of Baden alone, so late as 1822, 112 different yards. What an obstruction to trade! The metric system ought to become universal.

⁸ By the 'pipe line certificates,' which are simply warrants or titles to so many barrels of crude petroleum, oil is traded in, used for collateral, etc., as freely as bonds, stocks, or bank-notes. The system is now extended to pig iron, and will probably be to all other commodities durable in nature and susceptible of division into permanently fixed amounts.

⁹ See in Part III. Well-made and full-weight coins, paper at par herewith, monetary units having stable purchasing power, sound and widely-developed banking and clearing systems — all are needed. Helpful to international trade are established and familiar banking relations between different lands, the trustworthiness of stamps, labels and the like. A later age will see world-money and the international currency of personal checks.

¹⁰ Cf. § 54, iv. International expositions [Philada., 1876; Paris, 1889] doubtless have vast commercial value, informing nations about each other's products.

¹¹ Chief reference is to private international law, to the facile collection by private parties of debts due abroad. The industrial importance of this has been too little observed.

CHAPTER II

INTERNATIONAL EXCHANGE

§ 56 Initial View

Mill, bk. iii, ch. xvii. *Cairnes*, Leading Principles, pt. iii, ch. iv. *Perry*, chaps. xiii, xiv. *Ad. Smith*, bk. iv. *Bastable*, Theo. of Intl. Trade. *Gill*, Free Trade. *Somers*, 'Exchange,' in Encyc. Brit.

Nations as well as **individuals** have diversities of relative advantage, so that, *prima facie*, international exchange offers **all the economic benefits** of personal and domestic,[1] on a far **grander scale**. Such an impression is confirmed by the following considerations: i Were there no mutual profit in international exchange, it would **cease**. ii Should nations undertake to produce at home the things which they import, **effort** would obviously be **wasted**. iii Since the gain from international trade depends on the **relative cost** of the things exchanged, and not on the absolute cost of either, the traffic may be **profitable** though the imported ware could have been produced at home more cheaply.[2] iv The commodity exports and imports between any country and the rest of the world, must, in the long run, **pay for each other,** gold and silver being used but rarely.[3] v As wealth from abroad can be gotten **only** by the provision of a **domestic surplus,** foreign trade **enlarges** domestic industry instead of lessening it. vi Yet the **great advantage** of this trade resides not in mere extra bulk of goods produced for export, but in the **nature of the imports,** since in these each nation reaps some of the benefits which flow from the **peculiar advantages** enjoyed by the nations with which it trades.[4] vii A nation having every incentive to send abroad its **cheapest products,** those, namely, in the creation of which it has the greatest advantage over others, commerce is a sovereign agent in **cheapening production.** viii The benefits of exchange between nations cannot be confined to any class or section,[5] but reach all consumers, the poor, if anything, more helpfully than the rich.

[1] See §§ 52, 53, 54, and notes. Walker, P. E., 468 [n. fr. Sumner].

[2] No anomaly, impossible as it may seem and rarely as it may occur. The loss on the import over what it would have cost at home may be met *and much more* by the extraordinary price realized on the export. "The ship would return in ballast." Not necessarily. Captains often pay for the privilege of bringing iron or tin from England, as cheaper than to purchase ballast, the diminution of freight thus secured sometimes outweighing the American duty.

[3] No nation could long send money abroad in payment for imports. A very short continuance of the process would so deplete the stock of money as to lower prices, inviting buyers from abroad. They would of course bring money, and the former supply would reappear. Should a country begin exporting for money only, the reverse phenomena would have place.

[4] Fawcett, Manual, 386.

[5] True, even when free competition in importing is not permitted. Fawcett, Manual, 379. If any given import becomes monopolized, as by an international trust, the distribution of advantages will of course be so far rendered imperfect, just as in case of domestic monopolies. The importer, that is, or the set of importers, will retain an undue share of the gain. But not all can be so kept.

§ 57 Common Ground

<small>*Mill*, bk. v, ch. x, § 1. *Roberts*, Government Revenue. *Roscher* [Eng. Tr.], App. II.
George, Protection or F. Trade. *Gill*, and *Bastable*, as at § 56.</small>

Nearly all economic thinkers admit,[1] on the one hand, that: i A nation may sometimes with advantage **restrict purchases**[2] by its citizens abroad 1) to **diversify its own industry**, 2) as a **provision for foreign war**, to force the domestic **creation of war material**, or 3) in the way of **commercial retorsion**.[3] ii Tariffs for **revenue**[4] are **legitimate** and convenient, and withal as just as any form of indirect taxation can be. iii Theoretically 'it may be advantageous to encourage by legislation a branch of industry which **might be** profitably carried on, which is therefore **sure to** be carried on eventually, but whose rise is prevented for the time being by artificial or **accidental causes**.'[5] iv **Particular men**, trades, and localities often **profit** largely from restrictive measures. Few will deny, on the other hand, that: v **Commerce, involving wide acquaintance of nations with nations** through their interchange of **services** and **productions**, is a prime **civilizer**,[6] greatly lessening the danger of **wars** and **famines**, and disseminating infinite **moral and religious good**. vi A policy of restriction cannot possibly be entered upon, altered, or given up, without visiting considerable **hardship** upon certain individuals, classes, or sections.[7] vii **Intro-national** free trade is a priceless **blessing**, as international is destined to become **in the course of time**.[8]

<small>[1] Still another point on which probably all would agree is that mentioned at end of § 60. "Compensating duties," too, on imports the same</small>

in kind with articles bearing excises [internal taxes], if not unduly high, no one would condemn [Ad. Smith, bk. iv, ch. ii].

² By duties on imports or by the absolute prohibition of them. This puts up the prices of the things thus taxed, and induces domestic production. See § 58.

³ High duties, or prohibition, in revenge for the like by some other nation to the disadvantage of yours.

⁴ Perry, 427. *Low* and practically inappreciable duties, on *few* articles, *not produced at home*. So-called protective duties, on the contrary, must of course cover home products, while the higher they are, the better, as a rule, they fulfil their office. They may easily be so elevated as to yield the government no income at all, smuggling [Blanqui, ch. xxvii], false invoices [Lond. Times, Mch. 21, '84], and other dishonesty in merchants being among the reasons. If the revenue on articles not produced in the country is insufficient without making rates too high, some imports the same in kind with things created at home may also be dutied, an excise equal to the duty being laid on the domestic production to prevent unfair favor to home producers thereof. The system so sketched is Great Britain's and New South Wales's. Ancient customs systems were for revenue, not restriction. Carthage exacted tolls both at home and at provincial ports. Rawlinson, Man. of Anc. Hist., 80. Athens in t. of Pericles, had a 2 per cent duty on both exports and imports, besides harbor dues of 1 per cent. Ib., 178. Cf. Thucydides, II, 38. Egypt under the Ptolemies, Rawl., 232. Obviously, taxes thus raised are paid alone by the users of the articles taxed. In strictness this is unjust, all admit. H. George and his followers, besides a considerable party in England, therefore repudiate revenue duties along with all indirect taxes, advocating direct taxation as alone admissible. Revenues are by no means large in proportion as duties are high. Rather does the proportion tend to be an inverse one. The rates of U. S. import duties were about doubled in 1812 with no increase of income.

⁵ Taussig. To illustrate, Maryland, about 1670, would have done well to protect cereals. Tobacco was so high that all attention was devoted to it, so that some years colonists were in danger of starvation. Winsor, Narr. and Crit. Hist., vol. iii, 543. "But from the difficulty of securing in any actual government sufficient wisdom, strength and singleness of aim to withdraw protection inexorably so soon as the public interests require, it is practically best for a statesman to adhere to the broad and simple rule of taxation for revenue only" [Sidgwick]. A good general precept at least. Cf. *post*, § 59, n. 1, also Bastable, Intl. Trade, ch. ix, Cairnes, Leading Prin., 403, n, and George, Social Problems, 231.

[6] Cf. § 53, n. 2. Another consideration of this moral order is the loss, beggary sometimes, which one nation's restriction inflicts upon another's citizens. On the *constitutional* question [in U. S.], 'F. Trade,' in Lalor; Cooley, Const. Law, 57; Ihering, *Geist d. röm. Rechtes*, I, 7.

[7] There must be more or less discrimination between industries, involving them often in great mutual hostility. Ad. Smith, bk. iv, ch. ii. Any bar upon commerce of course tends to destroy the business of ship-builders and sailors. Wells, Our Merchant Marine.

[8] Even Professor Thompson says this. The freedom will be safe, that is, so soon as the same fraternity and substantial economic equality come to prevail between nations which now subsist between the parts of each. Only a few advocates of perpetual trade isolation still remain. On Fichte's "Exclusive State," Adamson's *Fichte*, 76. Max Wirth, on H. C. Carey's Prot. Theo., *Vierteljahrsch. f. Volkswirtschaft*, 1863, vol. ii.

§ 58 The Theory of Nutrient Restriction

Denslow, Prin. of Ec. Philos., chaps. xiv, xv.   *Thompson*, Elements of Pol. Econ.; 'Protection,' in Encyc. Brit. [Stoddart's ed.: full restrictionist bibliog.]. *Rogers*, 'Free Trade,' ibid.   *Laughlin*, ed. of Mill, 677.   *Wells*, 'Free Trade,' in Lalor. *de Molinari*, 'Protection,' ibid.   *Sumner*, Protectionism.   *Fawcett*, F. Trade and Protection.   *Bastable*, chaps. viii, ix.   *Patten*, Prem. of P. E., vii.   [Best list of works pro and con is in Rob. Clarke and Co.'s Catal. of Wks. on P. E., Cinn., 1888.]

There are those who believe in the **legal limitation**[1] of foreign commerce not merely as a prophylactic, a stimulant, or a tonic, but as a highly beneficial form of **industrial nutriment,** supposing it to give the body politic flesh and blood not indirectly alone but as an **instant consequence,** at the very moment of its astringent efficiency, and about in proportion thereto. The error of this view appears when one reflects that it is absolutely impossible for the required check on importation to take effect save at the **public expense,** by a **rise in price**[2] through the whole line of goods affected, whether produced at home or imported. Actual restriction, therefore, so long as it lasts, could not but involve **net loss, swelling** the **cost** at which the nation supplied its wants, and **retarding production** by the transfer of effort from more to less efficient lines. Should a business previously sheltered at any time begin to yield average profits without the aid from society,[3] that very fact would be **proof** that it had **outgrown** its need of legislative fostering. Nor does restriction have a happier effect on the **distribution** of wealth than on its **production.**[4]

[1] It is well to avoid so far as possible the terms 'protection,' 'protective,' etc., because of their ambiguity. Scientific discussion with them is impossible. Besides the form of restriction canvassed in this §, each of the three mentioned in § 57, i, is known as 'protection.' To dub a policy 'protective' settles nothing. The very question at issue is, What policy bids fair to be on the whole most 'protective'?

[2] Efficient restriction *must* raise prices. In no other way can it become efficient. Nor is the loss on what a man buys made up by the higher prices of what he has to sell. The result is, during the actual incidence and working of the restriction, an increase in the total amount of effort put forth by the nation for its total product, or else the loss of a part of that product [Cairnes, Leading Prin., pt. iv, ch. iv].

[3] *I.e.*, still *pay*, yet sell at rates as low as free foreign competition would fix. The restrictive law might remain but would be a dead letter as to the given species of goods. Notice that the mere tariff *rate* on an article does not show whether, or, if so, how much, the duty raises the price of the article. It may not affect the price at all, in which case it is nominal only; or it may raise the price by the full amount of the rate. The continuance of importations in any sort of goods proves that prices have been elevated by the full figure of the actual 'protection.' If a duty is prohibitive, the elevation may fall much below the tariff figure.

[4] If it did, this fact might justify the policy even though the nation were poorer thereby. Feudalists and socialists are wont to allege that freedom of commerce would crush out the middle class, leaving only millionnaires and proletaries. French Revolutionary history and policy disproved this. von Sybel, French Rev., I, 24.

§ 59 Continuation

See the authh. at § 58, esp. *Sumner. Prince-Smith*, '*Handelsfreiheit*,' in Rentzsch's *Handwörterbuch*.

The same conclusion is reached if we consider the various ways in which restriction has by different writers been thought to effect its end. i **Lowering prices**.[1] ii **Increasing or condensing population**.[2] iii **Inviting in foreign capital**. Results i and ii are possible at best only after loss of capital and lapse of time, which refers them to § 57 : iii can ensue sooner. But though in each of these cases net gain **may conceivably** be realized **at last,** it can never in any of them **be proved** beforehand that this will result, or afterwards that it has resulted.[3] iv **Raising wages**. This can occur, if at all, only as an incident of general industrial prosperity, and will not attend even this if immigration is free.[4] v **Keeping at home exchange-profits which else would go abroad**. But the existence of a **desire** to exchange abroad makes it certain that legal restraint could not but **lessen** the number or the profit of the total exchanges, or both.[5] vi **Making foreigners pay part of our taxes**. This would be **unjust** were it **possible, but it is not.** To impose or raise duties certainly decreases foreigners' profits from trade with you, but does not force from them the slightest **positive tribute**.[6]

---

[1] This may be i) *temporary*, a consequence of ruinous competition, involving depletion of aggregate wealth, or ii) *permanent*. The latter might arise through protection to young industries [§ 57, iii]. Or struggling manufactories some time in existence might be enabled to cheapen their line of product by a larger market [above, ii]. In any case loss would have to be incurred, which no one could ever so measure as to certify that it was less than the gain, though it might possibly be. Of

course cheapness may *accompany* or *follow* restriction without being *caused* thereby.

[2] In new countries population may be too thin for the utmost efficiency of its total labor [Mill, bk. i, ch. viii, § 3]. The thought is that it can, by legal measures, costly at first, which nurse manufacturing, be thickened from abroad, or, without this, assembled in towns and villages, so as to produce more *per capita*, and presently, casting aside protection, to defy foreign competition even in the articles at first imported. Free-traders too much ignore the possibility of this, restrictionists its uncertainty, costliness and practical difficulties.

[3] Many chances for loss would be about certain to be overlooked, among them the impoverishment of customer-nations and the limitation of market for unprotected industries. Lalor, vol. ii, 303.

[4] See § 60, 3. If immigration is unhindered, foreign laborers are in competition with domestic, forcing wages down toward the lowest level abroad. If it is prevented, the wages question depends for answer on the propriety of the restrictive policy at large.

[5] If you forbid a man who wishes to do so to trade across the line, it is conceivable that he may effect the desired exchange with equal profit at home, his home customer's gain being a clear increment to the nation's wealth in consequence of the hindrance. But it is perfectly certain that this would not be the case once in a hundred times [Ad. Smith, bk. iv, ch. iii]. In arguing from such mere possibilities, restrictionists are often worse doctrinaires than their opponents.

[6] Sumner, [London] Economist, Dec. 1, '83; Protectionism, 149; Sidgwick, 491 sqq. Full canvass of the proposition is too long for this place. Only transitory and highly improbable conditions can be conceived in which the nation would get in revenue as much as its citizens lost in advanced prices.

§ 60 Important Specific Points

i *Wayland*, P. E., 140. *Perry*, 460 sqq. *Taussig*, Prot. to Young Industries, 60, 64; Pres. Tariff, 90. *Fawcett*, F. Trade and Prot., chap. ii, pp. 9, 28. ii *Fawcett*, Manual, 390. *Farrer*, Free T. vs. Fair ['85]. *Giffen*, Contemp. Rev., June, '85. Westm. Rev., Feb., '88. *Ad. Smith*, bk. iv, ch. ii. iii *Fawcett*, Man., 386. *Walker*, Wages, 44; P. E., 470. iv *Andrews*, Quar. Jour. Econ., Jan., '89.

i **Bounties**[1] offer a more **economical** means of encouraging industry than duties, as by them 1) **prices** are not advanced, 2) **smuggling** is not induced, 3) the country is burdened only for the **actual production** secured, and 4) all the **cost is borne at home**. ii '**Fair trade**' is the cry of a party[2] in England, who speciously plead that, while they would be quite willing to forego restriction if other nations would, free trade is **ruinous** save on this condition of **reciprocity**. But for a nation to lay tariff upon imports does **not remedy**, it aggravates instead, the loss suffered in the taxation of its exports by other nations. Offending peoples are punished, but the **chief penalty** takes effect **at home**. iii Though lowering of wages may not spring from the **mere fact** of using foreign labor, since free importation does not employ that to the **exclusion** of domestic,[3] may it not ensue if wages abroad are **lower than at home?** **Never, wages in general,**[4] and not necessarily wages in the trades in question, since lower nominal, or even lower real, wages abroad do **not imply** smaller cost of labor there. And even in industries where **whole cost** of labor is less abroad, home laborers have nothing to fear from foreign competition, provided this disadvantage is offset, as is often the case, by **advantages.**[5] iv Contrary to free-traders' usual statement, it is in certain cases **possible** for a trade combination in one country to **crush** competitors in another so as then to **put up prices,** or for an **international trust** so to control prices as to render the customs laws of all countries **nugatory.** Such results bid fair to be henceforth **more and more common,** perhaps the rule, that regulation of trade hitherto accomplished by nations separately, through tariffs, necessarily becoming matter for **international compacts.** Meantime, while free international **competition** is commonly one **valuable safe-**

guard against these syndicates, yet where one of them belonging to a given country **oppresses** a **foreign** land, the latter may **well defend** itself by a tariff.

¹ Alex. Hamilton in his famous Report on Manufactures, to the IInd Congress, Dec. 25, 1791, favored bounties as against customs duties. Schouler's U. S., vol. i, 187. In 1885, some 270,000,000 lbs. of sugar were produced in the U. S., about 10 per cent of the consumption. Average cost price not far from $2\frac{1}{2}$ cts., average duty [encouragement] nearly the same. *I.e.*, we paid $2\frac{1}{4}$ cents on each of the entire 2,700,000,000 lbs., conferring a protection equally well secured by a bounty of the same height on one-tenth that number of lbs. — a loss, so far as protection was concerned, of $60,750,000. It might, of course, have been needed for revenue, but as a matter of fact was not.

² 'Reciprocitarians,' Giffen calls them. Even when retorsion [§ 57, i, 3)] is desirable, it is a costly process.

³ See § 56, v.

⁴ Save in the *barely conceivable* ways allowed in § 59.

⁵ Cf. § 48, and n. 4. Roscher [Eng. tr.], vol. i, 218, n. Distinguish the 2 cases, i) high efficiency to labor, keeping pace with high wages, so that *cost of labor* is as low as with smaller wages, or lower; and ii) high labor cost, compensated by specially favorable conditions of production in other respects, so that whole cost of production is no greater. Agricultural wages are higher in Australia and the U. S. than in Europe, owing to the advantages of rich and low-priced lands. Through cheapness of grain, whiskey is manufactured in the U. S. so as to undersell foreign distillers all over the world, though labor here, no more efficient, is paid 50 per cent higher. Eng. factory hands, with their greater skill, better climate and machinery, defy competition from the protected 'pauper labor' of the continent. "India, where the cotton spinner gets only 20 pence a week, is flooded by the cottons of England, where the spinner receives 20 shillings" [Walker]. Thomas' Hist. of Pennsylvania, 1698, p. 9, says, "Poor people, both men and women, will get near 3 times more wages for their labor in this country than they can earn in either England or Wales." Of course America had no protection then. Hamilton's Report [n. 1, above], giving a long list of industries already established in America, notes the then exceedingly high rate of American wages, and well argues that that need be no bar to successful competition with Europe.

CHAPTER III

VALUE: GENERAL

§ 61 Value and Value

Roscher, §§ 4, 5. *Clark*, Philos. of Wealth, ch. v. *Dubos*, Théo. de Valeur, Jour. des Écon., Mch., 1888 [cf. ib., Sep. and Nov., '82, Ap., '83]. *Mill*, bk. iii, ch. vi. *Knies*, Geld, i. *Rae*, Contemp. Socialism, 156. *Sharling*, in Conrad's Jahrb., Mch., '88. *Martello*, La Moneta, App. *Wolf*, in Zeitsch. f. gesam. Staatsw., 42, Heft 3. *Marshall*, in Quar. Jour. Econ., vol. i, 227, 359. *Cairnes*, Contemp. Rev., '76; Leading Prin., pt. i. *Courcelle-Seneuil*, Jour. des Écon., Ap., 1883.

The term **value** bears both in popular and in economic speech **three meanings**, which must be carefully distinguished: i **Utility in general**, the power, whatever its origin, of satisfying human needs.[1] ii **Value in use, economic value proper**, the useful character[2] of things which are actually utilized, however this is estimated, and whether they are destined for exchange or not: in still other phrase, the **immediate significance** which things possess for men's economic life. iii **Value in exchange**, the ratio at which commodities and services pass for one another in open market. The **second** kind of value is nearly identical with the **wealth-character** of things; usually, therefore, not originating gratuitously, though it may also attach to entities, like land proper, which are **not wealth**. The third form of value is closely related to the second, being the resultant of more or less numerous **estimates** placed by human minds on the relative use-values of things. Values of varieties ii and iii hence correspond in a general way, though by no means exactly. In **practical exchange,** we obviously have to do mainly with value in the **third sense,**[3] but this can be properly grasped only by a **patient analysis** of value in the second.

[1] Air and water in general have this. It were better not to use 'value' to name the idea, but only 'utility.' Ever since Adam Smith it has been common to identify senses i and ii. Clearly a confusion, since the mere power to serve us [potential service] is not the same as actual service, or being "in use." The portions which we [by effort] *appropriate* have more than utility, viz., value in use.

[2] See § 1, and n. 6, also § 62. Whatever is wealth has this value, of course. The other things which possess it are very few [§ 28, and n. 3].

[3] It is in this sense, and in this only, that

"The value of a thing,
Is just as much as it will bring" [Butler]. Exchange-value is manifestly in no sense *intrinsic* [§ 62, n. 1]. It is not a property of all wealth [yet see § 1, and n. 7; § 51, and n. 1], but only of such as can be exchanged [§ 63], and reaches beyond wealth just as value in use does [last note].

§ 62 Value in Use

Bonar, Quar. Jour. Econ., vol. iii, 5 sqq. *Jevons,* P. E., ch. iii. *Wieser, Ursprung, etc., des wirtschaftlichen Werthes. Böhm-Bawerk,* in *Jahrb. f. National-oekonomie,* vol. xiii, N. F. ['86]; *Kapital,* etc., bk. iii, sec. i. *Menger, Volkswirt-schaftslehre,* 77 sqq. *Roscher,* §§ 4, 5. *Marx,* Capital, pt. i, ch. i.

i **Objective or general,** the ability which a kind of product **normally** has to produce economic effects.[1]
ii **Subjective or personal,** the power which a **given piece** of wealth possesses to gratify a **particular human being at this or that time.** Not only men's **nature at large** in its various situations has here to be allowed for, but all manner of **individual peculiarities** still more. Every one consciously or unconsciously groups[2] his various wants in a certain **order of importance,** and over against each, its **satisfactions,** in a regular scale of

degrees, always gratifying first the **highest degrees of his foremost wants,** though probably not all the lower degrees of these till the upper degrees of less important wants are met. **Retrenchment,** on the other hand, begins with the **lowest degrees of the least pressing wants,** working upward and backward, reaching last the things **absolutely needful** for life itself. The **value which a man attaches to any article is seen from the grade and degree** of the **lowest want** which he uses it to satisfy.[3]

[1] Coal has heating power; food, nutrient power, etc. It need not mislead to style objective value in use *intrinsic*, though it, as well as every other form of value, is, strictly speaking, an affair of *relation* [§ 61, n. 3].

[2] This may be easily understood by the aid of the following diagram, adapted from Böhm-Bawerk and Menger: —

Degree	I, Food	II, Clothing	III, Lodging	IV, Luxuries
First	Necessary for life			
Second	do for health	First suit, necessary		
Third	Agreeable	Second suit, convenient	A bed	
Fourth	Still less keenly so	Third, desirable	A room	A plate of cream
Fifth	Still less	Fourth, not unacceptable	A suite of two or three	Two plates of cream
Sixth	Satiety	Fifth, satiety	A suite of four Satiety	Three plates Satiety

The supply of wants proceeds [irregularly, and this in different ways with different persons] downward and to the right; retrenchment upward and to the left. "The difference in degree of importance between one meal when it is the only accessible one, and one meal when it is *any* one of five, is not as 5 to 1, but as infinity to 1. When we draw near to absolute necessity, the increase in importance is geometrical rather than arithmetical" [Bonar, as above]. Even when a thing is made necessary only by some pet view or preference of the individual, its importance "often increases with decrease in its quantity, in far greater than arithmetical proportion" [ibid.].

[3] A western farmer may use corn to eat and to burn. Then its fuel value is to him the value of the corn. Subjective value is thus disclosed,

not by its utility at large, but by its *lowest* [often called final] utility. Let the farmer run short of supplies in both kinds, the fuel-use of his corn will be foregone the earlier. Notice that the value of a given *whole* is not told by the lowest use to which any of its *parts* are put, but by the lowest use made of it *as a whole.* Each of several interchangeable and equally worthful *parts* reveals the estimate its owner places on it by the lowest use he makes of *any.* The value of an article to you is also revealed by the utility to you of what you are willing to give for it.

§ 63 Value in Exchange

The authh. at §§ 61, 62. Also, *Perry*, ch. iii. *Macleod*, Elements, ch. ii. *Bagehot*, Ec. Studies, 101 sqq. *Mill*, bk. iii, ch. ii. *Gide, La Notion de la Valeur dans Bastiat, Rev. d. Écon. pol., Mai-Juin,* '87. *Marx*, pt. i, ch. ii. *Sidgwick*, bk. ii, ch. ii.

From these **variations** of value in use according to persons, places, and times, spring the phenomena of exchange[1] and **value in exchange.** To be valuable in exchange, a ware or a service must of course have **susceptibility**[2] to exchange, as well as **utility.** A single case of value in exchange always presupposes **two persons** and **two fourfold estimates,** each party subjectively valuing **what he offers,** and the suggested **return,** at the same time surmising how both are valued by the other. These estimates are determined by a great variety of circumstances: knowledge or beliefs touching the conditions of production, the number of would-be buyers or of would-be sellers, or the value in use of the article in question to any or all. When **many** potential exchangers come into vicinity, **forming a market,**[3] the market rate of exchange at that given time is fixed by the estimates of the **weakest actual buyers** and the **weakest actual sellers.**

[1] But for the different scales and degrees of value [§ 62, n. 2] put by different parties upon one and the same thing, exchange would be unknown. See § 52.

² Our intellectual capital cannot be exchanged, though many of its products may be. It is capital, and wealth, and has value [in use], none the less [§ 1, n. 6].

³ This is the most interesting case. On what forms a 'market,' Bagehot, Ec. Studies, iii [Ad. Smith]; Cairnes, Leading Prin., 17–40; Thornton, Labour, bk. ii, ch. i; Mill, bk. iii, ch. ii; Bonar, Quar. Jour. Econ., vol. iii, 15. Bonar has this diagram:

WOULD-BE BUYERS (subjectively)	WOULD-BE SELLERS (subjectively)
A^1 values a horse at £60	B^1 values his horse at £20
A^2 " " 56	B^2 " " 22
A^3 " " 52	B^3 " " 30
A^4 " " 48	B^4 " " 34
A^5 " " 44	B^5 " " 40
A^6 " " 42	B^6 " " 43
A^7 " " 40	B^7 " " 50
A^8 " " 36	B^8 " " 52
A^9 " " 34	
A^{10} " " 30	

The horses are supposed to be of the same quality. The As and the Bs are 'strong' in proportion to their eagerness to buy or to sell: *i.e.*, those willing to *give* the highest prices are the strongest buyers, those willing to *take* the lowest, the strongest sellers. Assuming, what is likely to happen, that the parties on both sides effect exchanges something in the order of their strength, 5 trades and only 5 will be made, viz., between the As^{1-5} and the Bs^{1-5}. A^6 will give but 42, which is under the figure demanded for any of the three horses remaining. B^6 asks 43, too high for any would-be buyers who are left. A^6 is willing to give 44 or less, B^5 to take 40 or more: the market value, till the conditions change, rests at one or the other of these figures, or between. A^5 is in this case the weakest buyer, B^5 the weakest seller, the two constituting the 'terminal pair.' On the worst day of the snow blockade in N. Y. City, Mch. 13, 1888, Tiffany sold only 80 cents' worth of goods; a certain retail grocer, $10,000 worth. Tiffany could not that day have raised his prices at all; the grocer could probably have doubled.

§ 64 Price

Marx, Capital, pt. i, ch. i, sec. 3. *Mangoldt*, §§ 63-74. *Garnier*, *Traité*, 667 sqq. *Marshall*, Contemp. Rev., Mch., 1887. LEHR, *Vierteljahrsch. f. Volkswirtsch.*, xxvi, i, 2. *Roscher*, §§ 100, 101. *Böhm-Bawerk*, *Kapital*, etc., bk. iii, sec. ii.

When of any article the value is expressed in terms of some other, that other may be called the '**value-form**' of such article.[1] The most common value-form attached to goods is **money,** and the money value-form is **price.** It will be seen that while **general** rises and falls of **prices frequently** occur,[2] such an event meaning only a **change** in the **purchasing power** of money, to speak of a general rise or fall in **exchange-values** would be a **contradiction** in terms.

[1] When, *e.g.*, it is said that 'a bushel of wheat is worth a dollar,' the expression is by no means an equation, though involving the idea of one. The terms could indeed be reversed without falsehood, but not without altering the meaning.

[2] Greatly infringing justice and discouraging trade. See, later, § 87, on Ideal Money.

§ 65 Normal Value in Exchange

Cairnes, Leading Principles, pt. i, chaps. iii, iv. *Ad. Smith*, bk. i, ch. xi. *Mill*, bk. iii, chaps. ii-iv. *Maine*, Village Communities, vi. *Senior*, Pol. Econ., 101, 102.

Of the commodities **producible at will** in indefinite amounts, much the larger part of all, **market values** and **prices**[1] are not fixed ultimately by the influences mentioned at § 63, but by **cost of production,** or, more strictly, that of **reproduction.**[2] This cost may be styled the **normal value** of commodities. Around it market values and prices will hover, sometimes **higher,** sometimes **lower,** according to circumstances, but never for any considerable period[3] very far away. If, in the case of a given article, different portions of the necessary supply offered in one and the same market have **unlike** costs of production, normal value coincides with the **dearest cost involved**.[4] Things like heirlooms, paintings of old masters,[5] etc., which **cannot be duplicated**, are subject to no law of normal value, but command a higher price or a lower purely according to the relations between **supply and demand**.[6]

[1] Why mention 'market values'? Why is not 'prices' sufficient? Because the law would hold equally if money had never been invented [§ 64].

[2] See §§ 47, 48. If classes of goods be taken, cost of reproduction and of production will not vary much. The strictly ultimate determinant is the metaphysical cost [§ 47]. Cf. Hyndman, Hist. Basis of Socialism, 105. The discussion contemplates primary sales, viz., by growers or manufacturers themselves. Cost of production at the retail stage of the process includes allowances for handling, tare and tret, interest, storage, etc. Cf. § 69, ii.

[3] Though temporarily perhaps a good deal above or below [scarcity prices]. During the snow blockade, Mch. 15, 1888, milk sold in N. Y. City for $5 and $6 per can of 40 qts. The next day it had fallen to $1. Henry George found flour at the Frazer River gold diggings, in 1858, worth $1.50 a lb.; bacon, $3. To Purchas's 'Pilgrimes' [vol. i, 118, 133, 275, 417: see Tylor's Early H. of Mankind, 223] the natives of Madagascar were glad to pay a sheep for 1s. silver; a cow for 3s. 6d. At Saldanha Bay, on the west coast of Africa, in 1598, the natives, ignorant how to work iron, offered John Davis fat sheep and bullocks for nails or bits of old iron. In 1604 a huge bullock was to be bought there for a piece of iron hoop. If competition is free [Senior, 102], variation from cost of production, in an article whose price is determined by this, always tends to annihilate itself. If prices exceed this cost, production will be the more profitable, and hence copious; if they are below it, production falls off.

[4] An important principle. See on Rent, in Part IV. All the wheat of a given quality for sale in Chicago bears the same price, whether from poor land or rich, raised with good machinery or none. Block Island poultry, though produced at less than normal expense, brings in Providence as high

prices as any. When demand diminishes, the costlier parts of the supply are dispensed with first, and the normal value falls [cf. § 27, n. 3].

⁵ And some others. See § 68 and § 69, i. Cf. below, n. 6. On prices of monopolized wealth, § 66. The famous sermon preached by John Knox at Edinburgh, in August, 1565, "for the whiche he was inhibite preaching for a season," was sold recently for $2,075. A few years ago a Madonna by Murillo brought in Paris 615,300 francs. One Banks, in N. Y. City, sold from his arm, for transfusion into the veins of an asphyxiated patient, 8 ounces of blood, containing 240 drops each, for 10 cents a drop: = $192. Gen. R. B. Marcy has seen, in camp on the plains, $10 offered for a quid of tobacco. Consul L. Mummius, having conquered Corinth, 148 or 147 B.C., on sending the pictures and statues to Rome, told the sailors that if they lost or injured any, they must furnish others of equal value. One of the choicest works of the painter Aristides he let them use as a draughtboard [Liddell, Rome, 479].

⁶ Mangoldt, §§ 64-66. Demand differs from mere desire. It is this coupled with the necessary goods or credit. Supply, too, is more than the simple existence of commodities. Their owner must be willing, at some rate, to exchange them. Cf. § 63, also Cairnes, pt. i, ch. ii. The market value of all things at times and, to an extent, of all ordinary commodities at all times, is regulated by the equation between supply and demand. Inequality at any moment between these is equalized by readjustment of value. Demand increasing, value rises; diminishing, it falls. Supply diminishing, value rises; increasing, it falls. The rise or the fall continues until demand and supply are again equal, "and the value which a commodity will bring in any market, is no other than the value which, in that market, gives a demand just sufficient to carry off the existing or expected supply." Mill, bk. iii, ch. ii, §§ 2, 3, 4. On de Molinari's law respecting the ratio at which change in supply acts on price, § 15, n. 5. The law is as follows: "When the relation of the *quantities* of two products or services offered in exchange, varies in an arithmetical ratio, the relation of the *values* of those two products or services varies in a geometrical ratio" [*Jour. des Écon.*, Feb., 1889, 188]. When the N. Y. Tribune reduced the price of its copies from 4 to 3 cents, 25 per cent, its circulation increased 30 per cent, though income therefrom fell off [as stated] 19 per cent. The Times reduced from 4 to 2 cents, 50 per cent, gaining 130 per cent in circulation and 15 per cent in income.

CHAPTER IV

VALUE: PECULIAR PROBLEMS

§ 66 Competition and Value

Cairnes, Leading Principles, Harper's ed., 87 sqq. *Sidgwick*, bk. ii, ch. ii. *Ingram*, Hist. of P. E., 158. *Clark & Giddings*, Mod. Distrib. Process, chaps. i, ii. *Bagehot*, Postulates of P. E.

That market value should absolutely conform to cost of production, in the way just described, would presuppose (i) general **information** touching all cases of profits,[1] (ii) **equality of advantage** among competitors, and (iii) perfect **mobility** of labor and capital.[2] Such conditions are **rarely** if ever realized[3] save in a very imperfect way. As to **labor**, not only do **poverty, ignorance,** their **distance** apart and **differences** of speech keep people from full competition, but not all those of a given vicinity compete for all **positions**. Instead, we everywhere find an arrangement of **groups**[4] **and sub-groups,** according to **occupation, ability,** and **training, within** each of which there is competition, between which, little or none. The tendency of **trades-unions** is to check competition still more. **Capital,** too, crowds capital only in proportion as (i) it remains **free** or non-specialized,[5] (ii) **profits** are known, and (iii) **monopoly** is prevented. A monopoly may be kept up either by the action of **government,** or by the sheer mass of **wealth** behind it [6]

VALUE: PECULIAR PROBLEMS   111

¹ As sucn knowledge is rarely direct or exact, and always incomplete, statements about the proportion of national income taking the form of profits are little but guesses. Rate of interest is no guide. Thus, ignorant of each other's prosperity, businesses will not uniformly so compete as to keep selling prices the closest possible to cost. Absence of (ii) and (iii) would also help prevent this.

² The fundamental postulate of English Economics, which, however, Bagehot correctly declared only hypothetically true for much of modern Europe, and not true at all for primitive society. He was mistaken in supposing that it would ever accord with facts in other than a general way.

³ Usually, therefore, all that can be said is that products *tend* to sell at cost of production [§ 65, n. 2]. The law is, however, little less valuable because inexact.

⁴

	ploughs	cutlery	wire	tack	nail	rail	steel	pipe	stove	wire	tack	nail	rail	iron	ore
responsible brain workers															
automatic brain workers															
responsible manual labor															
automatic manual labor															
						iron and steel									
							ore								

This diagram, modified from Giddings, as above, shows by way of example the non-competitive grouping in the iron and steel industry. Observe that competition is more widely possible the lower the grade of labor. Ore-diggers [unskilled] and smelters may compete with the lowest iron and steel workers, and both with the automatists engaged upon final products. Higher up, work is mostly more specialized. Notwithstanding all the above, a degree of competition, defying the lines of classes and industries, still persists through the supply of youthful laborers continually coming on to the stage, choosing this calling or that, as offers best remuneration. Machinery and education extend the scope of this process.

⁵ Cf. § 29, notes 6, 7.

⁶ Those who deny the possibility of maintaining a monopoly in the last way named, overlook (i) the extent to which profits are concealed, (ii) the progressive immunity from competition which comes with immen-

sity of resources and specialization of plant, and (iii) the temptation of formal competitors not to become real ones, they sharing all the advantages from the elevation of prices [next §, and its n. 4].

§ 67 Monopoly Value

Sidgwick, bk. ii, ch. x. *Marshall*, Ec. of Industry, 180 sqq. *Senior*, Pol. Econ., 103-114. *Sumner*, Essays, 46. Quar. Jour. Econ., vol. iii, 143.

Monopolies may be **natural or artificial,**[1] **exclusive**[2] **or partial.** A monopoly, again, whether complete or not, may be in an article whose **production can be swollen** (i) not at all, (ii) indefinitely, but at increasing cost, or (iii) indefinitely at the same or lessening cost.[3] The monopolist's power will vary accordingly, but it is important to mark that he **need never,** in order to dictate sale prices, **control the entire production.**[4] In case of a product so monopolized, the price is fixed not by cost but by men's **necessity.** It goes higher and higher till demand, and hence profit, begins to fall off, and then plays about the line of **what the market will bear,** just as in other cases about that of cost. The monopolist can be more or less exacting according to the **nature of the product.** If it is a **luxury,** he extorts little; if a **necessity,** he may bleed consumers to death.[5]

[1] Government is a monopoly, natural and exclusive. A railroad, once created, has a natural, though incomplete, monopoly of its strictly way traffic — natural in that, power once given it to be a railroad, monopoly arises without further legislation; incomplete, since means of possible competition remain. Land-holding, be it private or communal, naturally involves monopoly. So the ownership of mines, water-power, and the like. The legislation granting the titles in such cases does not create, it merely assigns, the monopolies. But when, as so often under Elizabeth and James I, public power grants the exclusive right to manufacture or

sell, the monopoly originates in the grant [artificially], not in the nature of the case.

² "Constantia (wine) owes its peculiar flavor to the agency of a few acres of ground, and would be destroyed if high cultivation were employed to force from that ground a larger quantity of wine. No person but the proprietor of the Constantia farm can be a producer" [Senior, P. E., 104]. Not so a railway. If it is too extortionate, some people will use wagons.

³ The owner of Constantia [n. 2] illustrates (i); the proprietor of a rare mine, (ii) : see § 34; the patentee of a manufacturing machine or process, (iii).

⁴ Immediate mastery of a decided majority is, as regards dominating the price, the mastery of all. That is, competition with a partial monopoly is formal only, and it does not become real until competitors attain power to supply the entire market. The law of dearest cost [§ 65 and n. 4] has here one of its applications. For illustrations, Quar. Jour. Econ., vol. iii, 142 sq. Cf. above, § 66, n. 6.

⁵ "The price cannot, of course, fall below the cost of production, but may indefinitely exceed it. . . . If fashion were to make it an object of intense desire among the opulent, a pipe of Constantia [n. 2], costing perhaps £20, might sell for £20,000" [Senior]. Imagine a monopoly over quinine in a typhoid epidemic. The parlor and sleeping-car service is a monopoly in a luxury. Rates must be moderate, else people will take the ordinary coaches.

§ 68 VALUES BETWEEN NON-COMPETING GROUPS

Mill, bk. iii, ch. xviii; Essay i, on Unsettled Questions. *Cairnes*, Leading Principles, pt. i, ch. iii, § 7. *Sidgwick*, bk. ii, ch. iii. *Cherbuliez*, bk. ii, ch. viii. *Nicholson*, Money and Mon. Problems, ch. vii. *Fawcett*, Manual, 390 sqq.

Products whose creators do **not compete**, exchange not in proportion to their **costs of production** but purely according to the conditions of **reciprocal demand**. International **commerce**[1] best illustrates this. At the opening of a trade between two countries there is usually a **greater demand** in one direction than in the other, at the prices first asked. Then the commodity, or line of commodities, least in demand must be **sold lower,** or the trade cease, and this every time demand becomes slack for any commodity at the old price. If the demanded reduction still leaves a profit, the exchange will go on; if not, not; but so long as it does go on, there is always a tendency toward an **equation of international demand.** The cost of **ocean freightage** rarely falls with equal weight on both countries. It is the **heavier** on that one the demand for whose commodity is the more **diminished** by it from what such demand would be were there no charge for freightage, and **in proportion** to that diminution. The same principles govern among **domestic groups** not in competition. Whatever **increases the demand** of any one for outside products, or its **supply** of things available for the purchase of them, renders **less favorable** the terms on which it will have to exchange, and *vice versa;* while all that **swells outside demand** for its products, or **lessens its supply, meliorates** for it the conditions of exchange, and *vice versa.*

[1] The principle of this section has ramifications difficult to follow, whose explication would be too lengthy. Mill's treatment [as above] is the best, to be read with Cairnes's reminder that the essential subject is broader than Mill saw, covering much domestic traffic, as well as that which crosses national boundaries. The main point to observe is that an exchange in such cases may profit the two parties very unequally.

§ 69 Complex Cases of Value
Mill, bk. iii, ch. xvi.

i **Wastes** utilized for purposes other than gain, also the products of labor **incidental** to main callings, usually sell at prices which are **independent** of their costs.
ii When, as often, there is for any commodity or service

a small, though permanent demand, that cost of production which determines prices, must be construed to include such items as insurance, risk, interest, storage, lessened economy in labor force, and the like. iii Many a single process of production yields a **main** and a **by** product, as gas and coke, or a cluster of joint products, as chickens and eggs, or beef, hides, and tallow. Cost of production will then, **supposing competition,** determine the value of the total product in relation to other things, but not of one of its elements in relation to another or others. Their **relative values** will be such as to keep the relative demand for them **proportionate to the relative natural supply**[1] of them. iv **Soil** which can grow **either** of two grains is often the better suited to **one.** In such cases, (i) if demand forces both on to **intermediate** soil equally good for both, their general costs here will fix their general values, and their **relative costs** their relative values; (ii) if either has to be grown on the soil best fitted for the other, this other will become **cheaper,** and the alien crop **dearer, in proportion to the stress** so created.

[1] By cheapening the one less in demand, or raising the other, or doing both. Suppose a special demand for coke. It can only be met by producing more gas. To market this its price must be lowered, though the cost of production of it, by itself, has not altered. Make other suppositions and **carry** through the analysis.

§ 70   A Measure of Exchange-Value[1]

Mill, bk. iii, ch. xv.   *Marshall*, Contemp. Rev., vol. 51, 354 sqq.   *Jevons*, Money and the Mech. of Exchange, ch. xxv.   *Yves Guyot, Sci. Economique,* bk. iii, ch. ii.   *Mangoldt*, §§ 75 sqq.

While **labor, corn, money,** or any other service or commodity, will serve as a measure of the relative values[2] of particular things at a given time and place, or of the changes in these between different times and places,[3] no even approximate gauge of **exchange-value in general** is furnished by **nature.** Art itself could not make such a measure **perfectly accurate**; but a **compound standard**,[4] formed by adding the values, ascertained from period to period, of **fixed amounts and qualities** of the world's **staple** commodities, each allowed weight according to the quantity of it consumed, would **closely** meet the requirement.[5] Then, by carefully expanding and contracting the currency, **money** could be kept in conformity with such composite standard, thus realizing a measure of general value in **one single commodity.**[6]

[1] The problem concerning a measure of value in use [§ 62] is very different. See Clark, Philos. of Wealth, 89. He thinks even that not insoluble. So Friedländer, *Theorie d. Werthes* [1852]. Ad. Smith's idea, bk. i, ch. v, where he argues for labor as a measure, is not exclusively that of exchange value. This theory of Smith, Franklin had stated and avowed so early as 1752. To-day the socialists are its great champions. Rae, Contemp. Socialism, 94 sq., 152 sq. Value, says Marx, is neither v. in use nor v. in exchange, but labor-quality.

[2] If one thing is worth 2 bushels of wheat and another 3, the first is obviously worth ⅔ as much as the second. The same if iron, coal, or money had served as measure. But after any lapse of time you could not reckon from mere equality in value between the first and 2 bushels of wheat, that it was still worth ⅔ the second. The value of wheat itself might have altered. See next n.

[3] If a bushel of wheat would buy a day's farm labor in 1850, and only ⅔ of this in 1870, we know that wages, in terms of wheat, went up during that double decade in the ratio of 2 : 3, or 50 per cent. But whether wages rose in general purchasing power, neither wheat, gold, nor any other commodity, left to natural fluctuations, would reveal.

[4] See Jevons, as above. He has wrought out the general idea more fully in his Investigations in Currency and Finance, section ii.

[5] In denying that we "can even suppose any state of circumstances in which this would be true," Mill does not take account of the possibility

here set forth. His is the common idea. See Fix, *Jour. des Écon.*, 1844, IX, 12. So Ricardo wrote, in Proposals for an Economic and Secure Currency, sections i, iii, "against such variation there is no possible remedy."

[6] See later, § 85. Mill, as above, well charges us to distinguish between a *measure* of value and a *regulator* or *determinant* of value, such as cost of production is. To conceive a measure of cost of production Mill [ibid.] thinks not difficult, though no such is forthcoming in nature.

§ 71 The Value of Futures

Böhm-Bawerk, Kapital u. Kap.-zins, vol. ii, bk. iii, sec. iii. *Gross,* 'Zeit in d. Volkswirtsch.,' in *Zeitsch. f. die gesam. Staatsw.*, 1883, 126 sqq. *Jevons*, Theo. of P. E. *Mill*, bk. i, ch. xi. *Menger*, as at § 62, 127 sqq. *Sax, Grundlegung*, 178 sqq., 313 sqq.

i Owing to (i) the **productive power** of present goods meantime, (ii) our **uncertainty** about future demand and supply, and (iii) our **undervaluation** of future pleasures and pains, **future goods,** per unit of quantity and quality, have for most men a lower **subjective value** in use than present goods. ii From these subjective valuations arise **corresponding objective values and market prices,** which, reacting upon present goods, raise the **subjective** exchange valuations of these even for the few in whose mere **personal estimation** futures might have seemed **superior.** iii The **levelling tendencies of the market** then bring it about that, barring special causes of disturbance, futures will in the market bear **prices less** than those of **similar spot articles,** by a figure proportioned to the **degree** of their futurity.[1]

[1] This is the very valuable pith of what is strictly original in Böhm-Bawerk's book. The thought is wrought out with great thoroughness in his section cited above, and must henceforth be regarded as an integral principle of Economics. For his application of it to the problem of interest, see § 109.

Part III

MONEY AND CREDIT

CHAPTER I

THE NATURAL HISTORY OF MONEY

§ 72 Barter

Knies, Geld, i. *Jevons*, Mo. and the Mech. of Exchange, ch. i. *Aristotle*, Politics bk. i, ch. ix. *Nicholson*, Mo. and Mon. Problems, 17. Macleod, Elements, 120.

Barter is a form of traffic in which **commodity passes for commodity** without any use of money or other tool of exchange. The infelicities of barter-exchange confine it in the main to the societies that are the **least civilized** and productive.¹ The chief drawbacks are i Necessity of setting a **price to every commodity** in terms of every other.² ii Want of **subdivisibility** in most articles.³ iii Limited **correspondence** between needs and commodities or services. A special degree of this evil exists in the case of **the laborer**, who can work only for such as have, and will spare, the things needed for his support. When **money of account** is used to reckon in, yet no money ever passes hands, we may call the practice **quasi-barter**.⁴

¹ Although it has nowhere ceased entirely. Swapping horses or knives, changing works or teams [among farmers], taking cows or work animals for their keep, commonly involve no thought of money. Macleod con-

siders the society described by Homer still in a state of barter. Iliad, ii, 448, vi, 234, vii, 468, xxiii, 703. It was primitive money [next §] rather, but the passages usefully illustrate the evil phases of barter.

[2] Between 100 articles no less than 4950 possible ratios of exchange exist, all which a retailer on the truck system would constantly have to keep run of. With money, the number reduces to 100.

[3] Many could not be divided at all, others not without impairing or destroying their value.

[4] The line between barter and money is passed when, in trading, men accept this or that as pay, *with the idea of recourse:* i.e., intending not to *use* what they get, but to *pass it off* for the thing wanted. This transition, when general, is a decisive step in the onward march of civilization.

§ 73 PRIMITIVE MONEY

Jevons, ch. iv. *Chapin's Wayland*, 289. *Ad. Smith*, bk. i, ch. iv. *Roscher*, § 118. *Lubbock*, 'Early H. of Mo.,' Contemp. Rev., 1879.

In the evolution of society upward through succeeding stages, very various commodities have served as media of exchange. Of these may be mentioned especially: (i) **peltry** in the hunting state,[1] (ii) **cattle**[2] **and slaves** in the pastoral, (iii) **corn**[3] and other cereals, with **beans, olive oil, tobacco,** etc., in the agricultural, (iv) **mats,** pieces of **cloth, nails**[4] and various other manufactured articles, in a more civilized state, (v) **cowrie shells,**[5] **wampum**[6] and other articles of beauty, in every state previous to the invention of regular money. Gold and silver probably first obtained currency through use for **personal adornment.**[7]

[1] According to the Bismarck *Tribune*, 1885, gopher tails were then currency in parts of Dakota.

[2] Cattle were the main money of Homeric times [§ 72, n. 1]. Also among the Hindoos in the age to which the earliest Rig-Vedic hymns relate, 3000–4000 B.C. 'India,' in Encyc. Brit. Our word 'fee' originally meant 'cattle' [so the Latin *pecunia*, money, and *peculatus*, property, from *pecus*, a 'herd' of cattle or sheep].

[3] So. Carolina, in 1687, made "corne, pease, pork, beef, tobacco, and

tars" general legal tender. The rôle of tobacco as money in early Virginia and Maryland is well known. Mexico, when the Spaniards arrived, had no gold money, though both gold and silver were wrought, but for money used cacao beans in little bags holding 8000–24000 each, cotton materials, gold dust in goose-quills with values according to size, pieces of copper 3–4 fingers wide, and little tin plates. Schoenberg, I, 38, n. [2d ed.]. Morgan, Anct. Society, pt. ii, ch. vii, says the Aztecs had no money, but barter only. In Thibet, cakes of salt and of tea were money and legal tender till somewhat recently. La Couperie, Silver Coinage of Thibet.

⁴ Ad. Smith [as above] had heard that nails were still in his time used for small change in parts of Scotland. There is tin money in China and the Malay Archipelago. In Senegambia iron is money, as in ancient Sparta, where Lycurgus's laws forbade the possession of gold. Iron was a precious metal among the old Turanians of Babylon. Maspero, *Hist. anc.*, 140 sqq.

⁵ A beautiful shell, about an inch long, white and straw-colored without, blue within, found nearly all over the world, especially in the shallow waters of the Indian Ocean. There are over 100 species. The one in question is the *cypraea moneta* — '*cypraea*' from the name of the mollusk which it clothes, '*moneta*' from its wide use as money. On parts of the coast of Africa it is the regular tender, and it still enjoys great currency in farther India. In Bengal, formerly, 3840 equalled a rupee [50 cents]. 'Cowry,' in Encyc. Brit.

⁶ On wampum as money in colonial times, Weeden, in Johns Hopkins Univ. Studies, 2d ser., viii–ix.

⁷ But F. A. Paley, Contemp. Rev., Aug., 1884, argues learnedly that gold was first esteemed in connection with sun-worship. In Genesis, ch. xxiv, gold is only a commodity, bought with silver. More, Utopia, ch. vi, represents the Utopians as eating from earthen and glass, while using gold and silver for gyves to bind criminals, earrings to brand infamous persons, and even for purposes namelessly vile.

§ 74 MONEY PROPER

Mill, bk. iii, chap. vii. *Sidgwick*, bk. ii, ch. iv. *Bastable*, 'Money,' in Encyc. Brit. *Nicholson*, Mo. and Mon. Prob., ch. iii. *Roscher*, vol. i, § 119; vol. iii [*Handel u. Gewerbefleiss*] § 40. *Schoenberg*, vol. i, VII. *Walker*, Money, ch. ii. *Mangoldt*, §§ 50 sqq.

All exchange by means of primitive currency must manifestly have labored under many of the disadvantages of barter itself. Exchange could not become facile or extensive until commodities were discovered so **uniformly desirable** as to possess, by universal consent, a **universal purchasing power,** in other words, exchange readily everywhere for all commodities and services whatever, thus becoming **money proper.**[1] **Gold and silver** proved such commodities. Long current at first by **weight and test,** they acquired far fuller usefulness with the invention and extension of authoritative **coining.**[2]

[1] 'A universally successful tender' is perhaps the best definition of [full] money. Cf. § 82. Other things are then money only in so far as they meet this criterion. F. A. Walker, 'Money,' followed by Bastable, calls money "that which passes freely from hand to hand throughout the community in final discharge of debts and full payment for commodities, being accepted equally without reference to the character or credit of the person who offers it and without the intention of the person who receives it to consume it or enjoy it or apply it to any other use than in turn to tender it to others in discharge of debts or payment for commodities." This, of course, includes bank notes. Defining so, you are forced to subdivide money into kinds. Sidgwick, and J. H. Walker [Mo., Trade and Banking] include checks and all bankers' liabilities in 'money.' There are advantages to this, also disadvantages, as to any terminology. Choice of definition is less important than consistency in holding to the one chosen.

[2] See next §, iii, (ii,) and n. 10.

§ 75 The Money Metals

Roscher, vol. iii, ch. vi. *Jevons*, chaps. v, vi. *Schoenberg*, vol. i, VII, III, IV. *Eissler*, The Metallurgy of Gold; do. of silver. *Walker*, Money, chaps. v–viii. *Bastable*, 'Money,' in Encyc. Brit.

Gold and silver possess various **attributes** besides universal currency which fit them to serve as money better than any other known material. They are: i **Convenient:**[1] (a) divisible, (b) durable, (c) impressible, (d) portable. ii **Steadiest of all things in value,** owing to, (i) size and regularity of demand,[2] (ii) largeness[3] of quantity in use, (iii) uniformity in cost of production,[4] (iv) facility of transportation,[5] (v) tendency of every rise or fall in value **to be checked** by change in, (a) production[6] of the metals themselves, (b) use of credit,[7] (c) exchange power of a given amount[8] of the money.   iii **Relatively independent, in value, of governmental act.**   (i) Legal enactments do not make them into money.   (ii) Government, though it may modify, **cannot fix** their value,[9] **coinage** only attesting the **quantity** and **quality** of the metal in each piece.[10]

---

[1] Diamonds, like gold and silver, present great weight in small compass, but lack qualities (a) and (c). The Regent or Pitt diamond is thought worth about 2.2 tons of gold coin, as much as 40 men could carry. Gold is in fact far from being the most valuable substance. It is worth per troy ounce $20.67183. Rare metals are quoted by the gramme. Reducing this to troy ounces we have per troy ounce, omitting fractions, Barium $124, Calcium $311, Osmium $93, Rubidium $622, Zirconium $496. [Scient. American, June, 1886.] There are said to be 19 metals more precious by weight than gold, and cocaine is more so than any metal. A pound of steel in the form of hair springs for watches is worth [1889] $140,000. Platinum, coined by Russia from 1828 to 1845, proved poor money, being lustreless, difficult to melt, and very fluctuating in value, owing to meagreness of supply. Quicksilver liquefies too easily. Copper, 900 times less valuable per grain than gold, is, for rich societies, not precious enough for full money, but lasts nobly. J. B. Say believed certain copper coins to be still current in France early in this century which had never been out of circulation since the days of the Roman empire [Blanqui, vol. i, 321]. As to weight, gold [spec. grav. 19.253] is the heaviest metal but two: platinum [21.5], and iridium [22.23]. Silver has a spec. grav. of 10.474; copper, one of 8.8.

[2] The demand for money consists of all goods, services, *etc.*, whatever, which are offered for money.

[3] Of gold the world's existing stock, coin and wares, is about 11,000 tons, worth $7,700,000,000. The usual yearly loss, literal and from attrition, *etc.*, is 2 tons, or $1,400,000. The mines yield yearly some $85,000,000,

of which, till lately, ¼ has gone into coin, the rest into wares. Now, the consumption for wares is greater, about $62,500,000 annually. The gold in the world in 1884, in form of coin or of bullion covering notes, was $3,700,000,000 [Del Mar.], $3,400,000,000 [Burchard], or $3,270,000,000 [Soetbeer]. The silver of the civilized nations in 1884, money and hoards, was estimated at $2,185,000,000, and the increase that year, not quite $130,000,000. Of silver the western nations use in manufactures some $22,000,000, and send to Asia about $72,000,000, hoarding or coining not over $35,000,000.

[4] Greater for silver than for gold, because of its wider and more equable distribution in the earth. Suess, *Zukunft des Goldes.*

[5] See § 76. Here gold, value for value, has enormous advantage over silver: $1,000,000 in gold weighing only about $1\frac{3}{4}$ tons, in silver $26\frac{3}{4}$ tons. For subsidiary silver, about 6.4 per cent lighter than the dollars, the figure would be 25 tons; for nickel half dimes, 100 tons.

[6] If gold, *e.g.*, ever becomes abnormally dear, mining it pays better, the output increases, and the extra preciousness disappears, or tends to. Also *vice versa*. Notice, however, that, with the growth of fixed capital in mining the influence described acts less promptly. Hadley, Railroad Transportation, 72.

[7] In general, as money increases in value, more credit transactions take place, so far dispensing with money, and hence cheapening the same again. If it decreases in value, the reverse results appear.

[8] That $1 will now pay for as much as $1.10 would a month ago, means that so much more exchanging can now be effected with a given amount of money. This possibility has little effect in practice, because, though the dearer unit could exchange more, it would not do so, owing to tendency of dear money [low prices] to retard circulation. This is why the text does not, as is common, name 'swifter or slower circulation' as an element in the automatism of money's value. Dear money, working as a brake on circulation, tends to grow dearer still: cheap money [high prices], accelerating circulation, grows ever cheaper. But should extraneous causes give quick movement to dear money, rise in its value would be checked; or a slow pace to cheap money, it would tend to be less cheap.

[9] A metal not so already, might, however, become more valuable by being made legal currency, and it is believed that several powerful governments could by coining upon a common ratio maintain the relative values of gold and silver free from essential change [next §]. Certain writers exaggerate, others underrate, the character of money as product of state action. See Horton's note, Rep. of Intl. Monetary Conf. of 1878, p. 741.

[10] This, *i.e.*, constitutes the political essence of coining. The embossing, milling and other artistic work are of great service against counterfeiting, and may also embellish. The alloy imparts hardness. The 'fine bars' of silver made by the U. S. mints and assay offices run 998–999 fine, usually 999. The U. S. and most of Europe, coin from metal 900 fine, and bars of this fineness are in these lands called 'standard' bars. Great Britain coins gold $916\frac{2}{3}$ fine, silver from her 'standard' silver bars, 925 fine. The silver quotations in London refer to such bars. There is thus no universally recognized 'standard' for bars of either metal, but $\frac{900}{1000}$ will probably come in time to be recognized as such. Russian coins are $\frac{11}{12}$ fine, like English gold.

§ 76 Mode of their Distribution

Mill, bk. iii, chaps. viii, ix, xix, xxi. *Ad. Smith*, bk. iv, ch. 1.

Gold and silver find their way over the earth partly as **commodities**, partly as **coin**. If gold is plentiful in any country, whether dug there or brought there, it is **cheap**, prices are **high**, and foreign commodities throng in, to be paid for by **sending gold** to the countries whence they come. On the other hand, every country where gold is **scarce** will have **low** prices, and gold will be tempted in to purchase commodities for exportation.[1]

[1] A fine example of the play of natural law in the social world [§ 15, n. 5]. During the potato famine of 1847 Great Britain had to import enormous quantities of grain from America, sending hither therefor the sum of £16,000,000 in bullion. Prices at once rose here and fell in England. Eng. merchants bought less in America, while Americans bought largely in England, so that, the next year, all the gold returned to Great Britain. Toynbee, Industrial Revolution, 82 sq. The processes described are of course more or less obstructed by tariffs, and by whatever hinders trade [§§ 54, 55].

§ 77 Bimetallism

Nicholson, Mo. and Mon. Problems, pt. ii. *Walker*, P. E., 406 sqq.; Money, chaps. xii, xiii; Mo. Trade, and Ind., chaps. vi, vii. *Laughlin*, ed. of Mill, 633 [good bibliog.]. *Jevons*, ch. xii. *Schaeffle, Für internat. Doppelwährung. Arendt, Vertragsmässige Doppelwährung. Wagner*, in *Zeitsch. f. gesam. Staatsw.*, 1880, IV, 1881, I. *Suess, Zukunft d. Goldes. Lexis*, in Conrad's *Jahrb.*, 1877, II; 1880, I; 1882, I. *Soetbeer, ibid.*, 1880, I; *Vierteljahrsch. f. Volkswirtsch.*, XXII, ii, 2. *Laveleye, La mon. bimetallique. Pütz, Graph. Darst. d. Metallpreise. Nasse*, in *Schoenberg*, vol. i, VII, xi, 3. U. S. Consular Rep., Dec., 1887.

Bimetallic money is money formed by opening gold and silver both to **free coinage,**[1] and making each an **unlimited legal tender** at a certain permanent legal **value-ratio**[2] to the other. Its **superiority,** supposing the scheme feasible, arises from two facts: i It will add **steadiness** to the value of the dollar or other unit of value, since this, as we have seen,[3] is complete in proportion to the **size** of the whole **volume** of unwrought[4] money-metal. Gold and silver together of course form a far **vaster reservoir** than either by itself. But a bimetallic money-unit will be less changeful than a monometallic, even if the whole money-metal volume is the same in the two cases, as **fluctuations**[5] **in both** metals at one and the same time are **less probable** than in one alone. ii Such a system would furnish a **common measure** of value between its members and gold monometallist or silver monometallist states,[6] and between these latter also. The serious question is whether the two metals **can be made a single standard** of value. We pronounce this **possible.**[7] Sufficient nations may unite upon a given value-ratio to render both metals, in those nations, current together at that ratio, all **natural tendencies** to alter the ratio, as by extensive losses or new discoveries of either metal, being instantly **checked** by the new demand thus originated for the cheaper metal wherewith to make payments.[8] This bimetallic scheme, never yet tried, entirely differs in principle from a **unigovernmental** one.[9]

[1] Coinage is technically known as 'free,' even when a 'seigniorage' is charged for coining [§ 85, n. 4]. Full legal tender quality in both metals as in U. S. since 1878, does not alone constitute bimetallism.

[2] Either 15 parts of silver to 1 of gold [U. S., 1792-1834], or 15½ : 1 [the Latin Union, viz., France, Belgium, Switzerland, and Italy], or 16 : 1 [U. S., 1834-1874, and 1878]. A ratio differing from any of these might of course be chosen. A grain of gold bullion is now [1889] worth nearly 20 of silver.

[3] See § 75, ii.

[4] Taking, as yet, no account of paper money. If considerable labor has been bestowed upon gold or silver, as in case of most wares, the portions affected no longer aid stability. They are only so much commodity.

[5] Through extraordinary discoveries or losses, exportation, or new uses or disuses in the arts.

[6] About ⅛ of the world's population uses gold only as full money [gold monometallists], between ¼ and ⅛ are bimetallists, and nearly ⅔ silver monometallists. On advantage ii, Bonamy Price, Contemp. Rev., Mch., 1884, Walker, P. E., 409, 411.

[7] On the basis of such considerations as, with the other writers named above, Walker [P. E., 406 sqq.] and Nicholson [228 sqq.] adduce. About ½ the precious metal is coin or bullion accessory to coin. This part, so far as present in their borders, the league of nations would monopolize, which would go far to *fix* the relative *demand* of the 2 metals, a political cause determining the action of nature. To drive either sort of money to a premium, not only must enough of the other be supplied to displace it in the circulation, but a market must be found for what is displaced. Were the league small, both infelicities might occur: should the U. S., Gr. Britain and Germany join the Latin Union [n. 2] and all coin both metals freely, neither would be possible. Significant, too, are (i) the monetary hist. of France, which from the beginning of the century till 1874, unaided by other nations, and amid the greatest changes in the relative values of the 2 metals, welcomed both to its mint; and (ii) the fact that variations in the relative values of g. and s. have never imitated variations in relative supply and output, save very slowly and slightly. The fairest plea for gold monometallism is Nasse's, in Schoenberg. His main arguments are the political difficulties of a bimetallic league, and people's dislike of silver

because of its weight. The political difficulty is great, perhaps decisive: the other would mostly disappear with use of certificates.

[8] Reference here is to ordinary and local variations, radical and wide ones being prevented by the agencies specified in n. 7. Units of one coin, being cheaper yet equally good for the purpose, would be sought [by carrying bullion to the mint] for use in payments [Walker, Mo., 253].

[9] Hence to show, as Laughlin, H. of Bimetallism in U. S., does, the ill working of bimetallism in one land, in no wise disproves the scientific bimetallist argument.

CHAPTER II

BANKS AND PAPER MONEY

§ 78 BANKS OF DEPOSIT

Juglar, Banques, in Say's *Dict. des Finances*. *Courtney*, ' Banking,' in Encyc. Brit *Horn*, ' Banks,' in Lalor's Cyc. *Wagner*, in *Schoenberg*, vol. i, VIII, II. *Jevons* ch. xvi. *Ad. Smith*, bk. ii, ch. ii. *Bowen*, American Pol. Econ., 316. *Walker*, Money, 409 sqq.

The use of metallic currency is attended with certain disadvantages, as (i) labor and expense of **counting**, (ii) labor, expense and risk of **transportation**, (iii) liability to **robbery**, (iv) difficulty of **identification**, (v) **dearness**. All these are lessened by substituting paper for coin.[1] As trade multiplied, therefore, it naturally occurred to merchants to **deposit** their specie with some responsible party and traffic with his certificates of deposit, the specie for each certificate being obtainable by the holder **on call**,[2] and, at the outset, a slight **premium** allowed for the care of the money. Hence arose **banks of deposit**, serving to facilitate exchanges not only between individuals but also between cities and nations.

[1] Touching most of the items this is obvious. As to (iii), compare in ease of concealment, $1,000,000 in gold and the same in thousand-dollar notes. As to (iv), notes can be numbered and marked, which would damage coins. Ad. Smith compares gold and silver mo. to a highway on the ground, paper to a wagon way through the air. In the matter of dearness, the use of *subsidiary* paper effects no saving. The necessary expense of keeping up our subsidiary paper circulation during and after the war was 5 per cent of its face value yearly, being equal to interest on bonds enough to purchase the silver which supplanted it. The coining of

this cost, indeed, 1½–2 per cent, but the part of such expense belonging to a single year would be slight, as few if any of the coins would show wear in less than 50 years. And in paper money at large the saving occurs in interest rather than in wear. It costs Gt. Britain $10,000 to coin a million sovereigns. In 15 years they need recoining, and have lost $25,000 in value. Total expense for manufacturing and wear in 15 years, $35,000. The paper and printing for a million 1 pd. notes would cost $40,000, and they would have to be replaced three times at least, probably 4–6 times, in the 15 years. The cost for larger notes would of course be much less, and for the largest, under that of gold. On present condition of the Brit. coinage, Quarterly Rev., April, 1883, and Quar. Jour. Econ., vol. i, 225. The British gold coin taken together loses 4.16 per cent in 100 years, or a trifle over 1 per cent in 25 years. Sovereigns naturally wear better than half sovereigns.

[2] The identical coins deposited, that is, were at first to be given back, the loan being a *commodatum* [Roman law] as distinguished from a *mutuum*, in which the lender can demand again only equivalence, not identity. It was a 'surrogate' [dollar-for-dollar reserve] note system.

§ 79 Developed Banking

Quar. Jour. Econ., vol. ii, 482 sqq., 251 sqq. *Macleod*, Theo. and Prac. of Banking, vol. i, ch. ix. 'Banks,' and 'Banks of Issue,' in Lalor. *Jevons*, chaps. xvi sqq. *Juglar*, as at § 78. *Yves Guyot*, *Sci. Économique*, bk. v, ch. iv.

Such an institution, once established, could not but have the effect of **bringing together borrowers and lenders.** All persons having surplus money would **deposit,** and no objection would be raised against the banker's **lending,** so long as he **promptly honored** his paper. Hence arose banks of **discount and loan,**[1] serving to render capital more efficient. But it proved a very rare occurrence for more than **one-third** of the average amount on deposit ever to be called out of bank, two-thirds the average being always on hand. Bankers, therefore, ran no appreciable risk in issuing promises to pay far **beyond the aggregate of their deposits,** and, as they could discount with these surplus promises no less readily than with money, **the issue of them became a great source of income.**[2] Hence arose **banks of circulation,** furnishing the public with a cheaper and more convenient circulating medium.

[1] Discount, subtracting the interest beforehand, is now the sole form of regular bank loaning, except in cases of over-drafts.

[2] To explain: instead of using $\tfrac{2}{3}$ the average deposit wherewith to discount notes, holding $\tfrac{1}{3}$ as reserve, the entire average deposit might be made a reserve, and double its amount in notes used in discounting, thus multiplying the bank's gainful resources by 3. No fixed rule is observed touching the proportion of reserve, and it is rarely so much as $\tfrac{1}{3}$. Before the rise of the German empire Leipzig banks used to keep $\tfrac{2}{3}$, those of Bavaria only $\tfrac{1}{4}$ [Walker, P. E., 176]. The banks of issue in the German empire have at present almost exactly $3 in reserve to every 4 in circulation, *i.e.*, only $\tfrac{1}{4}$ the circulation is uncovered.

§ 80 Government Paper

'Banking,' in Lalor. *Perry*, ch. xi. *Walker*, Money, chaps. xvi, xxi. *Knox*, United States Notes.

Promises to pay issued directly by a sovereign power differ essentially from bank notes, (i) not **representing**[1] **values** in the same way, (ii) basing no **legal claims,**[2] and (iii) **lacking elasticity**[3] at best in the direction of expansion, and, unless **convertible,** also in that of contraction. Midway between the two kinds of paper is that of the United States **national banks.** On failure of one of these, the **nation** undertakes to insure the payment of its notes, yet always from the **bank's own assets** placed beforehand in the national treasury for that purpose.[4]

[1] Bank notes, though not covered dollar for dollar, are still thought of as 'representing' the reserve. The nation's promises [greenbacks] bear no exactly similar relation to any monies in the treasury or other property. See next n., also § 86, n. 6.

[2] Greenbacks are not a legal lien on any part of the nation's wealth, whether in the treasury or out, not even when a reserve is by law kept for their liquidation on presentation [§ 86, n. 6].

[3] Contraction and expansion occur more or less arbitrarily, by legislative fiat, not likely to accord at all exactly with shifting monetary needs. This might, it is true, be remedied in part. We return to the subject in Part VI.

[4] The system is described somewhat fully in Part VI.

§ 81 HISTORICAL

Juglar, and other authh., as at § 77. *Garnier, Traité*, 727 sqq. *Macleod*, Theo. and Prac. of Banking, vol. i, ch. ix. Quar. Jour. Econ., vol. ii, 251 sqq. *Jevons*, ch. xvi. *Ad. Smith*, bk. iv, ch. iii. *Lenormant, La Monnaie dans l'Antiquité. Simonin*, 'Florentine Bankers,' *Rev. d. d. Mondes*, Feb., 1873.

Pieces of **leather,** each probably intended to represent a whole skin, were current money in ancient Russia. The Chinese,[1] Tartars and Persians, had leather and paper money as early as the fourteenth century. **Bills of exchange**[2] were known to Assyrians, Phoenicians, Carthaginians, Greeks and Romans. They seem to have been first used in modern times to pay **papal revenues** in the crusades, many being now known dated in 1200[3] and on till 1250. The first **bank of deposit** was erected in Venice,[4] 1171. The Banks of Genoa[5] and Barcelona rose in 1407. The Bank of Amsterdam dates from 1609, and **still exists,** though radically **reorganized** in 1814. It, like the Bank of Venice, was controlled by the state, and had origin in trouble from **depreciation** of coins.[6] The Bank of Hamburg was founded in 1619, on the same principles with that of Amsterdam, only not controlled by the state.[7] As yet there were no banks in England, but, during the **civil wars** of the seventeenth century, **goldsmiths** received deposits of the precious metals, either holding them subject to check,[8] or giving transferrible receipts. The

Bank of England,[9] established in 1694, was the first to combine the **three functions** of deposit, discount and circulation. It is at present the most powerful bank on the globe. Next stands the Bank of France, founded in 1800.

[1] Ruge, *Gesch. d. Zeitalters d. Entdeckungen*, beautifully reproduces the oldest piece of paper money in the world. The original is Chinese.

[2] Lenormant, as above, 117, translates an Assyrian bill of exchange belonging to the 6th century B.C. On Gr. and Roman bankers, Courtney, as at § 78, also Macleod, Elements, vol. i, 279 sqq.; Banking, vol. i, ch. iv, sec. 1; Blanqui, Hist. of P. E., ch. xv. [On the technique of the foreign exchanges, see § 95.] At Josephus, Antiqq., XII, iv, 7, end, one Joseph farms Egypt's revenues in Palestine. He keeps money with Arion, in Alexandria, and when the taxes are due, writes an order on Arion for their payment. This amounts to a bill of exchange, an international check or draft.

[3] Blancard, *Lettre de change à Marseille au 13 Siècle*. Saladin, famous in the 3d crusade, 1189-'92, used bills of exchange. Is it not possible that this institution [like so many others] came from the Arabs, not from the Jews, as commonly supposed?

[4] Lalor, vol. i, 227 sq., N. A. Rev., Sept., 1885, 205 sq., Garnier, 727. This bank perished with the Venetian republic, 1797.

[5] This, the Bank of St. George, was perhaps the oldest bank of issue.

[6] Perry, 276, well tells the story. See, more fully, Ad. Smith, in ch. iii, of bk. iv. The latter thinks all the continental banks named, and that of Nuremberg also, to have sprung from this motive. Amsterdam's current money having through clipping lost 9 per cent of its face value, so that bills of exchange on the city, destined to be paid in that money, were persistently so much below par, a bank was established under the city's guaranty, to receive coin upon deposit according to weight, and give credit therefor. This credit was known as 'bank money.' All bills of exchange on Amsterdam, above a certain sum, were ordered to be paid in it, whereupon [par] Amsterdam exchange speedily rose to par, and even above.

[7] It still remains, and under its original organization. Soetbeer, in *Vierteljahrsch. für Volkswirtsch., Jahrg.* V, vol. ii.

[8] See Macleod, as above. Ibid., vol. i, 281 sqq. [4th ed.] are several of these primitive checks, varying somewhat in form. One reads:

16th Nov., 1689

Mr. Jackson, — Pray pay to the bearer hereof, Mr. Daniel Croker, five pounds, and place it to the accompt of

Your loving friend,

John Wynyarde

To Mr. Roger Jackson,
At Sir Francis Child's, Goldsmith,
    just within Temple Barr

These drafts were sometimes payable 'to bearer' simply, sometimes 'to payee or bearer,' sometimes 'to payee or order.' At first they were written out fully with the pen, and might be sealed. The receipts, or promissory notes, were always issued if the depositor preferred, and these, too, passed from hand to hand as well as the drafts.

[9] Noël, *Les banques d'Émission en Europe*, 2 vols. [noble history, from the sources, of all the greatest European banks]. On origin of Bank of Eng., Bancroft's U. S. [author's last rev.], vol. ii, 184; Macleod, Banking, vol. i, ch. ix.

CHAPTER III

THE THEORY OF MONEY

§ 82 THE FIRST FUNCTION OF MONEY

Knies, Geld, v. *Walker*, Money, ch. i; Mo., Trade and Ind., ch. i. *Perry*, ch. ix. *Nicholson*, Mo. and Mon. Problems, ch. ii. *Nasse*, in Schoenberg, vol. i, VII, 1. *Ad. Smith*, bk. ii, ch. ii. *Mill*, bk. iii, ch. vii. *Hildebrand, Theorie des Geldes*. *Sumner*, 'Mo. and its Laws,' Internat. Rev., vol. x. *Bonamy Price*, 'How Mo. does its Work,' Contemp. Rev., Feb., 1882. *Bastable*, 'Money,' in Encyc. Brit.

The first[1] and on the whole the **chief** business of money proper,[2] or hard money, is to aid in effecting exchanges, to furnish a **medium of exchange**. With reference to it as fulfilling this requirement, the following propositions are all-important: i It is still essentially a **commodity**,[3] only having a universal or **generalized** purchasing power. Buyers of other things may be said to **sell money**, sellers to **buy**. ii The commodity's service as money is, however, entirely **different in kind** from that which it would render as an article of consumption.[4] iii Money itself is but a **small fraction** of the value which it directly and indirectly helps to exchange.[5] iv It so powerfully **stimulates production** by promoting exchange, that, far from being 'dead,'[6] it may be set down as the most productive of all capital.

[1] Both logically and [with little doubt] historically. Knies and Marx, however, make this function secondary to that discussed in § 83. Bring this § and the following §§ into relation with those of Chapter I.

[2] Cf. § 74, n. 1. Whatever scope we give to 'money,' the analysis of its character must begin with metal money, there being many things predicable of it which are not so of any form of paper. See §§ 86, 93.

³ Not a mere *token*, or an *order*, as Macleod and the advocates of fiat money vainly teach. How far adoption by government conveys to it its peculiar power in purchase cannot be confidently stated. Some exaggerate, others underrate this. Cf. § 75, n. 9, and Horton, as cited at § 83.

⁴ Knies, *Geld*, 2d ed., 184.

⁵ See § 77, n. 1. Cf. Perry, 237, and Ad. Smith, as above. A dollar might effect 1000 dollar exchanges in a day. Also, money aids to transfer vast quantities of goods merely through its denominations, without the slightest further intervention. At the N. Y. clearing-house, $200,000,000 are sometimes exchanged in an hour, and as much at that in London, no coin or bank-notes being used except for balances [§ 94, n. 1].

⁶ As Newcomb and many other able authors have called it, out of a mistaken idea of productivity. See Walker, *Mo.*, 22 sq., and n. 5, above.

§ 83 The Second Function

Roscher, bk. iii, ch. iv. *Marx*, Capital, pt. i, ch. iii, sec. 1. *Knies, Geld*, iv. *Yves Guyot, Sci. Économique*, bk. iii, ch. iii. *Horton*, Position of Law in the Doct. of Money [a pamph.]. *Perry*, 246 sqq.

This is that of a **scale** or **measure** of value, and is entirely **separate** in nature from the first. The two may and often do belong to different wares.¹ Of money viewed in this second character we are carefully to remember that: i It is at best only an **approximately invariable** measure.² ii It is a measure of value by virtue of being **itself a value**.³ iii It is a more **perfect** measure the more **steady and invariable** it is as to its own value.⁴ iv It inevitably **shrinks**⁵ in value so soon, and about in proportion, as it is multiplied beyond the requirements of exchange.

¹ In the U. S., 1889, gold is the measurer, while silver, nickel, copper and paper do the actual exchanging. If no gold at all existed in the form of money [coin] it might still be the measure of value. Nicholson, *Mo. and Mon. Prob.*, 20.

² Herein differing from most other measuring scales of units [§ 87 and n. 1]. Nicholson, 299. Marshall, approved by Nicholson, 34, deems a perfect measure of value unthinkable. In what sense this is so, § 70.

[3] Measure and the thing measured being of the same *kind* or nature. Most measures bear this relation to the things measured. Not so the thermometer, which consists in an arrangement for measuring *heat* by *length*.

[4] See §§ 75, 77, 85, and notes.

[5] More strictly, perhaps, it *tends* to shrink, and will do so unless counter-causes are in play. Various influences, too, may and usually do interfere to prevent the depreciation from following inflation [or *vice versa*] with perfect exactness. See § 85.

§ 84 OTHER OFFICES OF MONEY

Walker, Money, ch. i. *Knies, Geld*, vi, vii. *Jevons* [ch. iii], *Nicholson*, and *Bastable*, as at preceding §§.

Besides the two sovereign services just characterized, it devolves on money also: i To furnish a system of money denominations.[1] ii Legally to make payments and liquidate indebtedness.[2] iii To be a standard for deferred payments.[3] iv To transfer values in space and in time.[4] v To regulate, as a totality, the value of each unit of its mass.[5]

[1] Not at all to be confounded with either of the greater functions. Thus, in English America before the Revolution, the money of account, viz., the *colonial* pounds, shillings, pence, and farthings, a different system from the English, neither exchanged nor measured values, but was a mere means of book-keeping.

[2] This, too, as Knies well points out, is something quite separate from the exchange-function. Governments might make corn or horses the legal means-of-payment, instead of money.

[3] As in case of all time contracts and transactions, and outstanding debts. This is logically and in point of time a secondary function of money, but, in modern business, hardly so in importance. See § 87.

[4] Walker, Mo., 12, against Jevons, thinks this not an office of money as such. "When a commodity comes to serve as a store of value, it ceases to be money." This seems arbitrary. Money is often used thus. Hoarded silver dollars [1889], for example, do not drop to their bullion value. Notice that the use of money as a reservoir of value differs from that of iii. It is true that when gold and silver are used as the form in which to send value abroad, they cease to be money.

⁵ We see from § 83, iv, and § 87, that the total made up of money and unwrought money metal actually does have this effect, whether artificially manipulated or not. It is, indeed, one of the most significant of all the facts relating to money.

§ 85 THE VALUE OF MONEY

Walker, P. E., pt. iii, chaps. iii, iv. *Mill*, bk. iii, chaps. viii, ix. *Perry*, 241 sqq. *Fawcett*, Manual, 356 sqq. *Bastiat*, Pol. Econ., 202 sqq. *McAdam*, Alphabet in Finance, vi. *Bilgram*, Iron Law of Wages. *Wagner, Geld u. Kredittheorie der Peel'schen Bankacte;* also in *Zeitsch. f. gesam. Staatsw.*, 1881, 759 sqq. *Nasse*, in *Schoenberg*, vol. i, VII, x. *Sidgwick*, bk. ii, ch. v. *Mangoldt*, §§ 79 sqq.

This, by which, observe, we do not here mean **interest**, but **purchasing power**, is regulated as in case of those goods whose **supply is limited**,¹ almost entirely by the relation between **demand and supply**, cost of production rarely coming into the account. i Money behaves like a monopolized article without being such, viz., while remaining freely **open** to both **additions and losses**. ii The facts named at § 75, ii,² render money **more independent** than aught else of all ordinary changes in demand and supply. iii Given **money enough** already to do all needed money-work, and the value of a country's money-total is wholly **independent of its mass**.³ iv The influence which **bullion** may exert in maintaining the **value-parity**⁴ between itself and coin, is **not to be explained** by supposing bullion to represent cost of production more nearly than coin, since of cost both are in equal degree **independent**. v If different portions of the money supply have **unlike costs** of production, the cheaper will not displace the dearer unless it is **sufficiently abundant** by itself to answer the demand.⁵ vi An alteration in the value of money may be nothing else but **phase** of a change in the **values of general commodities**.⁶ vii In determining the value of money, paper money and all the other so numerous instrumentalities[7] of exchange, have, according to the amount of exchanging which they effect, the same influence as **money proper**.

[1] See § 65, end, 67.

[2] Most potent among those conditions is the vastness of the *supply* of money, and the uniquely broad and uniform *demand* for it, consisting in all salable commodities or services except money itself.

[3] After the point named is reached [Cernuschi, 'Nomisma,' 14], an important condition, overlooked in Mill's discussion, a greater total bulk of money will purchase no more than a smaller. Why, then, should any one longer produce precious metal? Because each new dollar, though theoretically less valuable than dollars were before, is worth as much as any old dollar is now. And from the point of view of society's interest it is well for the total to be as large as possible [§§ 75, ii, and 77].

[4] *I.e.*, seigniorage being left out of view. Since 1875 [it had previously been $\frac{1}{2}$ of 1 pr. ct.] the U. S. mint charges no seigniorage for coining, but the bringer of the metal must pay for the alloy. In England also there is no seigniorage proper, but a delay in furnishing the coins occasions, through loss of interest, a slight practical seigniorage, giving coin usually a trifling excess of value over the metal it contains [Mill, bk. iii, ch. ix. § 2, n.].

[5] Gresham's law [Sir Thos. Gresham, founder of the Royal Exchange, London, d. 1579] is true only with this limitation. See Walker, P. E., 142. It is usually quoted to the effect that poorer money will *always* drive out better. So Aristophanes, 'Frogs,' Frere's Tr., 893 sqq. [cited by Laughlin, Bimetallism in U. S.],

> "For your old and standard pieces, valued and approved and tried,
> 'Here among the Grecian nations and in all the world beside,
> 'Recognized in every realm for trusty stamp and pure assay,
> 'Are rejected and abandoned for the trash of yesterday."

In fact another modification of the law should be named. The people may refuse to handle the poorer, as on the Pacific coast during the civil war [H. George, Prog. and Poverty, bk. v, ch. i.]. Legal tender paper would not circulate and gold was retained.

[6] See § 87.

[7] On different forms of paper money, see § 80. The 'instrumentalities' are checks, bills of exchange, promissory notes, due bills, book accounts, barter, post-office notes and orders, express orders, telegram and telephone orders, etc.

§ 86 Paper Money

Walker, Money, pts. ii, iii. *Noël, Le billet de Banque* [cf., same title, in *Dict. des Finances*]. *Knies, Geld*, xi. *Wagner, Geld und Kredit*. *Mill*, bk. iii, ch. xii. *Jevons*, Mo. and the Mech. of Ex., ch. xiii. *Nicholson*, Mo. and Mon. Problems, ch. vi. *Mangoldt*, §§ 58, 59. *Papa d'Amico, Titoli di Credito surrogati della Moneta*. *Walras, Théorie mathématique de la richesse sociale*, 145 sqq.

To secure simplicity, this Chapter has thus far supposed the monetary material to be **metal only**. The same laws hold in the main for **any system**. i If, along with metal, **surrogate**[1] **paper bills** be put in use, the foregoing principles remain **perfectly** unmodified, convenience and perhaps some economy in wear and loss the sole changes. ii If instantly and surely convertible **notes not fully covered** be introduced, the extra convenience **adds**[2] somewhat to the entire **number of dollars** in circulation, this increment costing nothing.[3] iii If there is in circulation **promissory paper not convertible**,[4] it drives out more or less metal in proportion to its **depreciation**, the latter being great or slight according to a variety of circumstances, of which its **amount** and the issuer's **credit** are the chief. It will be seen that no one of these species of paper can entirely take the place of coin. Hence, to be scientific, we have to call paper currency **partial** or **imperfect** money.[5] The failure to distinguish it from **money proper** leads constantly into the gravest **errors** of view. Paper, it is true, (a) is a **medium of exchange**, and (b) has **value**, which (c) is **not** in every case merely **representative**.[6] Yet, i Paper has **no universal purchasing power**, since it usually[7] passes only in the country that utters it. ii It forms **no final measure** of value, but must itself be constantly measured, as to value, by coin. iii Its value is **adventitious**, not springing from intrinsic cost, as is ultimately the case with gold or silver, but entirely from some operation of the principle of **credit**.

[1] Viz., bills covered dollar for dollar, like gold and silver certificates. Gold surrogates are issued not by the government alone but also by the clearing-house banks of N. Y. City. On the question of saving by the use of such paper, § 78, n. 1. On the effect of paper money to increase the proportion of fixed capital, Walras, *Rev. du droit internat.*, 1884, p. 587.

[2] In the figure,

let the heavy line, *xc*, represent hard money, and the light one, *ad*, promissory paper. As the paper is launched, part of the hard money, say *bc*, will leave the circulation, some going out of the country, some into the melting pot to be turned into wares and trinkets. See J. B. Say, as cited by Macleod, Elements, vol. i, 99; also Ad. Smith, bk. ii, ch. ii.

[3] Except, of course, what the paper costs. Barring the difficulty which it may occasion in a crisis, this part of the paper has in all particulars the identical effect of so much gold [Walker, P. E., 178]. Suppose it added just when a larger circulation was needed to do the required money work [§ 85, iii, and n. 3], it would be no less a blessing than the same amount of precious metal [§ 1, n. 2]. Yet we do not deny the possibility of some local and temporary inflation in a mixed system of this sort [see § 91, and notes].

[4] Like U. S. greenbacks between 1862 and Jan. 1, 1879. On non-promissory or fiat paper money, see § 93. Also see '*Cours forcé*' in Say's *Dict. des Finances.*

[5] Cf. § 74, n. 1.

[6] Illustrated by government paper money [§ 80; cf. Farrar, Man. of the Constitution, 339]. If a greenback 'represents' property at all, it must be that which is to liquidate it by and by. This probably is not yet in existence. Of the bank bills now at par not 40 per cent in value could be paid were all presented to-day. What do the 60 per cent 'represent'?

[7] Yet Bank of England notes pass on the continent, as U. S. notes more and more do in Liverpool, London, and Paris. They are not, however, accepted strictly as money, but with the idea of swift recourse, as bills of exchange.

§ 87 Ideal Money

Knies, Weltgeld u. Weltmünzen. Nasse, in *Schoenberg,* vol. i, VII, v, § 10. *Andrews,* 'An Honest Dollar,' in Am. Econ. Ass'n Papers, vol. iv. *Marshall,* Rem. for Fluctuation of Gen. Prices, Contemp. Rev., vol. 51. *Grosvenor,* Prices, vol. i. *Jevons,* Investigations in Currency and Finance, II. *Ricardo,* Proposals for an Economic and Secure Currency. *Wasserab, Preise und Krisen.*

The best monetary systems yet used are **very imperfect,** permitting the most unhappy **fluctuations** in the purchase-power of their **units, discouraging enterprise** and **robbing** now debtors, now creditors.[1] **Bimetallism** would relieve, yet only **temporarily.** The time must come when governments will be authorized (i) to watch, through competent commissions, for each **rise** or **fall** in the **value of money** (fall or rise of general prices), and (ii) to correct the same by expanding or contracting the circulation. Operation (i) is feasible by the **critical summation,** at intervals, of the prices of definite quantities and qualities of numerous **staples,**[2] each having prominence in the result according to the amount of it consumed. If the sum as reckoned to-day **exceeds** the last one, **prices have risen,** the **power of money fallen.** A lessened sum will mean falling prices, dearer money. Operation (ii), the necessary contraction or expansion, may be effected in either of several ways, the best[3] of which, it is believed, would be to inject into or withdraw from a gold or a gold-and-paper circulation, the proper amounts of **full legal tender silver tokens.**[4] The gold and the silver should both be represented by **certificates.** Such a system would invite if not necessitate **international agreement,** and might easily extend to **all nations and ages.** An **international coinage** would follow it, and **cosmic money** be at last realized.

[1] Nasse, in *Schoenberg*, vol. i, VII, v, § 9. The precious metals vary enormously in value. [§ 83, i, n. 2.] According to Jevons, gold fell 46 per cent between 1789 and 1809, rose 145 per cent between 1809 and 1849, and fell again at least 20 per cent between 1849 and 1874. Since 1874 it has risen once more, about 30 per cent. When money falls in purchasing power [prices rise], debtors on outstanding contracts are wronged, receiving in the stipulated number of dollars less value than was covenanted. If money value rises [prices fall], creditors are wronged in the same way. Worse, economically, than this injustice is the disorder imported into business by such changes in the power of money [viz., in general prices]. Rising prices are wont to breed speculation: falling prices asphyxiate industry by making it profitable to hold on to, rather than employ, money and titles to money.

[2] The practical difficulty in making and using such a value-measure would be considerable. What are staples? How ascertain the consumption of any one? In averaging, shall we employ the arithmetical or the geometrical mean? No one of these questions has yet received final answer. But the simple addition, from time to time, of a carefully made and kept price list, disregarding variations of volume between the commodities consumed, would disclose the rise, fall or stationariness of money with a close approach to accuracy.

[3] See Marshall, as above. The equity of a composite value-standard [Jevons, Mo. and the Mech. of Ex., ch. xxv] would be, by the plan suggested, incorporated *in the money system itself*, the only way it can ever be utilized.

[4] Pieces [dollars, *e.g.*] worth less than face value, yet passing at that value, viz., at the value of gold, because limited in amount [§ 85, v]. They should never be permitted on the one hand to become of full face value, nor on the other to be too cheap. The superiority of such subordinate money over paper would lie in its labor-cost value. In a panic, the metal tokens, nearly as worthful as gold, could be paid out on presentation of their certificates, when holders of mere uncovered paper would be helpless. Why our system would excel Ricardo's, see § 93, n. 1.

CHAPTER IV

CREDIT

§ 88 THE NATURE OF CREDIT

Mill, bk. iii, chaps. xi, xii. *Knies, Kredit. Schraut, Organization des Kredits. Mangoldt*, §§ 53 sqq. *Papa d'Amico, Titoli di Credito*, pts. i, ii.

i **Credit** in Economics is the power to command wealth or service **now** in exchange for some assurance of a return **in future**. It is, in general, the same as a power to **market titles** or to put in use any of the **instrumentalities**[1] of credit. It may be utilized or not. ii The main instrumentalities of credit are, (i) **promises**, as book-accounts, deposits, stock certificates, bonds, promissory notes, bank-notes, and (ii) **orders**, as post-office orders, bills of exchange, checks, circular letters and mobilizing certificates[2] of all kinds. iii Credit has **value**,[3] and may also become **capital**, being among the most **active producers** of value,[4] (i) utilizing **small sums and savings**,[5] (ii) **transferring capital** from less to more productive hands, (iii) supplying a powerful **motive for** the **accumulation** of capital, (iv) making possible **enterprises** too **great** for individual resources.

---

[1] 'Instrumentalities' rather than 'instruments,' to cover cases of orders and promises by telegram and telephone. 'Titles' or 'instruments' would cover only paper documents. According to one's purpose, credit may be classified as public or private, as personal or real, as *mobilier* [based on personal property] or *foncier* [on real estate].

[2] Pipe line [petroleum] certificates well illustrate these. Each is an order upon given holders of oil to deliver such or such an amount to the

bearer on demand. Pig iron, whiskey, and other bulky wares are in the same way 'mobilized,' viz., put upon the speculative market. The certificates are like dock warrants, except that the latter are not intended to be negotiable [cf. § 55, n. 8, § 78, n. 2].

[3] This does not mean either (i) that rights, embodied in titles, are the essence of wealth [Macleod, followed by Minton, in Capital and Wages], or (ii) that property and titles to the same property are both to be reckoned into the community's wealth [§ 2]; but that the *fact* or *system* of credit is an economic advantage. As such it is valuable [§ 61], however it originates, and it is *wealth* [§ 1, and n. 3] and *capital* [§ 28] so far as it comes under the respective definitions of these categories. With Knies [*Pol. Oek.* 215], against Wagner, we decline to rank under capital, titles as a class, but it is hard to see why the notes referred to at § 86, n. 3, are not at once wealth and capital. Value in exchange is of course an attribute of all such papers, unless worthless.

[4] "Credit has done more, a thousand times, to enrich nations, than all the mines in the world" [Webster, in speech for re-charter of U. S. Bank, 1834].

[5] The savings banks of America contain $12,000,000 or $14,000,000, nearly as much as all other banking institutions in the country. Most of this, as well as much of the capital in the hands of building and loan associations and co-operative banks, is an aggregation of trifling amounts.

§ 89 Credit and Crises

Roscher, '*Zur Lehre der Absatzkrisen*,' in vol. ii, of *Ansichten*. *Wirth, Gesch. der Handelskrisen*. *Mangoldt*, § 61. *Cairnes*, Leading Principles, 179 sqq. *Yves Guyot, Sci. Économique*, bk. v, ch. iii. *H. C. Adams*, Public Debts, 207 sq. *McAdam*, Alphabet in Finance, xvii.

Credit has its disadvantages also, (i) promoting indebtedness on the part of the poor, (ii) sometimes transferring wealth from more to less productive hands,[1] (iii) sometimes unduly stimulating demand, thus raising prices and introducing commercial panics. This occurs because credit possesses the same **purchasing power** as money itself, and people with credit purchase too much. Demand, losing all relation to amount of true money and permanent property, **inflates prices,** which in turn **stimulates exchange**, creating **new demand** for credit, and indefinitely multiplying all forms of indebtedness, until, at length, the discreet **decline to give credit** further, and the **crash** comes.[2] This, in general, is the course of a **business crisis**.

[1] Apt to be the case in public borrowing. See the masterly discussion in Adams, Public Debts, esp. pt. i, chaps. iv, v. All the great works on Finance treat this.

[2] How far this evil is possible in case the government and all banks of issue continue to cash their notes on demand, see § 91. As a matter of fact, specie payments are at such times usually suspended. Besides credit-crises we have crises from mere lack of money, and crises from [specific] over-production.

§ 90 Further Abuses of Credit

Rae, 'Natural Hist. of Credit,' Contemp. Rev., vol. 50 [1886]. U. S. Consular Reports, No. 43, July, 1884.

From **70 to 90 per cent** of the world's business is done on credit. In Germany, Siam, and Canada the proportion is 90 per cent, in Belgium and China, 80. Credit-traffic has its feeblest development in **Holland**, its strongest in **Turkey and Yucatan**. Credit may be a **necessity** of life, therefore a sign of **poverty,** or an instrument of **production** and hence a mark of **wealth.** The difference lies mainly in the degree of its **organization,** which is higher for any nation in proportion to its **industrial advancement.** With progress in economic organization, the **sphere** of credit becomes less **extensive,** its **operation** more **intensive. Cash** payments, getting the mastery first in **wages,** in **retail** trade and in **raw** products, spread gradually over other fields, shutting up credit to its most helpful and least dangerous functions.[1] Latest to be overcome are unwise plans, stimulated by its immense undoubted advantages, for the use of **credit in exchange**. Of these, the three which follow deserve the most consideration.

[1] The assumption which so many have taken up from Bruno Hildebrand, of three great periods in the world's economic evolution, viz., barter, money, and credit, as if credit were to have its fullest development in the most perfect economic state, is now seen to be false. With nations as with individuals, those best able to get credit use it least. In all the wealthiest countries the proportion of cash payments to total volume of trade is steadily increasing.

§ 91 FREE BANKING

'Free Trade in Banking,' Westm. Rev., Jan., 1888. *Wagner, Geld und Kredittheorie der Peel'schen Bankacte. Walker*, P. E., 178 sqq.; Money, pt. iii. *James*, 'Banks of Issue,' in Lalor. *Horn*, 'Banks,' *ibid. Wesslau*, Rational Banking.

Many theorists have advocated that incorporation for **banking** purposes be as **free** as for other, and that every **bank**, like every private individual, be permitted **all the credit it can secure**, with the privilege of utilizing the same in **uttering bills** for circulation, to be used in discounting, leaving the receivers and holders of the bills to look out for the **security**.[1] But **experience**, notably that of the United States from 1814 to 1863,[2] has shown that such a plan is nearly certain to put into circulation vast amounts of **poor bills, swindling** the unwary and the poor,[3] driving hard money from **circulation**, raising and distracting **prices**, and provoking and aggravating commercial **crises**. It is believed that such **unhealthy inflation** may occur, at least **locally**, even when no bills are legal tender and all are instantly **convertible**.[4]

[1] "As long as the bank is bound to honor its obligations just as any other debtor, and redeems its notes in specie upon presentation, the public will be able to determine its solidity, and consequently measure its credit.

An excessive issue of notes will cause these notes to flow back into the bank and thus correct itself" Horn, [as above, p. 236].

² During this period probably 5 per cent of the entire circulation averaged to be lost annually. Walker, P. E., 177.

³ The acceptance of the notes may be to a certain degree compulsory although they are neither legal tender nor irredeemable. They may form so great a part of the circulation that people have to accept them for lack of other media of exchange. The poor are never in condition to refuse what is offered them as money, even when not too ignorant to suspect it. Many receivers are sure to be remote from the place of redemption. See James, as above, p. 245. The government must, he says, i) not make the notes legal tender, or anywise artificially favor their circulation, ii) forbid the issue of too small denominations, and iii) see to it that convertibility is real, and not made illusory by any unfair practices. The bank notes of small denominations are the most vicious as traps for the poor.

⁴ The question how far government should supervise banking is closely bound up with that between the 'banking principle,' to the effect that, if perfectly convertible, paper changes in no particular the behavior of the money system to which it belongs from what it would be if composed of metal alone [Walker, P. E., 178. Cf. § 86, ii, above], and the 'currency principle' [Walker, P. E., 179], according to which convertibility is no sure guaranty against local and temporary inflation. Wesslau, with Wagner and most European economists, favors the 'banking principle,' Walker the 'currency principle' [P. E., 190].

§ 92   THE JOHN LAW THEORY

Bilgram, Iron Law of Wages. *Perry*, 292 sqq. *Horn*, 'Banks,' in Lalor. *White*, Paper Mo. Inflation in France. *Sybel*, French Revolution, vol. i, ch. iv. *Nicholson*, Mo. and Mon. Problems, pt. ii, 1. *Blanqui*, Hist. of P. E., ch. xxxi. *Bryant and Gay*, U. S., vol. ii, ch. xxii. *Thiers*, Mississippi Bubble. *Whately*, Kingdom of Christ, 171 sqq. *Alexi, John Law u. sein System* [cf. *Vierteljahrsch. f. Volksw.*, XXII, ii, 230 sqq.]. *Rondel, Mobilisation du Sol en France*.

This maintains that bills may be put forth not only in lieu of gold and silver, but also in lieu of **all values**,¹ and hence, if called for, may be issued to the **whole extent of the property** of the issuer, such currency being a **self-regulating** machine, which, if left to itself, will adapt its volume to the public needs. But, (i) paper uttered against **anything else** than coin or bullion, not being instantly convertible into coin, cannot long remain at par, and (ii) having depreciated and raised prices, ceases to be self-regulating in volume, and goes on inviting further issues.

[1] A predecessor of Law was Francis Cradocke, publisher, in 1661, of 'Wealth Discovered' [Quar. Jour. Econ., vol. ii, 485 sqq.]. Law said: "5 oz. of gold is equal in value to £20, and may be made money to that value; an acre of land is equal to £20, and may be made money equal to that value, for it has all the qualities necessary in money" [Perry, 293]. Mr. Hugo Bilgram, in the pamph. named above, presents the same theory, recommending its application as a means of economic justice. Law's bank, which ran from 1716 to 1720, did not realize his principle with any exactness, but [at last] printed and marketed paper money practically regardless of security. Its shares, which had risen from the par, £500, to £18,000, and its notes, at one time better than gold, became valueless. In the final 'run' upon the bank, 12 persons were crushed to death. Truer to the theory were the '*assignats*' issued by the Revolutionary government in 1790, 1,200,000,000 francs face value in all, based upon confiscated church lands. They were legal tender, and receivable for lands at any public sale. By June, 1793, they had fallen to 83 per cent of par; by Aug., to 16 per cent. They finally stood at ¾ of one per cent. The '*mandats*,' immediate titles to lands, were issued to redeem the *assignats*, 1 in *mandats* for 30 in *assignats*. But, though their total face value was less than the value of the lands, after rising from 16 per cent of par to 40 and 80, they soon sank again to 5. Joined to Law's bank was the 'Mississippi Co.' or 'Western Co.,' which had a monopoly over Louisiana, and owned a tract of land 12 miles square on the Arkansas River. Collapse of the bank did not destroy the colony, though the settlers, mostly Germans, came down to the Mississippi near New Orleans, peopling what is still known as the 'German Coast.' Rondel's book defends the *assignats*.

§ 93 FIAT MONEY

Ricardo, as at § 85. *Knies, Geld*, xi. *Walker*, P. E., 153 sqq., also pt. vi, ch. viii. *Hume*, 'Do we Need a Metallic Currency,' Forum, May, 1886. *McAdam*, Alphabet in Finance, xi. *Prince-Smith, Uneinlösbares Pap. Geld*, etc., in *Vierteljahrsch. f. Volkswirtsch.*, 1864, III.

A school of monetary writers, inspired by certain teachings of **Ricardo**,[1] would repudiate all specie basis for currency and make government the sole issuer of it, the notes, full **legal tender** but strictly **limited in amount**,[2] to be convertible into **bonds,** and the bonds redeemable in the **notes.** The **plausibility** of this scheme to the **popular** mind lies in the fact that legislative acts may and often do in some sense **create value,** as when a precious metal, not so before, is declared to be money and legal tender.[3] But **its logic** resides in the principle of **limitation** to the circulation, and in the idea that, so long as the total money consists in **precisely enough** dollars to do the work, **additions** beyond this being wholly **impossible,** the value of the dollars has **no connection** with the **cost** of the material from which they are made. Could the **conditions be strictly fulfilled** the system would probably work.[4] We believe this, in any society hitherto known, **out of the question.**[5] Perception that the notes were **absolute,** not promissory, must awaken **distrust** of them, leading to **depreciation** and to larger use of bullion, **barter** and all forms of **credit.** This would **augment** the depreciation, and the new depreciation this, so by degrees **deranging** values beyond hope.

[1] Ricardo, however, proposed to continue gold as the standard and measure of value, only using paper as the medium of circulation [§§ 82, 83]. He would so limit the amount of paper as to conform its value-fluctuations to those of gold. Most fiat money men [greenbackers] at present abjure this guaranty. Ricardo has emphasized as strongly as any one the indispensableness of *some* standard by which the value of money shall be gauged. Without this the whole system is in the air. Suppose we tried to limit the circulation, by what criterion could we determine how or how much? Men fail to feel this difficulty because, applying in thought to their proposed fiat system the denominations of our present promissory one, they lose sight of the difference between the two. Let the bills not contain the word 'dollar' but bear the mere legend: "THIS IS ONE

KEHOE," "THIS IS TEN KEHOES," *etc.*, and the character of a no-standard system becomes plainer. Even Ricardo saw no way to *regulate the standard itself*, as suggested in §§ 70 and 87. Variations in the value of gold he considered wholly irremediable.

² According, that is, to the soberer theorists of this class. Many little regard any necessity of limitation.

³ Thus, all admit that, should the commercial nations resume the free coinage of silver, this metal would advance in value. It rose somewhat by the [Bland] Act of the U. S. alone [1878], ordaining the coinage of at least $2,000,000 worth and at most $4,000,000 worth monthly. The cause was simply the enlarged demand. Nearer to a creation of value by fiat is the phenomenon described at § 86, ii, and n. 3. Now, if value is thus imparted to gold, it is asked, why not to paper, and if some value, why not more? The answer is that the suggested parallel between gold and paper is precise. Paper will, by being made money on the basis proposed by this plan, appreciate in proportion to the wider market thus opened for it, *but no further*. A 'fiat' dollar would in time be worth precisely the [engraved] paper contained in it. See note 5. Another fallacy lurks in the idea that the uttering of paper money is analogous to the coining of precious metal, and proper function of government simply on that account.

⁴ This does not contradict the admission, at § 85, that money's cost of production is *at present* the ultimate regulator of its value.

⁵ The necessary confidence between man and man, and in the wisdom of government's action, could not be engendered. Even the fact that the notes were legal tender and receivable for customs and taxes would not quiet all concern. The state itself may fall. The minutest degree of such distrust would introduce more or less of the ancillary media of exchange, which it would be wholly beyond the state's power to prevent.

CHAPTER V

THE CLEARING SYSTEM

§ 94   Settlements by Check

Lloyd, 'Clearing,' in Lalor. *Jevons, Mo. and the Mech. of Exchange,* chaps. xx–xxii. *Rauchberg, Neueste Entwickelung des Clearing und Giroverkehrs, Statist. Monatsschr.,* June, 1887. *François, Clearing Houses et Chambres de Compensation.*

A vast majority of **inland payments** are made by checks, each debtor sending his creditor, however far away, a **check** or a draft on the bank with which he, the debtor, deals. Such a check, unless happening to reach the drawee bank **directly,** or (in a very small town) its neighbor bank, finds its way back to the drawee bank through some kind of a clearing institution. The clearing will occur at a **local** clearing-house, or the check have to pass through the **national** one,[1] according to the **location,** banking **relations,** etc., of the parties to the transaction.

[1] The following diagrams illustrate all this.

I   Single City System

[say] *Providence*

```
A B C D E F G H I
 \|/   \|/   \|/
1st Nat'l 2d Nat'l 3d Nat'l  etc.
      \   |   /
       \  |  /
        \ | /
     Providence
     Clearing House.
```

If Mr. A [or B, or C], who banks with the 1st National, wishes to make a payment to Mr. I [or G, or H], whose account is with the 3d [or to D, E, or F, dealing with the 2d], he draws a check upon *his own bank*, the 1st, bidding it pay to the order of Mr. I the desired sum. I turns in this check to *his* bank, the 3d, which gives him credit [or cash] therefor, and, at the clearing house, swaps it for a check or checks *drawn on* itself but *handed in* at the 1st. If the amounts, in checks, between any two banks do not match, the balance is paid in cash.

II THE NATIONAL SYSTEM

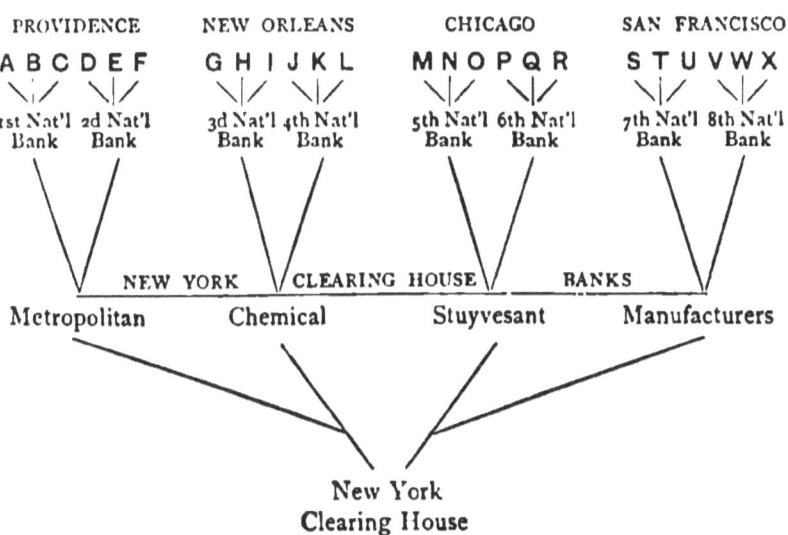

Suppose Mr. B [or A, or C] of Providence is indebted to Mr. X [or V, or W] of San Francisco [or to any one in N. Orleans or Chicago]. B, having a deposit with the 1st National in his own city, writes a check upon that bank, requesting it to pay the sum to X or his order, and sends this paper directly to X. The latter turns it over to his bank, the 8th National, in San Francisco. It is credited to him, and forwarded, as a debit, not directly to Providence, but to some bank in N. Y. This may possibly be in communication with the 1st National, of Providence, in which case the check is forwarded to its destination directly. Otherwise, unless itself one of the [about 60] banks of the metropolis in immediate relation with the clearing house [clearing house banks], the N. Y. bank first receiving it passes the check to a bank which is thus connected. In the clearing house it falls, through another debit and credit operation, into the hands of a clearing house bank which does business with some Providence bank, perhaps the 1st National itself. The grand circuit completed, and the 1st National having debited the amount of the check to B, the latter's account with X is closed, not a dollar in cash having been used [save for clearing house balances]. The N. Y. clearings for 1881 were $48,565,818,212. See also the following figures, for 1884.

NEW YORK CLEARING HOUSE

Clearings for the week ending May 3 .... $855,711,696
Clearings for the week ending April 26 707,078,332
Clearings for the week ending April 19 652,880,160
Clearings for the week ending April 12 576,804,205
Clearings for the week ending April 5 690,816,011
Clearings for the week ending March 29 610,332,765

LONDON CLEARING HOUSE

Return of Paid Clearings for the week ending April 23, 1884.

Thursday £17,172,000
Friday 16,920,000
Saturday 15,345,000
Monday 15,905,000
Tuesday 13,463,000
Wednesday 15,533,000

Total £94,338,000

In the corresponding week of 1883 the total was £98,078,000.

PARIS CLEARING HOUSE.

Dec., 1887 .... 397,897,335 francs.
Nov., 1888 .... 448,524,956 francs.
Dec., 1888 .... 488,916,294 francs.

§ 95 INTERNATIONAL PAYMENTS

GOSCHEN, Theo. of the Foreign Exchanges, *Ad. Smith*, bk. iv, ch. iii. *Macleod*, Theo. and Prac. of Banking, vol. i, ch. viii. *Mill*, bk. iii, ch. xx. 'The A B C of the Export Bus.,' Northwestern Miller, Jan., 1889.

Imports are, as a rule, paid for not by bullion but by **bills of exchange**[1] drawn on the **importing** countries and sold to brokers. There are[2] (i) time and sight bills, (ii) commercial and bankers' bills, (iii) direct and indirect bills, and (iv) accommodation and true bills. If New York is **importing** more from than **exporting** to London, bills on London bear a **premium** in New York, and bills on New York are at a **discount** in London. When this occurs, exchange and balance of trade are said to be '**against**' New York.[3] If bills in neither country bear either premium or discount, exchange is said to be at **par**. The par will be the **weight-relation** between the unitary coins of the two nations.[4] If the premium attains a higher per cent than the cost of the **freightage** and **insurance** of gold,[5] gold will be sent to pay debts; but this soon cures the necessity for it, by **lowering prices** and increasing exportations.[6]

[1] International checks or drafts. Several cases may arise. i A, in N. Y., both an importer and an exporter, owing B, in London, draws on his debtor C, in London, and sends the draft to B, who collects of C. ii A, of N. Y., exports to B, of London, and C, of London, to D, of N. Y. B buys of C a draft on D, and sends it to A, who collects of D. A and C are thus both paid without shipment of money. iii Two *brokers*, one in N. Y. and one in London, agree to honor each other's drafts. A, of N. Y., owing B, of London, buys of the N. Y. broker a draft on the London broker and sends it to B, in London, who collects from the Londoner. iv The world's clearing house is London. If a N. Y. merchant wishes to pay a debt in Italy he buys a draft on London and sends it to his Italian creditor, who gets the cash on it from Italian brokers in correspondence with London. Thus we are not obliged to have direct exchanges with every country, but the majority of exchanges are effected through the one great centre.

[2] Goschen, ch. iii. The 'time' allowed for the payment of bills not cashed at sight is usually 30 days, but may be 60 or 90. Time bills are cheaper than sight bills, in a proportion determined by the rate of interest in the drawee country. Banker's bills are simple international checks, such as a traveller might purchase on going abroad. Commercial bills are

those which a shipper draws upon his consignee against merchandise shipped, each accompanied by a bill of lading, 'to order,' covering the property against which it is drawn. This is called 'documentary' exchange. To illustrate indirect bills: from Hong Kong for tea to N. Y. the exporter draws on London instead of N. Y., and the London house charges to N. Y. This item often settles the state of exchange between two countries [Goschen, p. 32]. One day in Aug., 1882, 3,200,000 Marks [$800,000] went from Hamburg to London, to pay for wheat shipped from N. Y. to Hamburg. Bremen merchants used to settle for N. Y. tobacco by bills on London in favor of N. Y., and, to offset these, buy up bills on London, from Dutch cattle and butter dealers. Bombay even now, in getting pay from Bremen, draws on London against Bremen. Accommodation bills are like drafts on a bank when it does not owe you [Goschen, 37 sq., Macleod, Elem. of P. E., vol. i, 403. Cf. below § 96, v, and n. 4].

[3] It seldom happens that the mutual debts of two countries exactly balance. Then, by a terminology now well understood but originating in a mercantilist error [§ 7, n. 5], exchange is said to be 'in favor of' the country owing the less, and 'against' the other. Speaking generally, the following phenomena will all arise together and be phases of one and the same state of exchanges, viz.: preponderance of exports, favorable balance or exchange, tendency to import gold [or actual importation], good time to buy exchange. Also the following: preponderance of imports, unfavorable balance or exchange, tendency to export gold [or actual exportation], bad time to buy exchange. The expression, 'exchange favorable to America,' does not mean that it is favorable to American bill-*sellers*, exporters, *etc.*, but to bill-*buyers*.

[4] Exchange is at par between N. Y. and London, when, in one city, I can buy, for a given weight and fineness of gold, the right to have, in the other so soon as communication can be had, the same weight and fineness delivered to me or my representative. The par of £1 is $4.866; of 1 Mark, 0.2478\frac{3}{4}$; of 4 Marks, $0.9915; of 1 Guilder, $0.40; of 1 franc, 0.19305\frac{8}{258}$; of 5 francs, 0.96525\frac{25}{258}$; of 1 Florin, 0.4788335\frac{29}{508}$.

[5] Usually, the premium can go no higher or lower than the figure necessary to cover this cost. Not so in a great panic. When Napoleon left Elba [§ 96, n. 5], continental exchange in London rose to 10 per cent, much more than enough for transportation and even war insurance. Gold normally begins to move from London to N. Y. when London exchange in N. Y. is at $4.84½, and back again when it is $4.90. But see next §.

[6] See § 76.

§ 96 Special Modifiers of the Rate of Exchange

Goschen, Foreign Exchanges, ch. iv. *Macleod*, as at § 95.

i All monies of a country **laid out abroad**,[1] as by purchase of ships or armaments, foreign travel, interest on bonds held abroad, or principal for the liquidation of these, tend to turn exchange against that country. ii On the contrary, all foreign monies **brought into** your country[2] tend to set exchange in its favor, as the expenditures of travellers from abroad, or a loan effected or bonds sold there. iii **Ocean carrying**[3] by the ships of any country likewise turns exchange **in favor** of that country in relation to the country or countries for which the carrying is done. A country like England containing a great **commercial entrepot**, as London is, will also secure **favorable exchange** for itself by the receipt of commissions. iv Draft on, and payment in, London, of many **indirect bills** against New York, might set English exchange against New York, coincidently with a preponderance of American exports to England. v As the balance of trade **shifts** from one side to the other, shrewd brokers,[4] not to incur the **double expense** of exporting and soon importing again, let their **accounts run till naturally balanced**, diminishing thus the average **cost** of exchange. vi Large merchants, who can readily **extend the time** of their transoceanic debts by **paying interest**, if exchange is **high**, wait for it to fall and then buy drafts. Rates are thus kept from going either so **high** or so **low** as they otherwise would.[5]

[1] It is estimated that $86,000,000 go from the U. S. to Ireland yearly, in aid of distress and agitation there.

² Thus, in Jan., 1883, though exports from America increased, foreign exchange did not go down in N. Y., because Englishmen were investing vast amounts of money here.

³ The Cologne Gazette computes that Germany averages to pay England £25,000 a day in ocean freights and bank commissions. The immense ocean carrying trade of England, having the effect of so much exportation, explains in large part why the balance of trade is always apparently against that country. This and other items account for the fact that no country's imports and exports for a given period ever appear to balance. For the 5 years, 1880–1885, exports from the U. S. exceeded imports by $623,000,000; from 1876 to 1880 the excess reached $921,000,000. Total in 10 years, $1,544,000,000. What became of this vast balance? Net imports of specie for the same years account for only about $50,000,000. Some of it went to settle the balances against us of previous years, some to pay freight. Another portion was required for the interest and principal of foreign-held debts. But were all these and such causes away, the account would hardly ever seem even, owing to the different scales of valuation for imports and for exports. In fact, as, in trade, we prize more what we get than what we give, perfectly truthful figures would make exchange seem against us just in proportion as it was really the reverse. See Thorold Rogers, Econ. Interp. of Hist., 97.

⁴ Pairs of brokers, that is, one in one country, the other in the other. Bills on the country with an unfavorable balance would then be 'accommodation bills' [§ 95, and n. 2].

⁵ Many more such modifiers might be named. Exchange drawn upon a country engaged in or threatened with war is always high, owing to the risk [§ 95, n. 5]. If the money of any drawee country consists of depreciated paper, or of coins deficient in weight and fineness [§ 81, n. 6], exchange is below par. That is, a paper giving you the right to so many units of that country's money, can be gotten for a sum of the money of your country, which is less than an equivalent, nominally, of the sum drawn for. Degradation of your own money has an effect precisely opposite. Before the adoption of our constitution, $4.444 in [Spanish] American money was the established custom-house equivalent of £1. By 1837, deductions from the value of the dollar necessitated $4.866 as the equivalent of £1, an advance of just $9\frac{1}{2}$ per cent upon $4.444. Still it long remained habitual to reckon on the old basis of exchange, stating it as at $9\frac{1}{2}$ per cent premium when it was really at par ['Dollar,' in Am. Cyclop., at end].

Part IV

DISTRIBUTION

CHAPTER I

THE NATURE OF DISTRIBUTION

§ 97 General Statement

Sidgwick, bk. ii, ch. i. *Leroy-Beaulieu, Essai sur la Répartition du richesse. Mangoldt*, bk. iv, chaps. i, ii. *Mill*, bk. ii, ch. i. *Patten*, Premises of P. E.; Stability of Prices [Am. Ec. Ass'n Papers, vol. iii]. *Schoenberg*, vol. i, XI. *H. George*, Prog. and Poverty, esp. bk. iii. *Hertzka, Gesetze d. soc. Entwickelung*. *Cherbuliez*, bk. iii, chaps. i, ii.

Distribution, as a rubric in Economics, is that **substantive**[1] **department** thereof which canvasses the problems, **into what hands** the wealth created by production proper and exchange would naturally[2] fall, and **on what principles,** also wherein and why actual fortunes differ from those which strict economic causes would assign, — all of them important inquiries, to which economists have given relatively **too little attention.** It must not be assumed[3] that the shares fixed by natural or economic laws are therefore certain to be **just.** Whether, or how far, they are so is still **a question,** among the most vexing connected with the science.

[1] Sidgwick, pp. 25, 31, adverts to the new attention which this part of Economics has received since Ad. Smith. Till quite recently, in fact, it has been too much the habit of economists to treat Distribution as incidental, laying all stress on Production. The Professorial Socialists [§ 13] have nobly rebuked this.

[2] Mill, in his distinction [bk. ii, ch. i] between production as a natural process, and distribution as artificial, cannot mean that the latter is wholly given up to whim and custom. This would certainly be an error. But relatively arbitrary influences confessedly play here a great part.

[3] Sidgwick, 498 sqq. Cf. all the socialist writers. The assumption is made by orthodox economists almost to a man — a source of infinite confusion in their discussions. There is no necessary sacredness to mere operations of nature. Many of them it is the work of reason and civilization to correct. Progress largely consists in this. H. George, in saying [Social Problems] "The just distribution of wealth is manifestly the natural distribution of wealth, and this is that which gives wealth to him who makes it, and secures wealth to him who saves it," cherishes a purely *a priori* notion of 'natural.' So does Giddings [Mod. Distributive Process] in calling 'natural' that rate of wages which secures the highest productive power. These ideas are nevertheless very wholesome.

§ 98 CATEGORIES AND SHARES

Walker, P. E., pt. iv, ch. i. *Crehore*, Quar. Jour. Econ., vol. ii, 361. *Webb*, ibid., 188 sqq., 469 sqq. *Mangoldt*, §§ 85-95.

The **net product** of a people's industry for a given natural period, viz., the increment to wealth which **remains**[1] after **making good** the stock present at the outset, finds its way into **five**[2] theoretically separate **categories**,[3] determined thither by special causes. I The permanent **monopolist** of any **material** necessary to production receives **rent** in virtue of his **proprietorship**, II The **capitalist, interest,** for the same reason, plus **abstinence**, III The **laborer, wages,** for his **toil**, IV The **undertaker, profits,** for the use of his ability to **organize and superintend**,[4] and V The

anomalous recipient, anomalous fortune, for a variety
of reasons, often excessively hard to analyze.[5]

[1] The strict 'dividend' would of course embrace, what we here omit for the sake of simplicity, the products [including services] enjoyed in the course of the period. These seem to follow the same law as the rest. 'Net product' does not exclude all costs of production [§§ 47, 48], but only the wealth used up or worn out. It includes what goes for interest, wages, profits. See following Chapters. On the nature of national income, Mangoldt, as above, is best. It may be gotten at by summation of particular *products* or of particular *incomes*. With either method, much care is needed to exclude error. In general, a nation's income is simply the total proceeds of its own and its subjects' industries. But it may also receive tribute, indemnity, or interest from another nation, or enjoy a permanent net advantage over others in foreign trade.

[2] If, in a large and developed society, we look at any single industry by itself, a sixth category appears, viz., the general public, embracing the beneficiaries of all the five categories of every business aside from the one in question. In other words, the people immediately interested [as winners of rent, interest, wages, or profits] in cotton manufactures [either at a given factory or in general] are not the *only* ones interested. Through exchange [§§ 53, 54], it disseminates advantage everywhere, in more or less perfect return for its own extra profitableness in consequence of so great a market [§ 31, esp. n. 4]. It is obvious, however, that when the whole round of the industries is taken together, this extra category must in effect dissolve and disappear by a process of mutual cancellation.

[3] On Method in Distribution, or the logical order of its topics, George, Prog. and Poverty, bk. iii, chaps. i, vii.

[4] The words express but very inadequately the real nature of the undertaker's office. See Chapter V. On the close analogy, identity even, between the principle of rent and that of profits, see §§ 103, 119.

[5] The pupil must not expect satisfactorily to understand this § apart from the two following, and not exhaustively until the remaining Chapters in Distribution have been studied. The subject is complex, and cannot be truthfully expounded in the cursory and apparently simple manner hitherto so common. Observe, too, that upon many matters touching distribution authors are still divided and scientific opinion now in the process of formation. Its trend we propose to indicate in our sketch, referring for fuller light to the latest and best literature.

§ 99 Blending

Same authh. as at § 97.

While these functions and categories are really **distinct** and scientific analysis demands their separation, **two or more** of them are usually represented **in one person,** who thereby participates in the product under a **plurality of titles.**[1] Thus the **small farmer,** owning and himself working his capital and land, unites them all. A **socialist** community, viewed as a whole, would do the same. All laborers save the lowest receive, besides wages in the narrowest sense, earnings on **intellectual capital,** as well as **profits** or rent of ability.[2] In a society of low industrial organization, to a large extent in America even yet, **capitalists** are **also undertakers,** and *vice versa.*[3] In England these functions coincide more with **classes,** which has hitherto been the general tendency of industrial advance everywhere.[4] At present, however, both capitalists and undertakers more and more derive gains from **monopoly.**

---

[1] That is, we do not here have in view so much different classes of human beings as different industrial functions and their workings. See, more fully, § 101.

[2] See §§ 103, 121.

[3] In any joint stock undertaking each participant may be regarded as at once capitalist and undertaker, since the whole stockholding body is both. Every stockholder of course owns part of the capital: he also, at least indirectly, by voting upon directors and policy, has weight in managing the business.

[4] Now counteracted and negatived, somewhat, by the movement toward Socialism. See Webb, Socialism in England, Papers of Am. Econ. Ass'n, vol. iv. Whether, and if so, how far, this movement is healthy, perhaps no man living is wise enough to say.

§ 100 The Law of Equal Returns to Last Increments

Webb, 'Rate of Interest and Laws of Distribution,' Quar. Jour. Econ., vol. ii.

According to the **pure theory** of economic distribution, presupposing **omniscience** and the **perfect mobility** of the various means of production both to prevail throughout an industrial community, **competition,** in its effort to secure the **maximum utility** for given sacrifice, would so **dispose and arrange** capital, skill, and human energy, that the **last** application of any one of them at any point or in any way, would evoke as great a **return** per unit of the factor applied, as the last application made **elsewhere** or in **any other way**. And in actual fact, competition, though imperfect, is sufficient to maintain a **constant tendency** to the realization of this law.[1]

[1] In agriculture, *e.g.*, the operation of the law of diminishing return [§ 34] prevents all workers from concentrating at the same point, while each new comer will seek to work at the most advantageous point *all things considered*. There must be theoretically, at any time, a certain arrangement of labor, skill and capital upon the land, which will get from it the maximum of utility. That ideal order may never be actually reached, but so far as self-interest prevails, and is enlightened, there cannot but be a steady approximation thereto. Skill, capital, and labor, as well as land, will be put in requisition according to the same law. Webb, as above, p. 194.

§ 101 The Other General Laws of Distribution

Webb, as at § 98. *Clark*, 'Possibility of a Sci. Law of Wages,' Am. Ec. Ass'n Papers, vol. iv. *Patten*, 'Stability of Prices' [ibid., vol. iii]. *Mangoldt*, §§ 128 sqq.

These are two, (i) the **static** and (ii) the **dynamic.**
i Supposing, **at any given time**, a community where **perfect knowledge and competition** existed, with no **artificial hindrances** to the play of economic **causes**

in distribution, we should, partly *a priori*, partly from experience, expect the proceeds of its industry to be classifiable as follows. **Wages** proper would be the return to the **simplest form of labor,**[1] absolutely unhelped, or, if applied with aids, the reward of the proportion not owing to these. All surplus gotten by labor in virtue of **location, native fertility** or other not individually created advantages connected with **land,** would be **Rent,** which would also cover the proceeds of all **fixed material monopolies.** Excess proceeding from the use of native **skill superior** to that of the simplest labor, would be **Profits.** Whatever increase was due to the employment of **capital,** material or immaterial, would be **Interest.** Gains **not referrible to any of the above** sources, present to some extent in the best conceivable social organization, would form a **Fifth Category.** ii If, now, introducing the **dynamic element,** we consider the productive process as in **movement,** the various factors[2] in production will tend to be remunerative in proportion to the **slowness of their increase,** competition enabling the **hindmost,** especially by reaping the benefit of **improvements,** to enlarge its share at the expense of the others.[3]

[1] This is doubtless a somewhat indefinite conception. All labor, as we have seen [§ 25], involves an intellectual element. The labor here meant is that into which enter no training and no special native gifts.

[2] Land resources, capital, supervising and planning ability, and simple labor.

[3] Patten, as above [sec. iv, esp. p. 37], well develops the second law. It operates through competition. Overlooking the effects of diminishing returns [§ 34], suppose capital to be doubling in 30 years, the labor force [§§ 35, 36] in 20. Wages will fall, till population increases less rapidly than capital, that which is lost to wages, along with all gains from improvements, going to capitalists through rise in the rate of interest. So,

if land facilities are multiplying slower than either labor or capital, land rent will be swollen at the expense of both, most, however, to the loss of the one getting on the faster. Cf. carefully the following Chapters: also Patten.

§ 102 The Fifth Category

Wagner, Lehrbuch, vol. i, §§ 300 sqq. *George,* Prog. and Poverty, bk. iii, ch. iv. *Walker,* P. E., pt. iv, ch. vi. *Hertzka, Gesetze d. soc. Entwickelung.*

Rent, interest, wages and profits **by no means exhaust** the product of industry. **Non-producers** may share therein, or producers get an **undue** share, in almost **innumerable ways,** chief among which are the following: i **Gifts other than charitable,** as to one's family or friends. ii **Charity** in its endless variety of forms. iii **Gambling,**[1] in which stock and exchange gambling must be included. iv **Fraud, theft,** and **robbery,** of all sorts. v **Casual monopoly,**[2] whether natural, accidental or based on legislation or on immensity of financial power. vi **Unfair legislation** or administration in other things. vii Changes in the **value of money.**[3]

[1] See § 21, n. 7.

[2] See §§ 66, 67. A good illustration is the fortune amassed in London one day in June, 1815, by Baron Rothschild and Moses Montefiore, as sole possessors of the secret that Napoleon had left Elba and landed in France [§ 95, n. 5]. They bought, low, credits which appreciated immensely soon as the tidings became known. *Permanent* monopoly gains from any sort of material possession we reckon as rent [§ 103].

[3] See § 87.

CHAPTER II

RENT

§ 103   Rent in General

Mangoldt, §§ 120 sqq. *Schaeffle, Pol. Oek.*, § 300; *Theo. d. ausschl. Absatzverhältnisse*, iii–vii. *Wagner, Lehrbuch*, vol. i, § 301. *George*, Prog. and Poverty, bk. iii, ch. ii. *Cherbuliez*, bk. iii, ch. vi.

Rent, in the broadest sense, is any kind of **gain** arising from **monopoly**, whether in land, capital,[1] or talent — income which falls to the possessor of any **productive agency** simply because of its **rarity**. Rent forms **no part of the cost** of production,[2] and is payment for no **service**. It swells individual fortunes only at the **expense of society** as a whole. To the **total revenue** of the **world**, or of a **nation** or an industrial group not exchanging with any other, it therefore **adds nothing**, nor does it subtract, except as dissuading from industry. On the other hand, rent does not **cause** high prices, but **is caused** by them.[2] It is usual and well to restrict the term 'rent' to winnings from **somewhat permanent** monopolies, though the **idea** does not necessarily presuppose such limitation.

[1] Such cases as are mentioned at § 65, notes 4 and 5, are really cases of rent [on capital]. For land rent, or ground rent, see § 104. Profits and special wages [see Chapters III and IV] also involve the rent principle. English writers have usually confined the term to ground rent [§ 104]. Our use of the word, which seems to us to have very much in its favor, is that of Mangoldt and Schaeffle.

[2] See § 105.

§ 104 GROUND RENT

Ricardo, Prin. of P. E. and Taxation, chaps. ii, xxiv. *Mill*, bk. ii, ch. xvi. *Roscher*, bk. iv, ch. ii. *Maine*, Village Communities, vi. *Walker*, Land and its Rent; P. E. [either ed.], 'Rent.' Cf. Int'l Rev., vol. xii. *Rossi*, in *Cours d'Econ. pol. H. George*, Progress and Poverty. *Cairnes*, Log. Meth., 29, n., 50 sqq. *Wachenhusen, Untersuchungen ueber Grundrente. Hertzka, Sociale Entwickelung*, ch. vii. *Patten*, Premises of P. E., i.

Ground rent is the advantage accruing[1] to landowners from the use of certain uncreated or socially created[2] powers and utilities connected with land, including, besides mere fertility of soil, also mineral wealth, water-privileges, location, etc. Return from the occupation of land, as the most common form of ground rent, furnishes the most obvious and useful matter wherewith to illustrate the doctrine.

[1] The definition must be thus wide because the essence of rent is present whether land is owned privately or by the community. Of the spots which at any time have to be occupied, some are better than others. Both socialism and the mere policy of nationalizing the land would try to distribute this advantage, but nothing could abolish it. For varying and loose uses of the word rent, note 3, below, and § 106. Cf. Mill, bk. ii, chaps. viii-x.

[2] Capital inwrought into land will bear rent if the land does. This is strictly not *ground* rent, though inseparable therefrom. It differs from the normal return on such capital, which is interest [§ 106, iv, and n. 1]. Cf. § 19, i, n. 2. Let a considerable number of human beings settle in a new country: special value instantly attaches to particular localities, and this with no act of creation save the act of the people in coming there. But much land value is socially created. The Dutch purchased all Manhattan Island for 60 guilders, about $24. On the main street fronts in N.Y. City that sum would to-day not purchase a single foot. Store sites on Fifth Ave. cost in 1886 $65 per sq. ft.; $85 have been paid on Broad St., and $100 and $115 on Broadway. Shares of a land company at Birmingham, Ala., costing $1,100, recently paid a yearly dividend of $24,000. In London land has often sold for $240 per foot, and select spots, it is said, for as much as it would cost to pave them with English sovereigns laid upon edge. Such dearness, springing though it does from a sort of human agency, is not the product of conscious doing on the part of any one per-

son. In bringing it into being, A, B, and C were instruments, not agents. See 'Ground-rents in Philad.,' Quar. Jour. Econ., Ap. 1888.

§ 105 Rent and Price

Mill, bk. ii, ch. xvi, sec. 3 sqq. *Ricardo*, Principles, ch. xxiv. *Walker*, P. E., § 243.

Since, as a rule, all land will be cultivated just so fast and far as it pays the **cost of cultivation**, the rent of land always tends to represent the surplus of gain arising from cultivating **better land** over the gain of cultivating the **poorest** that is cultivated at all,[1] 'better' and 'poorest' here referring to **location** as well as to **quality**. It follows that so long as unused land is still accessible[2] and freely resorted to, rent can never become factor in the **price** of agricultural produce, for this price, as always where the law of **diminishing return** has begun to work, is fixed by the **dearest cost** of production, which falls precisely upon the **no-rent** tracts. Capital rents, in like manner, never enter into the **prices** of products.

[1] Compare with this, § 34. The margin of cultivation tends to move outward with the increase of population, land to-day bearing rent which did not do so years ago, etc. But new fertilizers, and new agricultural machinery and methods may hinder this. A particular new need for food might be thus entirely satisfied without extending cultivation at all. We may therefore speak of an 'intensive margin of cultivation,' as well as an extensive. Variety of appetites is a further element of irregularity in the taking up of land. Soil ill fitted for one crop may grow another; poor arable may be good pasture, etc. [Patten, as at § 104; also in Stability of Prices, Am. Ec. Ass'n Papers, vol. iii.]

[2] Suppose no more land to be obtainable. At once begins a competition, which did not exist before, for the poorest lands, which, under private ownership, owners will promptly utilize by charging rent. To pay this, the produce from these tracts too must be sold higher. Under these circumstances, therefore, rent *will appear in price*. The statement in the

first part of this §, as to the measure of rent, will, however, still hold true. That, normally, rent does not appear in price, Hume saw, though Ad. Smith did not [cf. Bagehot, Ec. Studies, iii].

§ 106 Peculiar and Nominal Rents

Walker, P. E., pt. iv, ch. ii.

Rents of **mines, water-privileges, building-lots,** etc., are determined by the **same general law** with agricultural rents. Yet notice here that: i The **location** of a lot, not its fertility, usually settles its rent, though, ii **Lowest** town-rents coincide with the value of the lots for **tillage.** iii The **so-called rent** of buildings themselves is usually not rent proper but interest of capital. iv The normal return for **improvements**[1] **on land** is also not rent, though often practically inseparable from it.[2] v With increase of the ground rent on a spot of land, **capital rent** often attaches to the **buildings** situated thereon, as well as to the **improvements** incorporated therein. vi The tendency of long working is, in **mines** toward, in **lands** away from, the **no-rent** condition.[3]

[1] Hedges, ditches, grading, roadways, artificial fertility, etc. Cf. § 104, n. 2.

[2] This fact seems to a considerable extent the occasion of the erroneous view referred to in § 107.

[3] Mines often become so deep that it no longer pays to use them. Any given piece of land, on the other hand, despite the law of diminishing return [§ 34], is likely, with the growth of population, to bear higher and higher rent. There is no necessity that a piece of land should be worn out by cultivation, though extended through centuries.

§ 107 Controversy

Mill, as at § 104. *Schaeffle, Bau und Leben des socialen Körpers*, vol. iii, 433 [also as at § 103]. *Wirth*, in *Vierteljahrsch. für Volkswirtsch.*, 1863, vol. ii. *H. C. Carey*, Prin. of P. E. *Yves Guyot, Sci. Écon.*, bk. v, ch. i. *Patten*, Premises of P. E., i.

'This is the theory of rent first propounded at the end of the **last century**[1] by **Dr. Anderson**, and which, neglected at the time, was almost simultaneously rediscovered twenty years later, by **Sir Edward West, Mr. Malthus**, and **Mr. Ricardo**.'[2] Most of the **leading economists**[3] still approve it. First challenged by **Hoffman**,[4] in 1831, it has since been earnestly opposed by three eminent writers, **Carey, Bastiat**, and **Max Wirth**, who reduce rent to **interest** and maintain that no mere **power of nature** can be made to yield a **price**. Their appeal to facts is **unsuccessful**: differences of rent do not at all coincide with differences in the amounts of capital applied to different lands. Nor is their doctrine a whit better than Ricardo's as weapon against **socialism**.[5]

[1] The pamphlet really appeared in 1777.

[2] Mill, as above. He adds: "It is one of the cardinal doctrines of P. E., and, until it was understood, no consistent explanation could be given of many of the more complicated industrial phenomena."

[3] Besides Walker, we mention Wagner, Schaeffle, de Laveleye, Roscher, and Mangoldt. Mill and Hermann argued for it stoutly. Schaeffle declares that its critics have not shaken it "in the slightest." Patten's criticisms do not touch the substance of the doctrine, and are not always just even to the Ricardian exposition.

[4] Chief of the Prussian statistical bureau, in an address delivered in 1831. Next came Carey, in 1837, probably ignorant of Hoffman's contention. Bastiat wrote in 1848, merely repeating Carey [*Harmonies Écon.*, xiii]. Carey's view is discussed by Wirth, as above, and by Mill, bk. ii, ch. xvi, § 5. It boots nothing to allege with Carey that improvements on

land [in U.S., *e.g.*] have cost more than the land would bring. Many of them have been foolishly made, and, what is more to the point, for particular lots and localities, *the statement is not true.* Equally vain is Hoffman's plea that land value always originates in labor [see above, § 104, n. 2]. Specially weak is it, with Yves Guyot, to think Ricardo all wrong because of his error in assuming that the richest land is always occupied first. But if these writers mean (which can hardly be the case) only that the product which mankind *as a whole* gets from the land is measured and determined by its toil, are they correct [§ 103]? The same is true of a nation having no foreign commerce, also of one which has, unless it possesses net advantage over those with which it trades [§ 68 and n.]. But this is no contradiction to the fact of rent.

[5] Wirth urges that the Ricardian theory makes rent-taking unjust, a winning which is not an earning, while his own view considers rent nothing but a form of interest. But in fact the title of the great British landlords [in question] to their income is ethically no clearer on the one assumption than on the other. It was the fact of rent [as privately monopolized] that led Proudhon to his famous thesis, "property is robbery" [*la propriété, c'est le vol*].

CHAPTER III

INTEREST

§ 108 The Nature of Interest

Webb, as at § 100. *H. George*, Prog. and Poverty, bk. iii, ch. iii. *Clark*, 'Capital and its Earnings,' Am. Ec. Ass'n Papers, vol. iii. *Böhm-Bawerk, Kapital u. Kapitalzins*, bk. iii. *Knies, Der Credit*, viii. *Sidgwick*, bk. ii, ch. vi.

Economic interest is that portion of the proceeds of industry which arises in consequence of the **employment of capital**: in other words, the wealth which, by the aid of **capital**, men with given native **skill**, given **energy** and felicity of **situation**, create **over and above** what they could create using those same helps but **without capital**. Interest varies according to the unlike **advantages** supplied to labor by the different forms, locations, and applications of capital, some pieces of capital assisting labor little, perhaps, temporarily, not at all, while others are absolutely **indispensable**. Economic interest differs more or less from **loan interest**,[1] whether (i) at the **current** rate for short loans or for long,[2] or (ii) at the **normal** rate,[3] to which variations in current rates tend, in any community, to conform for **considerable periods** of time.

[1] It will be seen that the essential fact of interest does not presuppose a loan, interest upon loans being a subsidiary and incidental phenomenon, growing out of the division of labor and the diversities of human ability and circumstance. Intellectual capital of course cannot be loaned, though its services may be hired [§ 113].

[2] Rates, *i.e.*, always being, if other things are equal, the higher the

shorter the term — higher at banks of discount, discounting only for days, weeks and months, than at savings banks, which loan for years.

[3] 'Rate' is not a happy form in which to conceive economic interest. 'Portion of product' is better. Yet to think of it as a percentage need not mislead if we bear in mind that its 'rate' may vary widely from the rate of loans, and is in fact a very different thing.

§ 109 LOAN INTEREST

H. George, as at § 108. *Atkinson*, 'What makes the Rate of Int.?', Intl. Rev., vol. xi. *Böhm-Bawerk*, vol. i. *Knies*, *Credit*, vii.

Nearly all theories of interest err in **narrowing** the problem to loan interest instead of viewing this as **incidental** to the larger one of interest in general. But of loan interest itself most accounts are very **defective**. i One set of writers mistakenly call interest **robbery**,[1] ignoring its natural source in **capital** and **production**. ii Others fail in **merely** referring it to the productivity of capital,[2] overlooking the elements of **abstinence, time**, and **risk**. iii Certain authors seem to conceive **abstinence** not only correctly as **indispensable** to interest, but incorrectly, as its **efficient cause**.[3] To the **elements of truth** contained in these three views needs to be added the one first put in its true light by **Böhm-Bawerk**,[4] that 'a loan is in fact an **exchange of present against future** goods,' so that, as 'present commodities normally command a **premium** over future ones of like kind and quantity, a definite sum of present wealth is to be had only at the price of a **greater** in futures.' This premium is the **pure loan interest**. Gross loan interest contains the further element of **insurance** against **risk**.

[1] Marx, and, in part, Rodbertus. See Marx, Capital, vol. i, pt. iii. Böhm-Bawerk criticises the view in his vol. i, ch. xi.

[2] Closely allied with this theory are 3 variants: i) the notion of James Mill and M'Culloch, that interest is nothing but the wages of the labor stored up in capital; ii) the 'fructification' theory, advanced by Turgot and in a modified form favored by H. George, that capital at large draws interest because some of it, as land [Turgot], animals, bees, wine [George], is actually or in effect *live* capital, bringing forth value without concurrent labor; and iii) the 'usufruct' theory, of J. B. Say, Hermann, and Menger, which derives interest from a supposed peculiarly profitable employment of it, yielding gain over and above its natural productivity. Böhm-Bawerk [vol. i] keenly and at length reviews all these.

[3] Senior and Bastiat are referred to, but one cannot agree with Böhm-Bawerk in supposing them to have meant all that many of their utterances would imply. Rees, in From Poverty to Plenty, also wrongly considers the truth of the abstinence theory to involve the falsehood of all productivity theories.

[4] Vol. i, 308; vol. ii, sec. iv. We must emphasize the truth that 'capital,' not 'money,' is the true correlative of interest. Contrary to Bilgram's thought [Iron Law of Wages], money is rarely, if ever, really the form of capital for the use of which interest is paid. Money usually only aids to mediate the transfer of capital to the borrower's hands. It may (i) be the full and sole agent of this transfer, or (ii), the more frequent case, only give denomination to credit-instruments serving the same purpose.

§ 110 THE RATE ON LOANS

Walker, P. E., pt. iv, ch. iii. *Mangoldt*, §§ 102 sqq. *Sidgwick*, bk. ii, ch. vi.

The **rate** of loan interest is determined by the ordinary law of **supply and demand**, except in this, that inasmuch as desire and reluctance to borrow and to lend are influenced by **every circumstance** that affects business,[1] supply and demand of loans, and hence the rate of interest, **vary and fluctuate** more than other prices do. The chief **modifiers** are (i) the state of **business**, (ii) the **abundance**[2] or scarcity of capital, (iii) the **risk**[3] or security of loans, and (iv) the strength or weakness of men's **motives** to accumulation. Rate of **interest** and amount of **saving** are not, however, in exact correlation.[4] Owing to the strong **conservatism** of certain money-lending classes, the **actual** market minimum, as in case of consols, government bonds, and bottom mortgages, is lower than either the **gross** or the **pure** loan interest of capital.[5]

[1] The slightest panic or insecurity, caused, *e.g.*, by the rumor of a war, though not affecting in the least men's wish to sell meat, bread, corn, or iron, will make many unwilling to sell the services of capital. Every financial crisis reveals how coy capital is at such times, and also how stupid, careless, and bold it is at others.

[2] It is the growth of capital which causes the rate of interest continually to fall in all prosperous industrial lands. Till 1868 12 per cent, or, better, 1 per cent a month, was the lowest rate of interest paid in San Francisco. In many districts on the Pacific slope, 1½ and 2 per cent per month were not considered excessive, and throughout the Mississippi valley, except in a few of the great business centres, the rates of interest did not run much below these figures. At present, on the average, interest west of the Alleghany mountains costs about one-half what it cost in 1868. The security is probably no better now than then. The likelihood of an advance in the value of the security upon a mortgage loan was even better then than now. The change has come simply because, in proportion to the demand, there is now a much larger amount of available capital. In London, while the official rates of discount have, in the last fifty years, sometimes averaged in twelve months considerably over 6 per cent, for fifteen years past the yearly average has been but once over 4 per cent. During 1888 a large part of the British debt was refunded at $2\frac{3}{4}$ and $2\frac{1}{2}$ per cent. Early in the 20th century the normal rate on loans in the richer countries will very likely not be over 2 per cent, the lowest point to which Bank of England discounts have ever yet gone. On the rate of int. in Germany since 1815, *Zeitsch. f. Volkswirtsch*, XXII, iii, 233. It is evident that high interest may or may not betoken financial prosperity, according to cause. Rise of the rate in consequence of increase in production is a favorable symptom; if resulting from greater risk, the opposite. Conversely, reduction of the rate may be a bad sign, of stagnation in business, or a good, indicating lessened risk. Save in panic, abundance of capital usually works low interest; paucity, high.

[3] A very influential condition. The low rate at which Gt. Britain and the U. S. can market bonds, while in part due to plentifulness of capital,

is largely owing also to the perfect credit of these governments. The Athenians at one time allowed 60 per cent upon marine interest, while on land the rate was but 12.

[4] The rate will go down in proportion as accumulation increases, but accumulation will not go down in proportion as the rate falls. Many would save were there no [loan] interest at all. Among the poor, in particular, the precise rate has but the slightest effect upon economy.

[5] "Any large lender, placing his risks judiciously, and spreading them somewhat widely, is mathematically certain to realize a larger return from his capital through a term of years, after deducting losses, than if he had invested in the most approved securities" [Walker]. The long time of these investments is part cause of this: also the peculiar ease of collection. We may say that in return for these advantages lenders *give back* to borrowers a part of the real loan interest. Elimination of the risk element through multitude of loans is the principle of the English Investment Trusts. What is lost in one investment is made up in another.

§ 111   Inflation and Interest

Rate of interest bears **no necessary relation** to the **quantity** or the **value** per unit of the money in circulation. Hence an **increase** of currency does not, in and of itself, affect the **rate** of interest.[1] It diminishes the power of a dollar to buy commodities, but not to hire its old multiple in money of the same kind with itself. Since, however, an **expansion** or **contraction** of **paper** currency is always an expansion or contraction of **credit,** the effects of the two are easily confounded. But the effect of paper issues on interest is not from their character as an **enlargement of the currency,** but from their character as **loans.**[2]

[1] Unless indirectly, by quickening business [§ 110 (i)].

[2] In a state of tense credit the rate rules high because you are not absolutely safe in loaning to any one, the monetary unit being so likely to fluctuate in value while the indebtedness is outstanding. Thus during the civil war all stocks rose and fell with the premium on gold.

§ 112 Usury Laws

Knies, Der Credit, vii. *Böhm-Bawerk, Kapital,* etc., vol. i, i–iii. *Perry,* ch. x. *Bentham,* On Usury. *Garnier, Traité,* 722 sqq.

The rate of interest determining itself **naturally, usury laws,** as distinct from **legal rates**[1] for the settlement of **old debts** when no rates were agreed upon, are **pernicious**. Aiming especially to protect the **borrower,** which is unjust, they in fact **burden** him instead, **raising the rate** by narrowing supply[2] and by compelling borrowers to resort to **indirect methods.**[3] Such legislation is relic of a **departed social state** or of **exploded economic ideas.** The **Mosaic code**[4] forbade interest because in its time only those in **distress** sought loans. Partly the same fact, partly **tradition,** led the **Church fathers**[5] without exception to retain the Mosaic scruple. The **Greeks and Romans** were set against interest[6] by the further thoughts of all wealth as consisting in gold and silver, and of these as 'barren.'[7]

[1] These are of course appropriate and necessary.

[2] The legal maximum is sure to be too low. Hence many try to use their capital rather than lend. This narrows the loan market immediately. It does the same also mediately, by keeping capital in hands not the most productive possible. Both effects raise the rate.

[3] One device often resorted to to evade usury legislation is this: A wishes to loan, and B to borrow, $1,000 at 10 per cent for a year — amount at the end of the year, $1,100. B deeds to A a piece of land or a building for $1,000, at the same time signing an agreement to buy it back at the end of a year for $1,100. The necessity of all this, and of breaking the law, will make such as resort to these means charge and pay high.

[4] Leviticus, ch. xxv, Deuteronomy, ch. xv. But the parable of the talents, Matthew, ch. xxv, shows that Jesus did not share this prejudice.

[5] See Gibbon, Decline and Fall of the Rom. Empire [ed. Milman], vol. v, 314, where reference is made to Barbeyrac, *Moral des pères.* The mediæval theologians were fond of using against the legitimacy of interest

the words of Jesus, Luke vi, 35, which read in the Vulgate, *mutuum date nihil inde sperantes.*

[6] Yet the theoretical opposition did not keep the institution from being legalized. The legal rate at Athens when the Roman conquest began was 18 per cent. Cf. § 110, n. 3. The Twelve Tables of Roman law made it 10 per cent for twelve months, viz., $8\frac{1}{3}$ per cent, or an *uncia* to every *as*, per year of 10 months. The latter was then the fiscal year, though the Romans were already beginning to employ the 12 months year along with the 10 months or lunar year. At Babylon, in the 6th century B.C., interest ranged from 13 to 20 per cent, paid monthly. Here only the lunar year was used.

[7] Shakespeare, too, calls interest the posterity of a sterile metal.

CHAPTER IV

WAGES

§ 113 DEFINITION

Walker, Wages [cf. his P. E., pt. iv, ch. v]. *Sidgwick*, bk. ii, ch. viii; also in Fortnightly Rev., Sept. 1, 1879. *Clark*, 'Possib. of a Sci. Law of Wages,' Am. Ec. Ass'n Papers, vol. iv. *Wood*, 'Theo. of Wages,' ibid.; also in Quar. Jour. Econ., vol. iii, 60 sqq. *Webb*, as at § 100. *Mangoldt*, §§ 109 sqq. *Thornton*, in XIXth Cent., Aug., 1879.

'**Wages**' means here (i) **pure** wages as distinguished from **gross**, viz., the mere reward for **common labor**, excluding all high **salaries and fees**, and also all forms of remuneration under the **name** of wages so far as earned by special **talent, education** or **training**,[1] (ii) **real** wages, which may in any case vary greatly from **nominal** through differences in the value of money and in the regularity, safety, and healthfulness of work, also through extras given or allowed to be earned.[2] We seek, chiefly, the laws of **general** wages, deferring the reasons for the **different levels** of wages within any group of competitors, to the end of the Chapter.

[1] Though we may stop short of Leroy-Beaulieu's avowal that "the *whole* theory of wages must be rebuilt," little, certainly of the older teaching on the subject can be accepted without sifting. New definitions are especially needed. Rewards earned by peculiar talent are profits [see next Chapter]; those bestowed in consequence of education and training are interest on intellectual capital [§ 98. Cf. Crehore, Quar. Jour. Econ., vol. ii, 361]. That the several elements all go by the name of wages is unfortunate, yet no nomenclature could avert the necessity for care in the mental analysis of the case, as the elements of gross wages are themselves to a great extent inseparable in fact. But gross and nominal wages do not usually so vary

from pure and real as to render reasonings about the one kind wholly misleading in respect to the other.

² Walker, P. E., 260 sq. A common instance is the custom in stores, of letting the clerks have goods at wholesale prices.

§ 114 Cause and Source

Walker, as at § 113 [his 'Wages' is devoted to the demonstration of the view we present on this point]. *H. George*, Prog. and Poverty, bk. iii, ch. vi. *Fawcett*, Manual, bk. ii, ch. iv. *Cairnes*, Leading Principles, pt. ii, ch. i. *Sumner*, in Princeton Rev., Nov., 1887 [also in his Essays, in Pol. and Soc. Sci.]. *Beauregard, Théo. du Salaire. Levasseur*, do., *Jour. des Écon.*, Jan., 1888. *McDonnell*, Hist. and Criticism of Theories of Wages [prize essay, Dublin, 1887]. *Marx*, Capital. *Marshall*, Econ. of Industry, bk. ii, chaps. vi, vii, viii, xi [cf. Quar. Jour. Econ., vol. ii, 218 sqq.]. *Roscher*, bk. iii, ch. ii. *Jevons*, Theo. of P. E., 1st ed., 256 sqq.; 2d ed., 289 sqq. *Thornton*, Labour.

The efficient **cause**[1] of wages is the **labor** from which they spring, a truth clearly apparent from a glance at primitive industry, and in no wise altered by the **complex** conditions which arise later. Equally manifest is it that the **source**[2] of wages is the **product** created by the same labor. This theory, now well-nigh universally accepted, opposes that of Fawcett and Cairnes, which speaks of a fast and rigid **'wage-fund,'**[3] existing at any given moment, made up of capital already produced, from which fund wages for the next ensuing period **must** be paid, so that, until there has been, through new production, a **new accession** to capital and the wage-fund, wages must depend absolutely and only upon the greater or less **competition** among the laborers, arising from their **numbers**.

[1] Bearing in mind the definitions of §§ 98 and 113.

[2] On this, H. George, as above, is best. Cf. Rae, Contemp. Socialism, 332. Cairnes, too, forgetting himself, well says, Leading Prin., 58, that "industrial rewards consist for each producer, or, more properly, for each group of producers, employed on a given work, in the value of the commodities which result from their exertions." "Freight the mother of

wages" [*i.e.*, no freight, no wages for sailors] is an old maxim of admiralty law [Prog. and Pov., 50].

[3] See Laughlin, ed. of Mill, 178 sqq., Cairnes, as above [the ablest presentation of the old view], Walker, "Wage-fund," in Lalor, vol. iii, Mill, bk. ii, chaps. xi–xiii, Fortnightly, May, 1869 [where Mill repudiates the old doctrine, taught in his Principles]. Mill was led to this by Longe's pamphlet, 1866, A Refutation of the Wage-fund Theo. of Modern P. E. Cliffe Leslie wrote, agreeing with Longe, in Fraser's Mag., July, 1868. Endless has been the discussion since, not all of it sober. If the wage-periods be considered very brief, and the reckoning carried over considerable time, the two theories would not differ in practical effect, since by both product would avail for the sustenance of labor at once after it was amassed. The wage-fund belief has wrought mischief in disseminating the false impressions that contract wages are the only wages, and that wage-earners are totally dependent on capitalists. But the new and better doctrine, while correcting these errors, leads many to the equally great mistake of supposing the portion of the proceeds of industry which can issue in wages to be naturally unlimited, so that, if wages are low, capitalists or the state must be to blame [cf. 119]. Further, (i) so far as wages are advanced, which is not common, they must be taken from capital, not from product, (ii) the amount of wages *promised* in any given bargain is according to *prospect* of production, and (iii) the total of wages *realized* on the whole and in the long run is as the *amount* of production.

§ 115 Developed Wages

Ad. Smith, bk. i, ch. vi; bk. ii, ch. i. *H. George*, as at § 114. *Clark*, Pol. Sci. Quar., vol. ii, 605. *Sax*, *Theoretische Staatswirtsch.*, 230, n., §§ 39, 40.

As industry **advances** it leans more and more on **capital**, which not all possess. Moreover, not only are the **precise shares** due to each man often no longer discoverable, but the product is usually **not divisible**[1] so early or often as the needs of workmen require. Those lacking capital therefore covenant with capitalists to **sell** them their wages, in the proper sense, for certain supplies to be paid at convenient intervals, so originating the **wage system** as now familiar. The **wages** proper we may term 'noumenal[2] wages,' as distinguished from the 'visible wages' actually received. Observe that modern wages are as natural in their time as primitive wages were earlier.

[1] In a cotton factory, for instance, each weaver's true wage for a given day's work is at the end of that day stored up in the web of cloth woven during the day. To save breaking bulk, the owner of the establishment *buys* the weaver's true wage, giving him money down. With many writers this transaction seems to be the beginning and the end of the wages-phenomenon. But wages take other forms than that of contract wages. Work in mills is not the sole kind of industry.

[2] The word is borrowed from Kant's philosophy, and means that which is real to thought though not to our senses.

§ 116 The General Rate of Gross Wages

Ricardo, Prin. of P. E. and Taxation, ch. v. *Clark*, as at § 113. *Webb*, as at § 100. *Cherbuliez*, bk. iii, ch. iii, sec. 2.

Competition pervades the entire wage-earning world, yet not at all **equally,** but in **tracts or groups of high pressure,** separated by **ridges of low.**[1] Why, in the world, a nation, or a group, does the **wages class** as a whole divide the joint social income on such and such terms with **landlords, capitalists** and **undertakers?** To this most difficult question different writers give the following several answers: i That the winnings of the laboring population tend to conform to the returns secured by such **unskilled workmen** as employ **no-rent lands** or **no-interest capital.**[2] ii That 'the natural price of labor is that price which is necessary to enable the laborers one with another **to subsist** and to **perpetuate their race** without increase or diminution,' according to the **standard** of **comfort** prevalent among them at the given place and time.[3]

[1] Cf. § 66 and notes.

[2] Tend to conform, that is, to *bare wages*, in the strict sense [§ 113]. The view counts all gains, in any cases, beyond those gotten by such unassisted labor, as interest or profits [§§ 101, 113, n. 1].

[3] Ricardo, as above. This is what Lassalle named Ricardo's 'iron law.' In fact it is neither iron, as the modifications show, nor Ricardo's. It originated with Turgot. He said: "In each species of labor it must come to this, that wages limit themselves to what is necessary for the support and reproduction of the laborer." But he insisted that this natural price of labor is in no wise *fixed* but varies greatly at different times in one country and more greatly still in different lands. The principle is that if the ignorant poor find themselves at any time unusually prosperous, they multiply till competition has destroyed the advantage. Fawcett, Manual, 234, declares that in the English agricultural districts wages fluctuate regularly with the price of wheat. This phenomenon Ricardo generalized somewhat too hastily, as if, which he after all denies rather than asserts, extra prosperity on the part of the poor absolutely could not be permanent. Cf. § 118. For H. George's interp. of Ricardo on wages, Social Problems, 201.

§ 117 THE RESIDUAL CLAIMANT THEORY

Walker, Wages, pt. ii; P. E., pt. iv, ch. v. *Atkinson*, The Distribution of Products; The Margin of Profit. *Chevallier*, Les Salaires au XIXième Siècle. *Giffen*, Progress of the Working Classes.

iii That the laws of **rent, interest,** and **profits** are at the same time **laws of wages,** wages consisting always in the total product of industry, minus what the operation of these laws apportions to landlord, capitalist and undertaker. According to this view, among the three divisions of social income which arise through **economic merit,** pure profits and interest constantly decrease, while wages increase, the **wages class,** not landlords, undertakers, or capitalists, being the **residual claimant.**[1] That this advantage shows so slight effect upon actual wage **rates,** is laid to (i) the **increase** of laborers in numbers, and (ii) the anomalous and partly **illicit gains** concealed in gross profits.

[1] We do not accept this view. Even the considerations at the end of the § do not bring it into accord with facts. Wages, both *per capita* and as a total [the one does not necessarily involve the other], are indeed increasing, as Chevallier and Giffen show, though the advance cannot be shown to keep pace with that in the means of production. The cause of the increase, however, we believe not to lie in any laws naturally limiting the other shares, but in such elevation, new self-respect, and new demands on the part of laborers, and such higher regard for them on the part of the public, as recent decades have developed [§ 118, and n. 1]. In proclaiming a natural limitation to the shares other than wages, writers are too apt to reckon interest by the mere rates of loans, and profits by mere statistics, forgetting, meanwhile, both monopoly gains and the steady growth of rents. On this, Hertzka, *Soc. Entwickelung*, bk. i, chaps. xi, xii.

§ 118 THE TRUTH

Giddings, 'Natural Rate of Wages,' in Mod. Dist. Process. *Gunton*, Wealth and Progress. *Patten*, in Am. Ec. Ass'n Papers, vol. iii, 406 sqq.

We take **Ricardo's law,** rightly understood and developed, as true, special emphasis being laid on the **last part** of it, which is usually ignored. In one direction, wages must **sustain life,** or work ceases. In the other, whatever the competition between employers, the figure will, up to the point where higher wages would begin to **discourage undertakings,** be fixed by the laborers' **standard of life,** their sense of what they **must have.** If **too high** wages are demanded, undertakers will **quit business:** if **too low** are allowed, laborers will **die.** Enforced **poverty,** or any other cause breaking wagewinners' **spirit, lowers wages;** all that gives them **pride, ambition,** and **courage, elevates** wages.[1] Two things are to be carefully noted, however. i After all, contrary to common opinion, the **portion** of the proceeds of industry which can during any **limited period issue in wages** is, to a great extent, not arbitrary but fixed,[2] and fixed by the amount of **capital** available for supporting labor. ii No **automatic action,** prompted by motives of self-interest, will heal the evil of **degradation** in the laboring population.[3] Hence the value (i) of a **public opinion** in sympathy with labor, (ii) of labor **agitation,** if at once **well planned,** temperate, and resolute, and (iii) of **education** wisely to devise, and moral character to make possible, **united action.**[4]

[1] Nor need this impoverish any one. Employers, to meet the demand, are forced to new economies and invention, which may even have the effect of increasing the total production. Gunton, as above, has well wrought out the idea. Touching the possibility of a sweeping benefit to wage-earners in this way he is probably too sanguine, but within considerably large limits his thought is correct [§ 117, n. 1].

[2] So Walker, Wages, 410. Wages are in some sense fixed, though not in the manner supposed by the wage-fund conception [§ 114]. The supply of capital influences them, but through its effect upon the productiveness of the labor. Many who here agree with Walker too nearly overlook this. H. George does, yet see Prog. and Pov., 62.

[3] See the noble discussion in Walker, Wages, chaps. xvi-xix. See also W.'s Address, in Am. Ec. Ass'n Papers, vol. iii, 157 sqq. Upon this point many earlier writers of repute held notions that experience has proved wholly false. Walker quotes some of these.

[4] We agree with Patten, as above, that a general advance in the incomes of laborers is not the necessary consequence of enlarged social production. It presupposes moral elevation, and must be a slow process at best. The ready optimism which studies the vast industrial progress of our time, assuming it "as an axiom that all the benefits of this progress pass quickly into the possession of the laboring masses," seems to us as mistaken as it certainly is honorable to the impulses of its subjects.

§ 119 Concluding Points

Ad. Smith, bk. i, ch. x. *Yves Guyot, Sci. Économique*, bk. iii, ch. iv.

I In spite of their **tendency** to equality through the action of supply and demand, wages **within any tract** of competition **differ** in the different employments, according as these are or are not (i) **agreeable,** (ii) **always demanding** labor, (iii) dependent on high **original gifts,** (iv) **easy** to learn, (v) **reputable,** (vi) **responsible,** (vii) **trammelled** by restrictive laws or customs.[1] II The amount paid for wages varies greatly, according to the nature of the business, in the **proportion** it bears to the value of **fixed** capital and in the proportion it bears to that of **circulating.** Fixed capital increases with the **advance of civilization,** out of proportion to both wages and circulating capital. III **Popular errors,** total or partial, are (i) that **good trade** makes high wages, (ii) that **high prices** have the same effect, and (iii) that wages must needs vary with the **price of food.**

[1] This influence sometimes raises wages above their proper level, sometimes has the reverse effect. The latter is many times the case with women's wages, which are often, though less and less so at present, lower than men's for the same amount and quality of work. Stated fees, too, tend to go unchanged through long periods, being fixed by custom.

CHAPTER V

PROFITS

§ 120 Terminology

Clark and Giddings, Modern Distrib. Process. *Mataja, Unternehmergewinn. Wirminghaus, Das Unternehmen. Gross, Lehre vom Unternehmergewinn. Schroeder, Unternehmen und Unternehmergewinn.*

All economic writers now agree in distinguishing **profits** from **interest**,[1] but another question still divides them, viz., whether, of the two elements making up **gross profits**, the **essence** of profits consists in (i) reward for **the exercise** of some peculiar **natural ability**, or rather in (ii) **risk**[2] and the accompanying haphazard and **anomalous gains**,[3] analogous with those of speculation. We prefer **nomenclature** (i), taking **pure profits**, or profits proper, as the remuneration of **special original**[4] **talent** exercised in any industrial direction. Profits manifest themselves most obtrusively in connection with the **management** of business, yet form an immense element in the sums nominally paid as **salaries, fees, and wages**.

[1] Ad. Smith, Ricardo, Mill, and Fawcett treat both under the one name of 'profits,' hopelessly confusing many important questions. See, for this, Mill's 4th Essay on Some Unsettled Problems in P. E. On Graziani's theory of profits, see in *Jour. des Écon.*, Oct., 1887.

[2] Risk cannot, as is so often thought, be the reason of profits. The risk of a business by no means falls, as a rule, entirely upon its manager. When authors so represent, they must have in mind the legal responsibility — a very different thing. The latter often protects the laborers, more often it does not, according to the manager's resources.

³ Monopoly profits, '*conjunctur*' winnings [as the German economists express it], mere good luck in business, etc. Cf. Progress and Poverty, 172 sqq. J. B. Clark cuts the undertaker function into two parts, the industrial and the mercantile. The returns for management he likens to wages, the rest, gain which arises from selling the product at more than its ingredients — ordinary wages, wages of direction, capital, taxes, etc. — have cost, he calls pure profits. But, as a rule, it is precisely the *management* which enables the gain to be made on sales. This gain, unless in case of some monopoly or peculiar feature removing the operation from the sphere of profits anyway, is brought about solely by *better management* than the poorest which still continues. It is reward to management. How else can such reward appear? Does not the gain of merchants come by managing wisely?

⁴ Acquired business ability is of course capital, and its remuneration interest [§§ 98, 108]. This, in the case of a profit-taker, would form a second element in gross profits, along with that suggested under (ii) in the text, above.

§ 121   Undertakers' Profits

Walker, Wages, ch. xiv; P. E., pt. iv, ch. iv. *Cherbuliez*, bk. iii, ch. iv. *Mangoldt*, §§ 96 sqq.

The **undertaker**,[1] as **capitalizer** or **user** of capital, fulfilling an entirely different office from that of the mere **lender** of capital, **profits**, the undertaker's share in the product, are governed by a law analogous with **rent**.[2] Power to **organize** industry and apply it to capital **varies** with different undertakers, as **fertility** of land with districts. By the law of **dearest cost** of production, the prices of manufactures, for instance, are fixed by the cost of the **poorest undertaker-talent** which demand forces into employment. This is **no-profit** undertaking. The returns of all **superior** undertakers are their **profits**, varying mainly with **ability**, partly with **opportunity**.[3]

[1] On the use and meaning of this term, § 46, n. 1. In the economic writings of Franklin and Alexander Hamilton it frequently occurs in just

this sense. An early minute of the trustees of Brown University authorizes the faculty to negotiate with some 'undertaker' for gowns to be worn by speakers at commencement. The real undertaker is often a composite body [§§ 46, iv; 99, n. 3].

² But beware of following the analogy too far. There is a scarcity of land relatively to need, and there is a scarcity of undertaker-ability relatively to need. But while competition for pieces of land can never so increase the productiveness of the best as to throw the poorer out of use, but rather poorer and poorer have to be occupied with the lapse of generations, competition cultivates undertaker-talent to an ever more and more perfect condition, so that poorer undertakers are thrust from the field. Degrees of fertility in the land used go on multiplying: degrees of talent in management go on decreasing. [Cf. Clark, Pol. Sci. Quar., vol. ii, 610.]

³ Of course, so far as the fortunate opportunity is thing of chance, of fraud, or of partial legislation, the profit is gross, not pure. Cf. § 117. Income of this sort might be rent, or belong in the fifth category [§§ 102, 103]. Hugo Bilgram finds the essence of profits to consist simply in the unfair advantage afforded by the ownership of money, the moneyless man being at 'the margin of opportunity,' etc. [for Bilgram too carries out the rent analogy]. But the gainful chance in trade may be created by natural ability functioning in purely economic ways, in which case the gain is pure profits. The theory of profits here set forth was first sketched by Bagehot, and then elaborated by Walker. It is now, in essence, the prevalent one. Ingram, Hist. of P. E., however, conceives it to be yet on trial. For good remarks on it, Hadley, 1st Rep. of Conn. Bureau of Lab. Stat., esp. p. 21.

§ 122 UNDERTAKER-TALENTS

Clark, 'Profits under Modern Conditions'; Pol. Sci. Quar., vol. ii.

The **reasons** for certain undertakers' superiority over others are **many** in both number and **kind**. **Force of will** and **strength of mind** are naturally the main determinants. All turns sometimes upon a cool, phlegmatic **temperament**, sometimes upon **courage** or **cheerfulness**. A gift for **administration** in general may tell the story, or, in particular, the power to **manage** men. So may economy, thrift, attention to business, memory, quickness at figures, accuracy, the ability to hold in mind many details at once. In not a few cases good health [1] or a rugged constitution will be the decisive characteristic.

[1] M. de Lesseps is able, it is said, to go days without sleep, and then, when opportunity offers, to make up by sleeping all day long, in a railway carriage if need be. Let pupils suggest as many other causes of profits as they can besides the above.

§ 123 Profits, Prices, Wages
The authh. at §§ 117, 118.

Pure profits, consisting wholly of wealth created by the **powers** of given undertakers **over and above** what would have been produced by the **same application** of labor and capital under **less efficient** leadership or management, neither (i) enter into the **prices** of products, nor (ii) lower or anywise antagonize **wages.**[1] On the contrary, wise and energetic undertaking is **absolutely vital** to the increase of wealth.[2] Anger at the great captains of industry on account of the **pure** profits which they acquire is not only **groundless** but **insane.** Rather is it the **stupid** and **unsuccessful** undertakers who deserve **blame,** sinking capital, starving laborers. The signal **importance** and unique character of the undertaker-function account for the present and probable **limitation** of **co-operation.**

[1] Gross profits may of course include illegal and immoral gains, to the injury of laborers as well as of others.
[2] As well, remarks Bagehot, speak of the compositors as 'making' the London Times as of laborers in the ordinary sense being the sole creators of wealth.

Part V

CONSUMPTION

CHAPTER I

NEED

§ 124 To Resume

Mangoldt, bk. v. *Chapin's Wayland*, ch. x. *Garnier*, *Traité*, ch. xxxiv. *Patten*, 'The Consumption of Wealth' [Univ. of Pa. Pubb., P. E. and Pub. Law Ser., No. 4]. *Lexis*, in Schoenberg, vol. i, XII.

The **general nature** of consumption was presented in § 49, where the subject received consideration so far as we found it to be a **phase of production**. Unproductive consumption, or consumption as an **independent department** of Economics, is now to be studied. Since man **produces to live** instead of living to produce, **unproductive** consumption is the **ultimate end**[1] of all **wealth** and hence of all **production**. Our economic **efforts** have their entire **occasion** and their essential **explanation** in the **needs**[2] of human beings. These may be (i) corporeal or mental, (ii) original or acquired, (iii) legitimate or illegitimate.

---

[1] But we do not agree with the authors who regard this fact a sufficient reason for treating Consumption before Production. A canvass of man's

needs would certainly not be inappropriate in an introduction to Economics, but consumption is not confined to a study of needs.

² It is a remark of the Italian economist, Fuoco, that man, "however great he may be, is nothing but a *living need*, a sum of needs" [*tutto quanto è puo chiamarsi un bisogno vivente, una somma di bisogni*].

§ 125 Elasticity of Need

Mangoldt, 197 sq. *Patten*, as at § 124. Cf., above, § 62 and the authh. there named. *Clark*, Philos. of Wealth, ch. iii. *Lexis* [as at § 124], § 4. *F. A. Lange, Arbeiterfrage* [4th ed.], 164 sqq.

Consumption **increases and decreases** with **plenty,** but very **unsymmetrically.** Although each **department** of the things which we desire is susceptible of great **expansion,** the **food** requirement has less latitude than that for **clothing,** this less than that for **shelter. Kinds** of food vary in the same respect. Any man's use of **salt** nothing could much extend, but new cheapness would greatly multiply **vegetable** dishes, and **meats, spices,** and **drinks** more still. In **dress,** each **season,** each change of **temperature,** and almost every occasion demands of such as can afford it some **modification. Dwelling accommodations** vary from wigwam to palace, while our demand for **immaterial goods** has a truly infinite range. Liking for variety develops most **rapidly** in food, next in dress, next in the appurtenances of home, last in the intellectual and spiritual realm. **Retrenchment** follows in general an order the **reverse** of the above, but with modifications largely determined by **pride**[1] and **habit.**

[1] The limitation of outlay is nearly sure to begin at points where it will be least noticed, since people do not love to advertise their poverty. Usually, therefore, economy will strike food before lodging, bringing one

to dispense with meat, *e.g.*, in favor of vegetables, and so on. This, in fact, when such partial luxuries as tea, coffee, and tobacco have not yet been given up, since habit powerfully co-operates with pride for the retention of these. Retrenchment in clothing comes last, — in the outer garments last of all. The possible *sweep* of retrenchment is greatest in housing, the whole of which may be surrendered, next most complete in clothing, a part of which, in temperate climates, must be retained, least complete in food [§ 62, n. 2, also Mangoldt, as above].

§ 126 Fashion and Progress

Roscher, § 89, n. 1.   *Patten*, as at § 124.

Presupposing **considerable resources** on the part of consumers, the **direction** assumed by consumption varies enormously with **class and station** in life, **custom, whim,** and **accident.**[1] As a rule, the **poorer** a family is, the **greater the proportion** of its total income which it expends for food.[2] Changes in **taste** render millions' worth of goods unmerchantable each year. In food the prime **delicacies** of one season may have **no sale** the next. The office of **sugar** at present was once fulfilled by **honey.** The middle age used enormous stores of **wax,** the head church of Wittenberg requiring, just before the Reformation, 35,000 pounds a year. In Catholic lands the consumption of **fish** noticeably varies with diligence in the observance of fasts. The **growth of civilization** and culture brings with it **increasing refinement** of needs, and a steady **advance** from coarser to nicer in the things which men consume.

---

[1] There are three ways in which wealth may cease to be such [cf. § 19], viz., change in (i) the *objects* constituting it, (ii) the *subjects* possessing it, or (iii) the *relations* between subjects and objects. Consumption in the

narrowest sense comes under (i). We have a case of (ii) whenever change in need leads to the casting aside of articles previously valuable, and of (iii) when war, revolution, or other cause renders possessions insecure [Mangoldt, § 134].

[2] The so-called 'Engel's law.' On this, and the numerous studies besides Engel's of the same problem, Lexis [as in § 124], §§ 21 sqq., and notes — very valuable. It may be regarded as a counterpart of this law that a man pays for house rent a smaller proportion of his income the larger his income is. It has been ascertained that in Breslau, Germany, a family with a yearly income of from \$300 to \$1000 pays about $\frac{1}{5}$ of it for dwelling accommodations, one getting from \$1000 to \$1500, about $\frac{1}{6}$, one with from \$1500 to \$3000, about $\frac{1}{7}$, one with from \$3000 to \$7500, about $\frac{1}{12}$, one with a higher income than this about $\frac{1}{20}$. Probably 90 per cent of the families in that city pay $\frac{1}{5}$. In the U. S. the proportion is doubtless somewhat smaller for the poor and much larger for the rich.

§ 127 Legitimacy of Need

Seneca, Epistle xxxix [moderate riches the best: useless wants]. *Hume*, Essay, Of Refinement in the Arts. The authh. at § 131.

Needs are not to be **recklessly multiplied,** but limited to those whose existence and supply are necessary to our best **producing power** and **largest life.**[1] Very often, however, the creation of **new need** will bring with it a **more than proportional** productive ability. This may occur **directly,** as when the ignorant and degraded acquire culture and the accompanying enlargement of **manhood,** or **indirectly,** by the limitation of **population,** rendering the laboring class more productive in proportion to its total need. There are also needs, **religious, moral, æsthetic,** whose existence is a good though they may not enhance productive ability at all.

[1] What this is Economics must find out from Ethics. In proportion as needs are fictitious and abnormal the gratification of them becomes destruc-

tive consumption. Economic law here agrees with ethical. Pre-eminently in the department of Consumption does Economics abut upon Ethics [§ 131, n. 2]. At many points the question whether an act or a process is productive or the reverse is absolutely unanswerable by Economics alone. Hume, as above, has good thoughts on the sorts of want-creation which ought to be encouraged.

CHAPTER II

ECONOMY IN SUPPLY

§ 128 Generic Principles

It is possible to **use up** wealth (i) in placating **legitimate** and proper needs,[1] (ii) as dead **loss,** answering no requirement at all, (iii) **disproportionately** to the necessities satisfied, or (iv) to meet cravings that, as **base and deleterious,** ought to be **repressed.** Obviously, with **given resources,** society will be prosperous economically in proportion as (i) expenditure is had only for **legitimate needs,** and (ii) all needs, these or other, which are ministered to at all, are supplied with the **smallest outlay adequate** to the end.

[1] See § 127.

§ 129 Specific Principles

Mangoldt, § 139. *Chapin's Wayland*, ch. x.

i In satisfying needs,[1] our own or those of other people, we should prefer if **equally efficient,**[2] (i) **reproductive**[3] to unproductive[4] consumption, (ii) **less unproductive** to more, and (iii) **high and lasting** gratifications to low and fleeting ones. ii It is important that (i) **every utility** connected with the consumed wealth should be **entirely** consumed, and that (ii) they should all be applied in the **most advantageous** manner. iii In case of any proposed **doubtful expenditure,** we should ask, (i) Will it **on the whole** and in the long run tend to **production or productiveness?** If not, (ii) will it inure to the **elevation** or to the degradation of character? If it will elevate, (iii) will the **whole good** attained by the consumption **exceed** that to be expected if the wealth remains **unconsumed**? In replying to (iii), remember that the **moral effort** of foregoing a benefit is likely to be **itself a benefit**.

[1] J. Tucker [Two Sermons, 29 sqq.: cited by Roscher, § 102, n. 2], lays it down that a man ought (i) not to spend beyond his income, (ii) to provide for himself and family, (iii) to lay by something for a rainy day, (iv) to be able to aid the poor, (v) to indulge in no pleasure injurious to body or mind, and (vi) to set in his expenditure no bad example.

[2] If the reproductive form is less efficient in the given case, then the question must turn upon the *character* of the proposed unproductive form. See iii, in this §, also §§ 127, 131, n. 2.

[3] A new coat to a feast or a concert, for instance. It is true that the need addressed would not be the same in the two cases, yet to a person with limited resources precisely such an alternative is often presented.

[4] A good coat to a fine one of poorer quality, for instance. Cf. n. 2.

§ 130 Prevention of Loss

Mangoldt, § 135. *Thomson*, 'Waste by Fire,' Forum, Sept., 1886.

While the vices specified at § 50,[1] causing **waste**, are responsible for enormous **destruction** of wealth, it is to be observed that much useless consumption is **inevitable**,[2] due to the very **nature of things**. Of this loss the volume can be reduced only by the **progressive mastery of matter by mind**, displayed in new arts and inventions. Our **resources** are: i Improved means for **preserving** perishable goods.[3] ii Wider knowledge, through more **general education** and **intelligence**, of such means as at any time exist. iii A more **durable construction** of buildings and other objects exposed to the destructive elements. iv Better-ments in **police,**[4] **veterinary,** and **sanitary science,** legislation, and administration. v A firmer grasp and wider observance of the **laws of life** in all its spheres, **social** and **moral** as well as **physical,** intensifying men's **productive power,** lengthening their average **productive period,** and **diminishing** the size of the **unproductive and dependent** class.

[1] See that §, and notes. In point is the incident related by J. B. Say, P. E., bk. ii, ch. v. A small latch was gone from a farmyard gate. One day a pig escaped into the woods, "and the whole family, gardener, cook, milkmaid, etc., turned out in search. The gardener, in leaping a ditch, got a sprain that confined him to his bed for a fortnight. The cook found the linen burnt that she had left at the fire to dry. The milkmaid forgot, in her haste, to tie up the cattle in the cowhouse, and one of the loose cows broke the leg of a colt that was kept in the same shed." Say figures at 20 crowns the loss of these minutes, all for want of a bit of iron which would have cost but a few sous.

[2] Professor Chandler Roberts, says the Engineering and Mining Journal, estimates the weight of the smoke cloud which daily hangs over London at about fifty tons of solid carbon, and 250 tons of carbon in the form of hydrocarbon and carbonic-oxide gases. Calculated from the average result of tests made by the smoke abatement committees, the value of coal wasted in smoke from domestic grates amounts, upon the annual consumption of 5,000,000 people, to $12,287,500.

[3] See § 54, n. 6.

[4] It was sheer neglect, nothing else, which caused the fearful Conemaugh disaster in and about Johnstown, Pennsylvania, May 31, 1889, when the bursting of an ill-made dam caused the loss of perhaps 10,000 lives and $10,000,000 worth of property [figures very uncertain].

§ 131   Luxury and Idle Wealth

Roscher, '*Ueber den Luxus*' [in *Ansichten*, vol i]. *Goldwin Smith*, 'What is Culpable Luxury' [in Lectt. and Essays]. *Vierteljahrsch. f. Volkswirtsch.*, XXII, i, 24 sqq. *Périn, Richesse dans les sociétés chrétiennes*. *Baudrillart, Histoire du luxe*. *Lexis* [as at § 124], §§ 11 sqq.

Consumption **beyond** the **actual requirements** of life may be termed **luxury,** 'luxuries,' of course, varying in their definition as the **standard of living** advances, and the luxury of one generation becoming a necessity of the next. It is clear from the principles already laid down that while certain species of consumption are always reprehensible, the use of luxuries is in itself never so. What luxury then is **culpable?** The foregoing paragraphs enable us to reply. i Consumption for luxuries is to be condemned from the point of view of one's own **personal life**, (i) when addressed to no **rational necessity**, or out of **proportion** to such necessity provided it exists, (ii) when addressed to **less pressing** or important needs to the neglect of those more so, and (iii) when it transcends one's **means.** ii It is an evil from the **social** point of view, (i) unless it **stimulates** rather than discourages labor, and (ii) unless it **elevates** instead of degrading the characters of men.[1] The **same principles** hold in cases where wealth is not immediately consumed, but **invested in idle forms**, as needlessly costly dress, houses, equipage, jewelry or plate, works of art to feed vanity or to please the taste of a select few, etc. In all such expenditures so much **capital is lost**[2] to the support of labor, as truly as by fire or hurricane.

[1] Baudrillart, as above, vol. i, § 98.

[2] The view characterized in n. 10, of § 20, is set forth by Bayle, Dictionary, vol. iv, 520. Arguing on the notion of the Stoics that evil is necessary as a foil or fender over against good to make it appear as good, he says: "Nevertheless it must be acknowledged that they were in the right in some respects, for, to give an instance of it, *can anything be more useful than luxury* for the maintenance of many families that would starve if the great men and ladies spent but little." On this specious but wholly untenable theory, study § 50, n. 1, and the references there made. Cf. also Lexis [as at § 124], § 19, and Mill, bk. i, ch. v. For the Cleopatra who drinks pearls, the Heliogabalus who feasts on nightingales' tongues, or the

modern spendthrift who gives an all-night entertainment costing thousands
and leaving only "withered flowers, rumpled vanities, deranged stomachs,
and overtaxed nerves," Economics finds no more justification than for the
Nero who burns Rome [Brown, Studies in Socialism, xii]. It will be said
that all these things furnish work. So does a conflagration. An uncle of
J. B. Say, the French economist, broke his wineglass after dining, remark-
ing, "the world must live." Say wondered "why he did not break the rest
of his furniture for the benefit of the world's workmen." That a product
wears out prematurely, and must be replaced is no industrial benefit, and
no more is extravagant expenditure. It furnishes immediate employment,
but it stops there [ibid.]. On needless wealth causing poverty at Rome,
Blanqui, Hist. of P. E., ch. vii. The consideration raised in the text and
dwelt upon in this note should be regarded in many cases of unproductive
consumption which are in themselves wholly legitimate, as building a
church, sending money to the heathen, investment in fine art though for
public behoof. Outlays of this kind certainly withdraw capital from the
support of labor. The man who loves his kind will in proposing an expenditure of this order raise the [ethical] question whether his capital is
likely to effect more good on the whole and in the long run laid out as
proposed, or productively. More imperative still is the query if I meditate
gratifying a merely personal need, however noble. So far as this life is
concerned, there may be an absolute conflict between my highest interest
and that of the laboring class [§ 15, n. 4].

Part VI

PRACTICAL TOPICS INVOLVING ECONOMIC THEORY

CHAPTER I

COIN CURRENCY IN THE UNITED STATES

§ 132   Colonial Times

Sumner, H. of Am. Currency. 'Dollar,' 'Cent,' and 'Coin,' in Am. Encyc. *Bryant and Gay*, Hist. of U. S., vol. iii, 131 sqq.

The earliest colonial coin is believed to have been one struck in **1612**, on the Bermudas, for the Virginia Company. The first coinage upon the main land issued from the '**mint howse**' at Boston, under act of the Massachusetts general court, 1652. There were twelve pence, six pence, and three pence pieces. The plainness of these exposing them to **washing and clipping**, the '**pine tree coinage**'[1] was the same year ordered struck from a new die. This Massachusetts mint stood about thirty-four years, and a new one went into operation in 1788. Coins for America were made **in England**, at first for Maryland alone, later for the colonies at large. The execrable '**Wood's money**,'[2] of pinchbeck, was among these. From 1778 to 1787, not only

Congress but **several states** as well issued copper coins,[3] Connecticut and Vermont in 1785, New Jersey in 1786 and 1787.

[1] This designation, the usual one, does not in strictness apply to the whole coinage, as part of the pieces bore the likenesses of other trees. The assumption by Mass. of the right to coin was one of the things which at this period so incensed Charles II against the colony.

[2] In 1722 George I commissioned one William Wood to coin pinchbeck money for the colonies. A pound of the material [3 oz. zinc to 16 of copper], which somewhat resembled gold, was coined into 13 shillings. Little of the money circulated.

[3] These are now rare. The Jersey copper wore on the obverse the inscription *Nova Cæserea*, a horse's head, and under it a plough; the reverse, a shield and the legend, *e pluribus unum*. The continental copper of 1787 had 13 rings on one side, representing the 13 original states. Each ring had the initial letter of a state. "Tempus Fugit," sun dial with rays, and "Mind Your Business" were the other insignia. On the continental copper of 1793 was a head of Liberty, with full, streaming hair.

§ 133   Earliest National Coinage

McMaster, U. S., vol. i, 189 sqq.   *Bancroft* [author's last rev.], vol. vi, 119.   *Laughlin*, Bimetallism in U. S., pt. i, ch. ii.

A plan for a **national decimal** coinage, which **Robert** and **Gouverneur Morris** and **Jefferson**[1] had devised, was approved by Congress in 1785–'6, its unit a **dollar,** virtually the same as the **Spanish,** in which the Continental Congress kept its accounts.[2] Jefferson's dollar contained $375\frac{64}{100}$ grains of fine silver. Half-dollars, double dimes, dimes, cents and half-cents were to be coined in proportion, also gold eagles and half eagles, but **no value-relation** between gold and silver was fixed. These gold coins, with the addition of double and quarter eagles and three dollar pieces, all reduced to **somewhat less** than the original amount of gold to the dollar,[3] still remain, mechanically and artistically among the best in the world.

[1] According to McMaster, vol. i, 195, the real work was done by Gouverneur Morris.

[2] Because in Pa. and N.J., where the old Congress sat, this had come to be the most common money. The Spanish milled dollar, 'pillar' dollar, or 'piece of 8' ['Reals,' 'Ryalls,' or 'Royals'], is one of the most interesting pieces ever coined. It began to be used in our southern colonies by 1650, and gradually worked its way before the Revolution to the extreme north. None of our histories have any adequate account of colonial metal money or colonial money of account. The colonists at first used not only English money denominations but English money itself. By 1650, however, the colonial pounds, shillings, and pence had become depreciated in comparison with sterling, so that from this time on the colonial pound was at no time or place the equal of the pound sterling. Moreover, the depreciation was different in different groups of colonies. If, about 1760, we call the pd. sterling 100, the Ga. pd. would equal 90; the N.E. and Va. pd., 75; the pd. of the middle colonies [N.J., Pa., Del., and Md.], 60; and the N.Y. and N.C. pd., 56¼. Corresponding to these various degrees of depreciation, the Spanish dollar, which was the equal of 4s. 6d. sterling, passed for 5s. in Ga., for 6s. in N.E. and Va., for 7s. 6d. in the middle colonies, and for 8s. in N.Y. and N.C. Colonial pds., sh. and pence were nothing but money of account, there being *under these names* no corresponding coins. Very various coins, English, German, Dutch, French, Portuguese, and Spanish, circulated, but far the most common by 1750 was the Spanish dollar with its halves, quarters and eighths. It was common and for legal purposes necessary to name each of these in terms of the shillings, pence, etc., of each group of colonies. The eighth part of the dollar [the 1 Real piece = 12½ cents], e.g., happened in N.Y. exactly to equal the shilling. In N.E. it was very nearly 9 pence, and was so called. In the middle colonies, where the dollar contained 90 pence [7s. 6d.], it was 11 pence and a fraction, and was hence called the 'levy.' Correspondingly, the half Real, or 6¼ cent piece, was known in N.Y. as 'sixpence,' in N.E. as 'fourpence' or 'fopence,' and in Pa. and N.J. as the 'fippenny bit' or 'fip.' When ninepences and levies became much worn they passed for dimes, whence the dime came to be sometimes called, in N.E. a ninepence, in Pa. and N.J. a levy, names heard in country parts so late as 1860.

[3] For the variations in the weight of our gold money, see next §, ii, and 'Dollar,' in Am. Encyc. As noted at § 85, n. 4, the U. S. now takes

no seigniorage for coining gold, the change having been introduced by the act of Jan. 14, 1875 [sec. 2], for resuming specie payments [Revised Stat., §3524].

§ 134 THE DOLLAR OF THE FATHERS

Laughlin, as at preceding §, pts. i, ii. 'Money,' in Am. Encyc. *Bolles*, as at § 139, bk. ii, ch. v.

i By the mint law **of 1792**, framed under the surveillance of **Hamilton,** the silver dollar was made to contain 371.25 grains of **fine** silver, 416 of **standard,**[1] the **alloy** constituting $\frac{179}{1664}$ parts of entire weight. The amount of pure silver in this dollar has remained **unchanged** ever since, but, in 1837, by the reduction of the alloy-fraction to the **more convenient** one of $\frac{1}{10}$, the coin assumed the weight which it now has, $412\frac{1}{2}$ grains, $\frac{9}{10}$ fine.[2] ii The law of 1792 had fixed the **value-relation** between silver and gold at 15:1, which proportion of silver being **too small,**[3] gold retired. The gold bill of 1834 **changed** the proportion to 16:1, **over-valuing gold** in turn and retiring silver. iii In 1853, on account of the still **further appreciation** of silver through the **discovery** of gold in California[4] and Australia, not only had the silver dollar totally **passed from circulation,** but, to retain in the country the **subordinate** silver, it was necessary to render this a **token** coinage by extracting a seigniorage of $6\frac{10}{11}$ per cent [5] the face-value of each coin, token silver being after this **legal tender** only to $5.00. The silver dollar, however, remained full legal tender till 1873, when, having in relation to gold greatly **depreciated**[6] again through large increase in silver production, lessened exportation to Asia, and the assumption by the German Empire of the gold standard, it was silently **demonetized.**[7]

¹ Or, as figured by Perry, 330, it was 8924 fine.

² Our gold coins have, also since 1837, this same fineness. They are intended to contain $\frac{90}{1000}$ of copper, and $\frac{10}{1000}$ or less of silver. If less than this silver, the lack is made up in copper, such margin being known as the 'tolerance' [see Lalor, vol. i, 509]. On fineness of Eng. coins, § 75, n. 10. The Canadian coins agree in this respect with the English.

³ It was at the time exactly correct, but silver was already growing cheaper relatively to gold, so that in the London market almost immediately over 15 parts of silver were required to equal 1 of gold. Less and less gold of course came to our mints [Gresham's law, § 85, n. 5], some years hardly any. After 1834, precisely the reverse conditions prevailed, the silver which had circulated gradually hiding itself away. A lively business was done at buying up the dollars from ignorant holders and selling them as bullion.

⁴ Cf. von Holst, Const. and Pol. Hist. of U. S., vol. iii, 405.

⁵ Our subordinate silver coins [tokens] were somewhat enriched again in 1873. Before that, the weight of 2 halves, 4 quarters, or 10 dimes was 385.8 grains, or 25 grams, and their value $.93\frac{1}{15}$ that of the full weight dollar. Now the value is $.93\frac{23}{45}\frac{75}{25}$ of full weight, giving a seigniorage of about $6\frac{4}{15}$ per cent. Our present half dol. exactly equals in weight and value half of a French silver 5 franc piece. There are now 66 Eng. shillings in a Troy pound of silver. Eng. silver money consists of tokens, legal tender only to the sum of 40 shillings, each piece having a bullion value $6\frac{2}{33}$ per cent less than its face value.

⁶ This phenomenon is more truthfully characterized as an *appreciation* of gold. The power of silver to purchase general commodities did not sensibly, if at all, decrease, but that of gold increased. General prices, *i.e.* [the only sure test, see §§ 70, 87], fell in gold countries, remained stationary in silver countries.

⁷ The act was popularly but with little doubt erroneously believed at the time to have been carried through Congress in guile, that knowing parties might realize from the rise of gold.

§ 135 Remonetization

Laughlin, Bimetallism in U. S., pt. iii. 'Bullion,' in Encyc. Brit. *Grier*, The Silver Dollar. *Bolles*, as at § 139, bk. ii, ch. v.

On the ground that the government **bonds** issued during the war had been made payable in '**coin**'¹ and that the demonetization of silver, if persisted in, would work **hardship** to taxpayers in liquidating the national debt, Congress, in 1878,[2] restored to the old silver dollar its full **legal tender quality**, ordering, however, instead of free coinage, that only a **given amount**, not under two or to exceed four million dollars' worth,[3] be coined **monthly**. Although still for many years the value of the gold dollar continued to **gain** over that of the bullion in the silver,[4] silver dollars and certificates have inflexibly held to the **gold par**. But the position, all admit, is **anomalous**.

[1] Which of course at the time legally included silver as well as gold.
[2] The act passed, over President Hayes' veto, on Feb. 28.
[3] Not so many *dollars*, but so many dollars' *worths*, very different conceptions. If the bullion in a silver dollar cost but 75 cents, $1,000,000 *worth* of silver would, ignoring alloy, yield $1\frac{1}{3}$ millions of dollars. The original bill provided for free coinage. The limiting clause originated in the Senate, with Senator Allison, and was dubbed 'Allison's tip.'
[4] May 15, 1888, and on one or two other occasions, the London price of silver fell to 42d. an ounce, corresponding to a bullion price for the silver dollar of about 71.5 cents. By noting in any report of the London market the price of silver bullion there, the bullion value of the silver dollar is easily figured according to the following rule. By whatever per cent silver in London goes above or below 58.98008 pence an oz., the bullion in the silver dollar is worth more or less than one hundred cents in gold. For another rule, see Rep. of Paris Monetary Conf. of 1878, early pp. The relation between the prices of pure gold and pure silver, or of gold and silver of any given fineness, provided it is the same for each metal, may be found by dividing 943 by the no. of pence per ounce which the silver costs. This rule is developed as follows: Gt. Britain makes 1869 sovereigns from 40 pounds Troy, $\frac{11}{12}$ fine (nearly). Hence an ounce Troy of gold $\frac{11}{12}$ fine is worth $\dfrac{1869}{40 \times 12} = \pounds 3\frac{128}{160}$ or $\pounds 3$ 17s. 10$d.$ = 934$\frac{1}{4}d.$; and the val. of the oz. Troy of *pure* gold is $934\frac{1}{4} \times \frac{12}{11}$. An oz. of pure silver at x pence per oz. $\frac{37}{40}$ fine w'd be $x\frac{40}{37}$ or $\dfrac{40x}{37}$. Now to find how many times more valuable a given weight of gold is than a given weight of silver, divide $934\frac{1}{4} \times \frac{12}{11}$ by $\dfrac{40x}{37}$ which $= \dfrac{934\frac{1}{4} \times \frac{12}{11} \times \frac{37}{40}}{x}$ or (nearly) $\dfrac{943}{x}$. *I.e.*, if $1

gold weighs 25.8 grains, $1 silver weighs $25.8 \times \frac{943}{x}$ grains. Also, if that weight of silver is worth but $1.00, 412.5 grains will be worth proportionally less. *I.e.*, as $25.8 \times \frac{943}{x}$ is to 100 cents, so 412.5 will be to the value of the dollar of the fathers in gold cents. French and German discussions usually describe our coins in terms of the Metric System. A grain Troy is .0648 of a gram. Hence the gold dollar, of 25.8 grains, weighs 1.67184 grams, and the silver dollar, of 412½ grains, 26.73 grams. A kilogram of gold contains very nearly $690, or £139 10s. A kilogram of silver, at the ratio to gold of 15½ to 1, contains about $43.80, or £9.

§ 136 THE FUTURE

Laughlin, ed. of Mill, Appendix [good bibliog. on silver qn.]. Cf. our §77, above, and its authh., esp. U. S. Consular Rep., Dec., 1887. *J. W. Sylvester*, Bullion Certificates: The Safest and Best Money Possible [a pamph., 1884]. *Knox*, United States Notes, ch. x.

i The **gold monometallists** would at once and forever **demonetize** silver. ii The more pronounced **friends of silver** cling to the **present law**,[1] willing, apparently, that the worst possible should come, allowing silver, if need be, the **monopoly** which gold has enjoyed since 1873. iii The advocates of **rated or proper bimetallism**[2] hope that the United States will assume no **final attitude** against silver as full money till effort for a **bimetallic league** of nations has been exhausted. iv A fourth party would realize M. Joseph Garnier's theory of **unrated or formal bimetallism**, further proposing that gold bullion as well as gold coin be made **legal tender** and the **standard** of value, silver likewise legal tender but only **at its market value in gold**, calculated and published daily by government. With numerous great merits, this plan[3] has in kind the defects of gold monometallism. International bimetallism, of which there is little hope,[4] would relieve us for a time, but only for a time. Wise action must look toward ideal money.[5]

[1] Except that many wish the free coinage of silver.

[2] See § 77.

[3] This is the scheme of Sylvester's pamph. named above. It allows to the dollar all the fluctuations in value to which gold alone is subject, this metal being the only ultimate standard, but it would somewhat limit the range or sweep of these, in that a good deal of silver would be in use as medium of exchange.

[4] See the Consular Report named above, esp. Appendix D, by the learned Soetbeer. Comparable with these invaluable "Materials" given us by Soetbeer on the Silver Question, is the memorandum by R. H. Inglis Palgrave, printed as App. B to the final Report of the [1886] British Commission on the Depression of Trade and Industry. It is based on Soetbeer, but adds much that is valuable. Germany would probably join a bimetallic league but for the opposition of England, who, as the great creditor-nation, declines to take a step destined to cheapen the sort of coin in which debts are to be paid her.

[5] See § 87.

CHAPTER II

PAPER CURRENCY IN THE UNITED STATES

§ 137 Early

Knox, United States Notes, chaps. i, ii. *Bryant and Gay*, U. S., vol. iii, 107, n. 132 sqq. *Greene*, Historical View of the American Revolution, 143, and Lect. v [best brief account]. *Bancroft*, U. S. [last revision], vol. vi, 167 sqq.

Down to the Revolution the paper money of America consisted in various kinds of credit bills issued by the colonies, which became so depreciated[1] that Massachusetts gave up, and Parliament finally forbade, their issue. After the Declaration of Independence both Congress and the states returned to them, putting forth such amounts that at the close of the Revolution they were $99\frac{9}{10}$ per cent below par.

[1] The pupil must bear in mind to distinguish colonial paper money from colonial hard money [§ 133, n. 2]. The depreciation mentioned in the present § [cf. Walker, Wages, 16], was in nearly all or all cases additional to that spoken of in § 133, n. 2. Mass. first uttered credit bills in 1690, after the attack on Port Royal. Greene, 143, Bancroft, vol. ii, 262 sq.

§ 138 Thence to the Civil War

Macleod, Dict. of P. E., vol. i, 170 sqq. 'Banking,' in Lalor; do. in Encyc. Brit.

i From this time till 1863 banking was practically free, any banking corporation being permitted to issue bills on condition of obeying certain easy requirements, and promising to redeem in coin on demand. Paper was over-issued. Immense numbers of banks failed, particularly in 1814, 1819 and 1837. Suspensions of specie payment were frequent. The **loss** in bills of broken banks is thought to have averaged during these years some **five per cent** of the circulation annually. ii About 1840, a plan was adopted in **New York** State, which became in 1863 the basis of the **national bank scheme**.[1] It arranged that any person depositing with the **state government** good securities to the minimum amount of $50,000, and any corporation depositing $100,000, **might issue** an amount of notes equal to the deposit. This plan was far **preferable** to the policy of the other states, yet liable to many objections. The **Suffolk bank system** was another step in the right direction, New England banks **depositing** funds with the Suffolk, in Boston, for the **redemption** of their notes. If funds from any bank failed, notes were declined and the state of such bank became publicly **known**.

[1] See § 141.

§ 139 Government Paper

Knox, United States Notes, chaps. iv sqq. *Powers*, 'Greenback in the War,' Pol. Sci. Quar., vol. ii. 'Money' in Am. Encyc. *Atwater*, Princeton Rev., Jan., 1882. *Rönne*, 'Zwangscours der Nordamerikanischen Tresorscheine,' in *Vierteljahrsch. f. Volksw.*, 1863, vol. ii. *Bolles*, Financial H. of U. S. 1861-'85, bk. i, chaps. iv, v.

United States **treasury notes** had been issued in 1812, 1837 and 1857, bearing interest, but **not for general circulation** and **not legal tender**. In 1861, at the opening of the civil war, Congress allowed the issue of fifty million in **similar notes**,[1] payable on **demand**, without interest, heralds of those immense greenback issues, amounting at one time to more than **four hundred million** dollars, which, being made **legal tender** for all payments save **duties** on imports, did so much to place and keep our national finances, till January 1, 1879, on a basis **other than coin**, thus greatly **aggravating the nation's burden**.[2]

[1] On the character of these old demand notes, Knox, 71 sqq.

[2] The government made a great mistake in not, by marketing bonds at any price, keeping our money at the gold par. The debt was nearly all contracted [bonds sold] in depreciated dollars, which had to be paid in coin or its equivalent. Besides this the national banks [§ 141] should have been forced to buy *new* bonds. Adams, Pub. Debts, 166 sqq. See also 'The Currency Debate of 1873-'4,' N. A. Rev., Jan., 1874. The greenback was at one time, July 11, 1864, 65 per cent below gold par. When the national bank act was passed in 1863, $450,000,000 in greenbacks were already authorized and $300,000,000 out. Gold stood at $1.70. In 16 months gold was $2.80—due in part, it is true, to national reverses, not wholly to greenback issues. Specie payments were first suspended in view of war with England over the Trent affair, just at the end of 1861. On greenback prices of gold during the war, see chart in Bowen, Am. Pol. Econ. Best brief account of government paper issues in the war down to 1879, is in Appleton's Annual Encyc. for 1879, where the pupil will also find an excellent history of the national debt at large to the same date.

§ 140   Government Banking

Bancroft, U. S., vol. vi, 25 sqq. *Atwater*, Princeton Rev., Jan., 1882. *Sumner*, Andrew Jackson. *Royall*, A. Jackson and the Bank of the U. S. *Hildreth*, U. S., vol. iv, ch. ii.

Of national banking projects there have been three.[1] i The **Bank of North America** began operations in Philadelphia, June, 1782, but after a most **successful** career of two years it **changed** its character to that of a state bank. This was done chiefly because of the **incompetency** of the then Congress to **create corporations**. It still exists in the city of its birth, under its original name.[2] The Massachusetts National Bank, in Boston, is of equal age. ii The first **United States Bank** went into operation in 1791, upon the plan of Alexander Hamilton. The national and state debts, the latter having been already assumed by Congress, were **funded** into six per cent bonds, and **three-fourths** of every private **subscription** to the stock of the bank were required to be in these bonds. This raised **national credit.** The bank, with its branches at various points, was also a source of great **profit** to stockholders, and, after twenty years, ceased to exist only because **denied a new charter** through the **hostility** of the now numerous state banks.³ iii The second **United States Bank** was chartered in 1816, on the **same principles** as the first. It was resorted to partly on account of the **depreciation of national credit** caused by the war of 1812, partly by the terrible **depreciation** of state bank bills. **Bad management** at first, coupled with odium toward banks in consequence of the numerous failures in 1819, rendered the bank **unpopular.** It was particularly obnoxious to **President Jackson,** who in 1832 **vetoed** a bill for the renewal of its charter, to expire in 1836, and in 1833 caused it to **relinquish**⁴ all the government's **deposits,** amounting to $10,000,000. These blows were **fatal** to the bank as national, though it secured a charter from Pennsylvania in 1836, and existed, languishing, till 1839. After 1836 there was **no national paper** money in circulation till the treasury notes of December, 1861.

¹ Not counting the national banks [§ 141], since the banking done by them is not the government's work. Government merely supervises it.

² Now again a national bank. It had been under a state charter ever since Jan. 1, 1774, and so had the Mass. Nat. Bank.

³ See Schouler, U. S., vol. ii, 316 sqq.

⁴ The deposits were not removed all at once. The new policy consisted in depositing no more, and gradually checking out, as needed, what was there. Sumner's Jackson has an interesting account of this controversy.

§ 141 The National Bank System

Richardson, The National Banks [Harper's Half Ho. Ser.]. *Bolles*, as at § 139, bk. i, ch. xi, bk. ii, ch. iv. *McCulloch*, Men and Measures of Half a Century, chaps. xv, xvi, xvii. The National Bank Act, and other laws relating to Nat. Banks [Gov. Printing Office, 1889].

The **present system** of National Banks had origin in 1863, again in the interest of the **national exchequer,** suffering the drain of war. It was a plan for raising money by **marketing government bonds.** By it: i Notes of **private** and **state** banks are prohibitively **taxed.** ii At least **one-fourth** the capital of each bank must be in United States **bonds** deposited in Washington. iii The notes constitute a **uniform currency, furnished** and if necessary redeemed by **government** with the bonds in its possession.[1] iv The **circulation is limited** to ninety per cent in value of the bonds, and to the same proportion of the paid-up capital stock, whatever the **size** of the bank. v Each bank must keep a **reserve** of lawful money proportioned in size to the amount of its circulation, viz., twenty or thirty per cent[2] of this. vi The notes are **legal tender from government** except for principal and interest of the public debt and **to government** except for customs, but not between **private parties.**

[1] So that should a bank fail its notes would still be good. Notes thus often circulate some time after the banks issuing them have suspended. The U. S. treasury does not in such a case surrender to the creditors of the bank the last of its bonds till all the notes are redeemed.

[2] In the reserve cities, viz., those in whose banks the banks of smaller places may deposit, it is 30 per cent, elsewhere 20 per cent. In all cases 5 per cent of the outstanding circulation has to be in the treasury at Washington for the redemption of notes there. This is part of the reserve.

CHAPTER III

OUR PAPER CURRENCY IN FUTURE

§ 142 Present System

McCulloch, 'Our Future Fiscal Policy,' N. A. Rev., June, 1881. *Allison*, ibid., June, 1882. *Scott et al.*, ibid., Sept., 1885. *Atwater*, 'The Fut. Paper Mo. of this Country,' Princeton Rev., Jan., 1882. *Neill*, 'Legal Tender Question,' Pol. Sci. Quar., June, 1886.

The **theoretical** faults of the national bank, (i) its **basis,** credit[1] instead of cash, (ii) temptation to **over-issue,**[2] (iii) **double interest,**[3] (iv) admission of **balances** and of clearing-house and United States deposit **certificates**[4] as part of the 'lawful money' **reserve,** have not wrought sensible mischief **in practice.** On the other hand, (i) the unchallenged **currency** of the bills all over the land, (ii) their steadfastness at **gold par,** (iii) the difficulty of **counterfeiting** them, and (iv) the infallible certainty of their **redemption,**[5] have inspired a very general wish to perpetuate the system.

[1] Viz., in the form of bonds. See § 141, ii. In the panic of May, 1884, all sorts of government bonds fell several per cent, materially altering the status of banks. But recovery was very speedy. Any political event abroad which sends home our foreign-held bonds has the same effect.

[2] No single bank can issue more than its share, but there is no legal limit to the number of banks in the country. The danger here signalized must be slight so long as the government maintains specie payments, since, if too many national bank notes are at any time in circulation, they can be presented for redemption, and if this takes place in greenbacks [one form of 'legal money'] instead of gold, these, too, may be turned into gold. Whether or not under these circumstances there can be inflation is the same question we touched at § 91 and notes.

[3] The bank draws interest on all the bonds constituting its capital

[§ 141, ii], and at the same time uses its notes in discounting. This was at first a source of exorbitant profits, but for many years has not been so, as shown by the widespread disposition of banks to surrender their bonds for cash to use in discounting, this assuring them greater gains than the bonds yield.

⁴ Balances due from other banks, and the gold certificates mentioned at § 86, n. 1.

⁵ See § 141, iii.

§ 143 DIFFICULTIES
Reports of the Secretary of the Treasury, December, 1888 and 1889.

Growth of national credit having advanced the value of **long bonds** and made possible the **refunding** of the others at a low rate, banks begin to prefer **relinquishment of circulation** to the interest of the bonds needed to retain it. Several measures have been propounded for the **prevention of contraction** from this source, and for the **maintenance** of the national bank **circulation** till the entire debt shall have been cancelled. Of these the following most deserve mention: (i) to **remove** the ninety per cent **limit**[1] on circulation, fixing this at the **par** or perhaps at the market value of the bonds deposited, (ii) to **refund**[2] the fours and four and a halfs into two and a halfs with an equal time to run, recouping holders by the **present worth** in cash of the interest given up, (iii) to **repeal** the one-half of a per cent **tax** on circulation, (iv) to transform the entire **annuities** now attaching to the fours and four and a halfs into **separate bonds**, in accordance with their present worth, then to **unite** these with the present fours and four and a halfs and issue **new bonds** to cancel both: the latter to be paid in **series year by year**, thus affording an **outlet** for the accumulating **surplus**.[3]

[1] The McPherson bill, passed by the Senate Feb. 28, 1884, killed in the House Jan. 15, 1885.

[2] The Aldrich bill, brought before the Senate of both the XLVIII and the XLIX Congress, but never passed. The Potter bill, contemporaneously moved in the House, proposed to exchange the 3's [now paid off] as well.

[3] Plan set forth by H. C. Adams, in the Forum for Dec., 1887. Its very great advantage over the others lies in the steadiness and regularity with which it would utilize the government's needless revenue for the lessening of the debt.

§ 144 Proposed Change of Basis
Report of Secretary of the Treasury, December, 1886.

The **last** of our national bonds, the fours, being **callable** on July 1, 1907, and the bulk of the others, viz., the four and a halfs, on September 1, 1891, and it being **unlikely** that the debt will be kept in existence merely to **furnish basis for banks,** none of the above schemes offer other than **temporary** relief. Various suggestions are therefore made of possible **substitutes** for national bonds as security to bank circulation: consols, rentes or other foreign public paper,[1] state, county or city bonds, bottom mortgages on real estate, etc. None of these could **fully replace** the present security. The best plan[2] yet propounded would (i) **restrict the circulation** of each bank to ninety per cent of its stock, (ii) make bills a first **lien** on all the assets of their banks and also on **other property** of stockholders to the value of 100 per cent of each one's stock, (iii) force each bank to keep with the United States Treasurer a **coin reserve** equal to 10 per cent of its circulation, (iv) force the united banks to **guarantee** each individual bank, and so (v) have bills of broken banks **infallibly redeemable** at Washington, as now.

[1] Mr. John Jay Knox, formerly Comptroller of the Currency, at one time favored the acceptance of foreign securities for this office.

[2] Drawn up by Hon. A. S. Hewitt. The essence of it was adopted by President John Thompson of the Chase Nat. Bank, N. Y. City, in his circular of Jan., 1885, intended to influence public opinion and so Congress.

§ 145 Probable Outcome

Adams, Pub. Debts, pt. ii, ch. ii. *Sylvester*, as at § 136.

This plan is **ingenious**, but has the defects of **intricacy** and of giving government too little real **control** over bank assets to **assure redemption** in all cases. Preferable to it, people more and more believe, would be some scheme for the issue of notes **directly by government** as greenbacks are issued now, only modelled more after the issue-department of the **Bank of England**.[1] The great **merits** of such an arrangement would be **efficiency, simplicity,** and **profitableness to government** both negative[2] and positive. Objections: It would be **unconstitutional.** But the Supreme Court has decided otherwise.[3] **Inelastic.** Somewhat, but could easily be made **less so** than our present paper system. Facile means to **inflation.** It could add nothing to the **power** or to the **inducement** which Congress had to create the present treasury notes. Such a paper circulation could readily be made tributary to a plan for **ideal money.**[1]

[1] Without, of course, the inelasticity of the Bank of England issues. There we find, (i) the circulation restricted to 15 million pounds above specie in vaults, otherwise free, (ii) every bill legal tender save from the bank itself, and instantly convertible. It would be advisable to have no absolute maximum or minimum of circulation. The business should be regulated by an able and impartial commission, a majority of them not bankers, empowered to suit the volume of notes to the needs of the country

according to the principle of § 87. This idea is as old as Ricardo [Proposals for a Secure Currency], who moved to vest the power of issuing paper money in commissioners appointed by the ministry but removable only on address by one or both houses of Parliament.

[2] The negative advantage would consist in relief from the expense and risk of supervising the present complicated system. For the positive, see § 78 and n. 1, § 86 and notes.

[3] Virtually, in Julliard *vs.* Greenman. See Knox, U. S. Notes, chaps. iii, iv, xi; James, in Pubb. of Am. Ec. Ass'n, vol. iii, 49 sqq.; Bolles, as at § 139, bk. ii, ch. i; McCulloch, as at § 141, ch. xv. This case to be sure related directly to the legal tender quality of notes redeemed and paid out again under the act of 1878. It pronounced that act constitutional. More certainly so would be the notes we propose, which *ought not to be legal tender at all.* It is the non-observance of this which creates so much prejudice against government paper money. People mistakenly conceive such paper as necessarily a forced loan. That Mr. Goschen, Chancellor of the Eng. Exchequer, intends an issue of English greenbacks, may perhaps be taken as some proof of the innocuousness of such money. See Budget Speech, Lond. Times, Ap. 19, 1889. Observe in particular that we advocate only *promissory*, not fiat greenbacks [§ 93]. We need not remark that the execution of the above proposal would in no wise interfere with the regular and most profitable business of banks, viz., that of discounting.

CHAPTER IV

TAXATION

§ 146   General Principles

Ad. Smith, bk. v. *Leroy-Beaulieu, Théo. des Finances*, bk. ii. *Schoenberg, Handbuch der Pol. Oek.*, vol. iii. *Cossa*, Taxation. *Cooley*, Law of Taxation. *Mill*, bk. v, ch. ii. *Nicholson*, 'Taxation,' in Encyc. Brit.

i Taxation, as topic in Economics, relates partly to **Distribution**, partly to **Consumption**, to neither exclusively.[1] ii The **generic principle** to be followed in taxation is : sufficiency of **revenue** in highest possible consonance with the **general good**. Subordinate abstract **principles** of so-called right, as **mortmain**, customary **privilege**, etc., are hence to be respected[2] only within the above limit. Also, while the **equalization** of wealth is no part of the **purpose** of taxation, incidental **tendency** to this in any plan of taxation should, *ceteris paribus*, give it **preference** over competing plans. iii Taxes should be, so far as is possible and consistent with their main aim, (i) **definite** in amount and as to time and manner of payment, (ii) levied and collected in the way most **convenient to payers**, (iii) made to take from the payer as **little** as possible **beyond what reaches the treasury**, (iv) arranged to **encourage**, not discourage, **industry, inventiveness, intelligence, taste,** and whatever ennobles national life.[3]

---

[1] The civil, military, and naval *personnel* is made up, theoretically and largely in fact, of producers, who receive [gross] wages. Taxation to meet this outgo comes under Distribution. But all waste through governmental

act, as well as all outlays on behalf of art and science, are referrible to Consumption.

[2] By legislators, that is. Assessors and collectors must of course proceed according to the laws, whatever they are.

[3] These are in substance the rules which have come down from Adam Smith, book v, ch. ii, pt. ii, reproduced by all subsequent writers upon finance. Cf. Walker, in P. E., ch. on Taxation, for one or two excellent modifications.

§ 147 Direct and Indirect Taxes

Mill, bk. v, chaps. iii-vi. *Cossa*, Taxation, pt. iii. *James*, 'Customs Duties,' in Lalor.

Taxes are **direct** or **indirect** according as they are assessed upon the **very parties** from whom they purport to be **collected,** or upon **other** parties, as manufacturers, importers, etc., who **indemnify** themselves out of the consumers by adding taxes to prices. **Indirect** taxes, viz., **customs** and **excises,** are in favor because, being identified in the minds of consumers with the **prices of commodities,**[1] they are easy to collect. They are objectionable as unduly **burdensome to the poor,**[2] particularly if **specific** instead of **ad valorem,** since they are rated rather according to **population** than according to **property.** If laid, they should bear lightly on **necessaries,** moderately on **comforts,** more heavily on **luxuries.**

[1] People pay, falsely thinking them to be part of the cost-and-handling prices of the articles bought, not surmising that they are settling their tax-accounts with the nation.

[2] To yield much revenue they must be placed on goods that are somewhat popularly consumed. Specific duties aggravate the evil because, being fixed at about so much on the value of the medium quality of the article, they are of course unduly high on the poorer qualities, which alone poor people can buy.

§ 148 Norms of Direct Taxation

Walker, 'Principles of Taxation,' Princeton Rev., July, 1880. *H. George,* Prog. and Poverty, bks. vii sqq. *Ely,* Taxation in Am. States and Cities. 'Taxation in U. S.' [4 artt.], New Englander, 1884. *Ford,* 'Reform in Taxation,' Int'l Rev., vol. xiii.

Five specific principles easily suggest themselves as possible bases for direct taxation, (i) **property** in general, (ii) **expenditure**, (iii) **productive ability**, (iv) **income**, (v) **non-capital** property. Taxation upon any of the first four is either **unjust**, or **impracticable**, or **both**.[1] The main category of non-capital property is **land** proper, viz., land aside from improvements — an eminently fit bearer of heavy taxation.[2] However, (i) to keep taxation **perceptible** by the people,[3] (ii) to avoid the inevitable **injustice** of any single tax,[4] (iii) to compass the requisite **elasticity** of revenue,[5] and (iv) to insure **disciplinary power** over refractory or extortionate businesses, **other taxes** besides a tax on land are needed: customs duties, excises, and taxes on general income.

[1] Not to mention the injustice in principle of a general property tax, which would in effect involve a penalty on thrift, such a tax absolutely cannot be equitably assessed or collected, such is the proportion of personal property which can easily be, and will be, concealed. See Ely, as above, also in Rep. of the Md. Tax Commission, 1887. See, too, the 1872 Rep. of the N. Y. State Tax Commissioners. The exact expenditure of families is rarely known even to themselves. A tax on productive ability, were it only feasible, would certainly involve much justice. But suppose, as is too often the case, the ability has been unused? Much is to be said for an income tax, and it is the favorite of all the great writers on finance, some of whom advocate it to the exclusion of every other form. But experience in Gt. Britain shows that even this tax cannot be fairly collected, so easy is the falsification of income returns.

[2] To this extent H. George is clearly right. Land cannot be hidden, while its true value can in most cases be determined with relative ease. Moreover, all people are dependent directly or indirectly upon the land,

and hence must, through the principle of 'repercussion' [Cossa, Taxation, 62], help pay part of a land tax whether themselves land-owners or not. A good deal of this equity obviously attaches to a real estate tax, which would be an infinite improvement over the general property tax now sought to be carried out in most of our states.

[3] That popular institutions may prevail government must be forced to solicit the people for funds, which would not be necessary so long as taxes were furnished in plenty by economic rent, as H. George and the single land tax theorists propose. This principle, ably discussed by Adams, Pub. Debts, 22 sqq., we have not seen appealed to in the land tax controversy.

[4] No particular tax can possibly be levied save with injustice here and there, weighting this man too heavily, the next too lightly. A single-tax system exaggerates every such unfairness to the utmost, while by burdening many things you tend to offset losses by gains.

[5] Any tax can on occasion be reduced, but few are the sorts of taxes which can be at once suddenly and safely elevated, producing no shock. Liquor taxes well answer this requirement. So do income taxes, which Gt. Britain has usually resorted to in such emergencies. Not, however, in the most recent case, Mr. Goschen's budget of April, 1889, introducing instead a death tax on estates of over £10,000.

§ 149   Taxation of Income

Cohn, 'Income and Property Taxes,' Pol. Sci. Quar., vol. iv.   *Mill*, bk. v, ch. ii, secs. 3, 4.

The **following rules**[1] should govern the incidence of an income tax: i Up to a given amount, income should **not be taxed** at all.   ii The **percentage** should **slowly increase** according to the amount of income.   iii Income from **capital** should pay a **greater percentage** than salaries or wages.   iv Income arising **without labor and risk** should pay a greater percentage than other.   Thus, all considerable **legacies**, except to nearest relatives, should be **well taxed**, the rate increasing with prospect of their **unproductiveness**.

[1] Involving the so-called 'progressive' [or 'degressive'] principle of income taxation. Fawcett in his Manual opposes this, but on insufficient grounds.

§ 150 Emergency Taxation

Mill, bk. i, ch. v, secs. 8, 10. *Adams*, Pub. Debts, pt. i, ch. v; pt. ii, ch. i.

Extraordinary public expenditure should, unless very great, usually be covered by immediate **extra taxation** instead of by loans, as slight extra taxes will be to a great extent paid out of **non-capital wealth**, not abstracting from the support of **labor**, while loans commonly **prey upon capital**. But if the projected outgo is **vast**, resort may well be had to a **loan**, more particularly if this promises to be largely taken up **abroad**.[1]

[1] This is not the place for full discussion. Read Adams, as above, or the proper chapters in any of the regular works on Public Finance.

CHAPTER V

POVERTY

§ 151   THE FIRST CLASS OF REMEDIES

Davis, ' Labour and Labour Laws,' in Encyc. Brit. *H. George*, Prog. and Poverty; Social Problems. *Cherbuliez*, pt. ii, bk. iii. *Mill*, bk. iv, ch. vii. *H. Spencer*, Man vs. the State. *Sumner*, What Social Classes Owe Each Other. *Rae*, Contemp. Socialism, last 2 chaps. ' Charity ' [several artt.], in Lalor. *Graham*, The Social Problem. *Warner*, Pop. Sci. Mo., July, 1889.

Of the remedies popularly suggested for poverty, some are expected to **raise wages,** others to operate **directly.** The latter are **poor laws** and **private** charity. Experience, especially in England, has proved the absolute **necessity,** both economic and moral, of **refusing** charitable aid **except to prevent actual and decided want.** To make **sturdy paupers** comfortable is to put a **premium on indolence, a penalty on industry.**[1] The work of **organized charity,** on the other hand, hunting out and shaming or punishing **impostors,** finding — not making — **work** for the healthy workless, and **prudently aiding** those truly needy, is in the highest degree advantageous both **economically and morally.**

[1] See § 16, n. 6. H. Spencer [also Sumner], as above, vividly shows the inexpressibly baneful results of coddling worthless human beings so as to enable them to propagate their kind. But society has a duty to such. It should, if possible, reform them both economically and morally. Peck, in Contemp. Rev., Jan. and Feb., 1888, and Manning, ib., Mch. The Charity Organization Societies in several of our largest cities are doing excellent work toward this end. On this interesting subject, Warner, as above, writes well.

§ 152 The Second Class

Mill, bk. ii, chaps. xii, xiii; 'Claims of Labour' [in Dissertations]. *Leroy-Beaulieu*, Question ouvrière au xixième siècle. *Ely*, Labor Movement in America. *McNeill, et al.*, The Labor Movement. *Gunton*, Wealth and Progress.

Here come the measures intended to **raise wages**: (i) **strikes**, (ii) **trades-unions**, (iii) **legislative enactments** upon wage-rates or hours of labor, (iv) demand that **wages be paid** when business can go on only with loss, (v) demand that **idle wealth** be turned into capital. Strikes and trades-unions are *per se* both **legitimate** and often **useful**, but call for the utmost **discretion** and **self-control** in management. i Strikes, unless **general**, fail, usually fail if general unless on a **rising market**,[1] and at any rate when not **successful,** possibly even then, **limit production**[2] and so **wages**. ii Trades-unions, so far as they endeavor to **control wage-rates** simply by **limiting the supply of labor, hinder** general **prosperity,** and hence general **wages**,[3] in the same way as most restrictive tariffs do. iii The **legislation** referred to, **important** and **desirable** as it often is, may easily be so framed as to prove either **futile** or **mischievous** like the above. iv Paying wages at a loss is **charity,** also the **destruction of capital,** putting farther off the day when wages proper can be paid. But firm, temperate and wise labor **agitation,** with or without these particular means, may do much to better wages, in the way pointed out at § 118.

[1] In March, 1888, during the greatest snow blockade ever known in N. E., when 12 locomotives were stalled in New Haven and no trains passed between that city and N. Y. for 3 days, 200 shovellers employed by the N. Y., N. H. & H. R. R. at Meriden struck for an advance of from 21½ to 50 cents pay an hour. It is needless to say that they were retained. How modern

systems of industry favor the success of strikes, see § 45. To the considerations there mentioned we may add this that nearly all manufacturers now work on orders, which they are under contract to fill at such and such times. A greater proportion of strikes [38 per cent] and strikers [50 per cent] succeeded in 1888 than in any preceding year [Bradstreet's, Feb. 2, 1889], due, however, in large measure to greater moderation in striking, and the consequent greater justice of demands. From 1881 to 1886, inclusive, strikes occurred in 22,304 establishments in the U. S., and 1,323,203 employees were engaged in them. At the same time 160,823 employees were locked out. Of all these strikes 9,439, or 42 per cent, were for increase of wages, 4,344, or 19.48, for reduction of hours, 1,734, or 7.77 per cent, against reduction of wages, 1,692, or 7.59 per cent, for increase of wages and reduction of hours. Wages or hours had most to do with more than 77 per cent of the strikes, and nearly 4 per cent more were influenced by the same causes coupled with others. Of the strikes for higher wages 66 per cent were successful and 8.43 per cent were partly successful. Of the strikes to secure a reduction of the hours of labor about 47 per cent were entirely or partly successful. On the responsibility of both employers and employees to the public, Carl Schurz, in N. A. Rev., Jan. and Feb., 1884. Why laborers cannot compete with landowners in a strike, Prog. and Poverty, 282 sqq.

[2] The aggregate losses caused by the stoppage of work during the three weeks of struggle in the southwestern strike of 1866, were placed at $30,-300,000: $3,000,000 in wages which 250,000 strikers threw away, $2,500,000 sacrificed through interruption to the business of employers, $4,400,000 lost in deferred industrial contracts, and $20,400,000 in building contracts.

[3] Advantaging their members at the expense of the laboring population in general.

§ 153   Ultimate Help

Patten, The Consumption of Wealth [see, above, § 124]. *Bilgram*, Iron Law of Wages. *Fawcett*, Manual of P. E.

The **capitalizing of idle wealth**[1] promises much, and would promise far more but for a sadly convincing induction which teaches that when **material betterment** does chance to come to the **ignorant poor,** as through a rise of wages or the cheapening of bread, it is instantly **checked** by increased **population.** However great relative relief[2] may be hoped from the measures named above, or from co-operation[3] in its various forms, private and public, and zealously as all should strive to multiply and promote such helps, the economic elevation of the poor will prove to be **ultimately** an **ethical** and an **educational** work.[4] Their great wants are, (i) a **moral** one, the **will** to restrict population where necessary,[5] check vicious appetites, and act unitedly,[6] (ii) an **intellectual** one, **knowledge** of economic and social laws, that they may assert claims **wisely**. Aids to these, the only **final relief** of indigence, are, (i) the **Christian religion**, which, rightly understood, includes all true **morality**, (ii) **sympathizing public opinion**, and (iii) **compulsory education**. This last is equally called for by the logic of **free schools**.

[1] See § 131.
[2] Cf. § 118, n. 4.
[3] On co-operation, Somers, 'Co-operation,' in Encyc. Brit.; Block, do. in Lalor; Holyoake, H. of Co-op. in Eng.; Marshall, Ec. of Ind., bk. iii, ch. ix; Giddings, in McNeill's 'Labor Movement'; Fawcett, Man., bk. ii, ch. x; Cairnes, Leading Prin., 289 sqq.; Co-op. in U. S., Johns Hop. Univ. Stud., VIth ser. Very much more has been written. A great deal may be expected from the co-operative movement, though probably less than many think [§ 123, end]. Profit sharing is the most promising phase of co-operation [best treated in Gilman, Profit Sharing between Employer and Employe; cf. Quar. Jour. Econ., vol. i, 232, 367] except perhaps co-operative banking and [virtually the same thing] co-operation in building and loaning [Dexter, Co-operative Building and Loan Associations]. On the excellent working of the various sorts of Friendly Societies, as the Odd Fellows, etc., a sort of co-operation, see Quarterly Rev., April, 1888.
[4] The more necessary to emphasize this because the fact is so commonly ignored in favor of nostrums or at best partial measures. Indefinite credit utilized as money is Hugo Bilgram's remedy [§ 92, n. 1].
[5] The general question of Malthusianism ['Population,' in Lalor] we do not here touch. All apart from this, it is perfectly obvious that very many

families would be in every way better off with fewer members. For the intelligent and well-to-do not to be celibates is, even by the principles of Malthus, a duty.

[6] How many strikes and promising labor movements fail through selfish ambition and treachery! While these prevail the employer will have laborers at his mercy.

www.ingramcontent.com/pod-product-compliance
Lightning Source LLC
Chambersburg PA
CBHW031751230426
43669CB00007B/572